AND THE LIFE EVERLASTING

By JOHN BAILLIE

———

OUR KNOWLEDGE OF GOD

A DIARY OF PRIVATE PRAYER

THE PLACE OF JESUS CHRIST IN MODERN
CHRISTIANITY

THE INTERPRETATION OF RELIGION

THE ROOTS OF RELIGION IN THE HUMAN
SOUL

INVITATION TO PILGRIMAGE

AND THE LIFE EVERLASTING

By

JOHN BAILLIE

D.Litt. (edin.), Hon. D.D. (edin., toronto, & yale)
Hon. S.T.D. (dickinson coll., u.s.a.)

PROFESSOR OF DIVINITY IN THE UNIVERSITY OF
EDINBURGH

Geoffrey Cumberlege
OXFORD UNIVERSITY PRESS
LONDON   NEW YORK   TORONTO

OXFORD UNIVERSITY PRESS
AMEN HOUSE, E.C.4
London Edinburgh Glasgow New York
Toronto Melbourne Wellington Bombay
Calcutta Madras Cape Town
GEOFFREY CUMBERLEGE
PUBLISHER TO THE UNIVERSITY

'*I believe in God* . . . . . .

. . . *and the life everlasting*'

THE APOSTLES' CREED

First English Edition 1934
Second Impression 1936
Third Impression 1941
Fourth Impression 1943
Fifth Impression 1948

PRINTED IN GREAT BRITAIN

PREFACE

THIS book had its origin in the conviction, which has established itself with increasing emphasis in my mind during recent years, that a large part of the current discussion of the problem of eternal life proceeds on entirely wrong lines. This is true not only of the more popular thought of our time but also, and even especially, of the writings of professional philosophers. It is a fact of curious interest that almost every philosopher who writes a volume of any considerable scope thinks it necessary to make some pronouncement, if only in passing, on the subject of immortality. Such pronouncements have constantly seemed to me to be involved in misunderstanding of the most serious kind. Many of them, I have felt, could not possibly have taken the form they did if the actual course of human reflection on this problem had been steadily kept in mind and the culminating Christian solution of it fairly and intelligently grasped. Not only the nature of the desire men have for eternal life and the nature of their reasons for believing that their desire may be satisfied, but also the nature of the eternal life towards which their desire has been directed, have been radically misrepresented.

What I have tried to do is to lead the reader's thought towards sounder ways. My book is not speculative, and hardly attempts to carry Christian thought farther than it has already advanced. For not only is the literature of past ages still full of rewards for the explorer in this field, but in our own day also—and this in spite of the numerous hasty and shallow deliverances to which I have referred—much wise thought and ripe scholarship have been devoted to the whole matter and their fruits generously placed at our disposal. From these contemporary writers I have myself learnt much, and it has been no small part of my aim to enable the reader to do the same. I have tried to be of service to him in the none too easy task of cutting his way through the tangle of conflicting opinions, ancient and modern, with which every phase of the subject is surrounded. In many cases, instead of expressing what I have learnt in different words of my own, I have preferred to quote representative passages from the works to which I have desired to direct the reader's attention—particularly from the writings of such authors as Sir James Frazer, Erwin Rohde, R. H. Charles, John Burnet, Archbishop Söderblom, and Mr. Edwyn Bevan, and of such other thinkers as Baron von Hügel, T. E. Hulme, A. S. Pringle-Pattison, Philip Wicksteed, Professor A. E. Taylor, Professor C. C. J. Webb, and the German writers Karl Adam, Karl Barth, and Paul Tillich.

The book contains the lectures delivered by me under the terms of the Ayer Foundation in the Colgate-Rochester Divinity School, Rochester, N.Y., in the spring of 1932. I have to thank the trustees of the Foundation for their courtesy in choosing me as the lecturer for that year, and especially for their considerateness in permitting me, and indeed urging me, to expand what I was then able to say in such a way as to make the printed volume more complete.

For the correction of the proofs I have once more trespassed upon the kindness of my friend, Professor J. Y.

Campbell, of Yale University, and of my brother, Dr. D. M. Baillie, of Kilmacolm, Scotland. Their criticisms and suggestions have proved most valuable, and I thank them very warmly.

JOHN BAILLIE

NEW YORK
September, 19.3.3

IN
MEMORIAM
MATRIS DILECTISSIMAE

CONTENTS

I. CONTEMPORARY QUESTIONINGS
I. THE MODERN REVOLT AGAINST OTHER-WORLDLINESS   3
II. AND ITS HISTORICAL ORIGINS   9

II. THE PROPER CLAIMS OF EARTH
I. THE INSIGHT OF MODERNITY   17
II. THE GLORIES OF THE SECULAR   24
III. THE HOPE OF EARTHLY PROGRESS   27
IV. SOME NECESSARY DISCRIMINATIONS   38

III. APPROACH TO THE ETERNAL PROSPECT
I. THE ASCENT OF MOUNT PISGAH   47
II. WHERE NEW TESTAMENT THOUGHT BEGINS   57

IV. A TALE—AND SOME COMMENTS
I. GHOSTLY SURVIVAL AMONG SAVAGE PEOPLES   62
II. IN THE CLASSICAL WORLD AND IN ISRAEL   68
III. A SCIENTIFIC RATHER THAN A RELIGIOUS DOGMA   76
IV. ITS PRESENT SCIENTIFIC STANDING   86

V. THE SEQUEL OF THE TALE
I. THE BEGINNINGS OF HOPE   100
II. IN GREECE   101
III. IN INDIA   113
IV. IN PERSIA AND IN JUDAEA   118
V. THE HOPE OF JESUS   132
VI. THE CHRISTIAN HOPE   137

VI. THE LOGIC OF HOPE
I. HOPE'S SYLLOGISM: ITS MAJOR AND ITS MINOR PREMISS   157
II. THE TRIBALIST ALTERNATIVE: CORPORATE IMMORTALITY   164
III. THE INDIAN ALTERNATIVE: REABSORPTION   180
IV. A RIGHT OR A GIFT?   191
V. WHAT LOGIC CANNOT DO   196

CONTENTS

VII. THE NATURE OF ETERNAL LIFE

I. GNOSTIC AND AGNOSTIC ELEMENTS IN CHRISTIANITY   198

II. ETERNAL LIFE AS A NEW QUALITY OF BEING   204

III. AND AS, IN FORETASTE, A PRESENT POSSESSION   207

IV. WHAT THE NEW QUALITY OF BEING IS   211

V. THE HEAVENLY REST AND THE HEAVENLY TASK   228

VI. ETERNAL LIFE FOR SOME OR FOR ALL?   237

VII. INDIVIDUAL AND SOCIAL CONSUMMATION   246

VIII. EMBODIMENT OR DISEMBODIMENT?   251

VIII. STRANGERS AND PILGRIMS

I. A FINALLY SATISFYING VIEW   256

II. THE TRUE RELATIONS OF SECULAR AND SACRED   257

III. AND OF TIME AND ETERNITY   268

IV. AND OF THE LOVE OF MAN AND THE LOVE OF GOD   273

V. 'NO CONTINUING CITY'   280

INDEX   289

AND THE LIFE EVERLASTING

Chapter I
CONTEMPORARY QUESTIONINGS

I

AMONG the very earliest pictures my memory provides is one which, though I see it but dimly, has come back to me again and again during the preparation of the following pages. I am sitting on my father's knee in the day-nursery of a manse in the Scottish Highlands, contentedly gazing into the fire which burns brightly on the hearth. My father asks me what is the chief end of man and I reply, with perfect readiness, that man's chief end is to glorify God and to enjoy Him for ever. This is, of course, the first question and answer of that Shorter Catechism which, having been agreed upon a few years previously by a notable body of divines assembled at Westminster, was prescribed by the General Assembly of the Kirk of Scotland at its meeting in Edinburgh in July 1648, as a 'Directory for catechizing such as are of weaker capacity'. My own infant capacity must have been very weak indeed, for 'chiefend' was to me a single word, and a word whose precise meaning was beyond my imagining. But I did grasp, I think, even then, something of the general teaching that was meant to be conveyed, and I grew up understanding and believing that only in the everlasting enjoyment of God's presence could my life ever reach its proper and divinely appointed fulfilment.

Such a belief is, I need not say, an entirely essential element in the Christian religion that has been known to history these nineteen hundred years. It was by no accident that the Westminster divines put the conception of eternal life into the first response that was to be demanded from their lisping catechumens; for it is one of those underlying presuppositions of Christian teaching that colour and determine almost everything that follows. It would not indeed, I believe, be true to say that nothing at all would be left of the Christian system if eternal life were denied; but what would be left would certainly not be Christianity. How much, for example, would remain of the great classics of Christian literature—of the *Imitatio* or the *Divina Commedia*, of *Paradise Lost* or *The Pilgrim's Progress*—if we were to take away from them all mention or implication of eternity in the soul's relations with God? From the beginning the Faith has been one with the Hope.

Yet it is impossible to disguise the fact that in our own time we are confronted with a certain failure of belief in regard to eternal life. Our forefathers, a hundred or five hundred or fifteen hundred years ago, habitually regarded their threescore years and ten as but a prelude to something immeasurably larger and grander. In proportion as they took serious thought about their lives at all, they envisaged them in the vast setting of a 'world without end'. It was around this eternal world that all their hopes and fears revolved, and the relation of their doings here to their destiny hereafter was their constant preoccupation. But nowadays we are confronted in many quarters with an outlook of quite a different kind, an outlook narrowly bounded by the limits of our present earthly and bodily existence and from which the hope and the fear of immortality have alike disappeared. It is the prevalence of this outlook that has suggested the writing of these chapters, which will therefore be devoted to an inquiry into the nature and grounds of the Christian hope of eternal life.

Let me, however, try to characterize somewhat more definitely the outlook of which I have spoken. At first sight it may seem to admit of very simple characterization, as no more than a frank facing of the fact (here taken to be a fact) that there is no real evidence of the survival of the soul after the death of the body, or even (as others would have it) of the still more damaging fact that there is real evidence against such survival. That these opinions have much to do with the fading out of the conception of eternal life from the minds of many of our contemporaries there can be no possible doubt, and hence we must be closely concerned with them in what is to follow. But it would be the greatest possible mistake to regard this as the whole of the story. What has happened is certainly not merely that a body of evidence which to our fathers seemed conclusive has to our contemporaries come to seem insufficient. The change is not merely, and perhaps it is not even chiefly, a change of intellectual persuasion; it is also a change of emotional and practical orientation. It is not merely a change in the fortunes of debate, it is a change in the direction of living interest, a change of temper and of mood. 'The difficulty about religion at the present day', writes the late T. E. Hulme, 'is not so much the difficulty of believing the statements it makes about the nature of the world, as the difficulty of understanding *how if true* these statements can be satisfactory.'[1] How far the changed mood has affected the weighing of the evidence, and how far the altered balance of evidence has given rise to the new mood, is a delicate question. But obser-

[1] *Speculations* (1924), p. 32.

vation and experience have at least convinced me that any mere argument aimed at the establishment of a continued existence after death is little likely of itself to meet the present need. 'Neither will they be persuaded, if one rise from the dead'—the words are literally true of many men to-day, if the persuasion in question be anything like the Christian hope; and this is natural enough, because, as we shall soon have occasion to see, that hope has always been in something much more than mere continued existence and has never claimed to rest on such evidence as is here suggested. And it is at least possible that if only we could share our forefathers' attitude towards the *question*, we should be much nearer than we are to returning their *answer*.

The new mood of which I am speaking may be most summarily described as a revolt against the other-worldliness of the traditional outlook. There is nowadays among us a greater measure of satisfaction than there was formerly with the possibilities and promises of the present life as bounded by the decay and death of the body and the general conditions of earthly existence. Not only has the belief in the eternal world failed, but the need felt for the belief has likewise failed. It is as if the present-day experience of living did not give rise to the same urgent demand for a further and heavenly completion as did the experience of earlier ages. We belong to a time which, as Professor Tillich of Frankfurt put it in his admirable survey of the present religious situation, 'has no symbols left to it in which Time is made to point beyond itself'.[1] The prevalence of this mood among our young men and women is particularly striking. I have myself heard many

[1] *Die religiöse Lage der Gegenwart* (1926), p. 25.

a young man go so far as to say, 'I have no desire for immortality. I do not want eternal life.' The question whether immortality is possible has long been familiar to us, but it must be admitted that the question 'Is immortality desirable?' comes as something of a surprise. I have heard others vary the sentiment a little and say rather, 'Eternal life does not *interest* me. My concern is with the life I know, and I cannot persuade myself to take an interest in an unknown future.' While some have varied it again and said, 'It is *morbid* to think about death and what comes after death. There was something radically unhealthy about out forefathers' concentration on the prospect of another world. The only healthy temper is one which is resolved to make the best of our present passing day, looking forward not to a new dawn in another kind of world but to an improved condition of the present world, in which our children and our children's children will have part after we ourselves have gone out into the dark.'

Such sentiments as these are no doubt of an extreme kind, and the number of those who share them is perhaps not enormous; yet I think it will be agreed that they represent only the furthest limit of a tendency that has made itself very widely, and increasingly, felt among us during the last and the present generation. Here is what one observer, Professor Clement Webb, wrote a dozen years ago: 'It must be allowed that there is a very large and perhaps an increasing proportion of thoughtful people to whom the prospect of a continuance of a personal life beyond the grave, which to a former generation it seemed the chief recommendation of the Christian religion that it set in a clearer light than other creeds, does not possess its old attraction. Not only are they dissatisfied with the evidence offered in its behalf; it is, if I may so put it, quite out of the picture which they have formed of the plan of the universe and of human existence. What charm it may be made to wear in fancy has for them as little influence upon their serious concerns as the glamour of a fairy-tale, which we may take pleasure in reading, yet about which it scarcely occurs to us even to ask whether we wish that it could be true, still less whether we could believe that it was so.' Professor Webb goes on to confess frankly (and how many of us will find it necessary to make a similar confession!) that this drift of opinion is to some extent reflected in his own sentiments. 'My imagination', he writes, 'is not easily persuaded to reach forward into a world so different from this as must be any reserved for us after death; it is rather repelled than attracted by the phraseology, so familiar to us in our religious literature, which expresses exultation in the expected catastrophe and overthrow of the present order of nature.'[1]

It can hardly be denied, then, that within the last half-century a notable share of men's attention, in these Western lands, has been diverted from the future to the present life. Even in quarters where the fact of immortality has remained unquestioned, the interest in the fact has lessened. Even where the existence of a future state has been regarded as a matter of course, there has been far less wistful brooding about its nature and far less eager looking forward to its joys. Even where hope has retained a place with faith and love in the trinity of Christian graces, its relative prominence has been greatly diminished. In a word, men's belief in another world has come, of late years, to have much less effect on their atti-

---

[1] *Divine Personality and Human Life* (1920), p. 254 f.

tude towards the present world, and their demeanour in it, than was formerly the case. Another life—yes; but 'strangers and pilgrims' in the life that now is—we do not like that quite so well. The next life as a fulfilment—certainly; but this one as only a prelude, a preparation, a time of training—that is not nearly so welcome. Death as the door to another room —we agree; but death as the end of the trial and the beginning of the judgement—that, increasingly, has become unfamiliar ground.

II

I have spoken of this change as having accomplished itself within the last fifty years. But the ultimate roots of it are to be sought much deeper down in the soil of Western thought than the thin topmost layer which has so recently been contributed. To reach them we must burrow through the thought-deposits of at least five hundred years until we find ourselves in the intellectual stratum of the Renaissance.

The Renaissance was above all a rediscovery of the engrossing character of certain purely secular and earthly human interests. Literature and classical lore, architecture and sculpture, painting and music, craftsmanship of every kind, science and invention and travel—these and the many other amenities of a cultured society had throughout the Christian ages been drawn into the service of religion, and they had also been indulged in for their own sake as providing harmless relaxation from the one serious business of life, which was of course the preparation of the soul for its eternal destiny. But now the tendency arose to find in these terrestrial occupations a quite serious importance of their own. There appeared what was for the Christian world a strange phenomenon—the spectacle of men gravely and eagerly devoting themselves to the pursuit of knowledge simply for the sake of knowing and to the pursuit of beauty simply for the sake of enjoyment. It was natural that such men should soon come to be known as 'the humanists'; for had they not added to the old Christian absorption in God a new absorption—in the secular and temporal life of man?

It must, however, be realized that in the period of the Renaissance itself the number of men who were affected by such an outlook was relatively very small indeed. And, moreover, even those who were most affected by it were far from thinking of themselves as having made any radical departure from the traditional outlook of the Church. A few, indeed, there were who declared themselves in more or less open rebellion, appearing as champions of a pre-Christian paganism. But the common state of mind among the humanists was a much more complicated one. It did not occur to them to dispute the accepted Christian teaching that while the whole earthly order of things is transient, there is another world which is eternal; and that one's standing in relation to that other world must in the last resort be the only thing that matters. They would have allowed that the claims of earth shrank into nothingness before the 'deserts of vast eternity' that stretched ahead. And yet they were keenly alive also to the dignity and authority, as well as to the irresistible charm and lure, of the secular interests; so that they were fain to claim that these were of some importance too.

Clearly a compromise of so inconsistent a kind could not long continue undisturbed. What happened was that with the passing of the centuries the humanists became more and more humanistic. The secular or cultural interests tended gradually to become all-absorbing, while the interests of eternity receded more and more into the background. Indeed the beginnings of such a deliberate *preference* of earthly to heavenly interests may be traced back, if not to the literature and philosophy, at least to the pictorial and plastic art, of the High Renaissance itself. It was one of the favourite historical generalizations of T. E. Hulme, from whose posthumous volume of *Speculations* I have already quoted and shall, I am sure, find myself impelled to quote more than once again, that a revolutionary change in human ideas never scores its first success by means of a direct frontal attack, but rather gets in its wedge in some outlying flank of our position where we are, so to speak, off our guard. And that, he says, is what happened at the Renaissance. When an attempted secularization of Christian *religion* or Christian *philosophy* would have been resented by all and sternly dealt with by the constituted authorities, the secularization of Christian *art* was far advanced before anybody realized what was happening. Indeed to this day we are slow to grasp the whole meaning of the change. Recently, for example, it was my good fortune to visit the exquisite little Chapel of the Arena at Padua, where in 1305 (or thereabouts) Giotto, being commissioned to decorate the walls with representations of the evangelic history, laid, as we are often told, the foundations of modern painting. Here at last is free-hand drawing come into its own. Here instead of the Byzantine gilt and azure are the bright natural colours, and instead of the stiff Byzantine symmetry the flowing natural lines, of homely human garments. Here for almost the first time are real men and women—not indeed as they could have been in Palestine thirteen centuries before, but as they were (townsfolk and *contadini*) in the Padua of that day. And I dutifully rejoiced, at Herr Baedeker's bidding, that art had at last been set free from restraining convention. Yet even my guide-books drew my attention to another aspect of the case. *The Italian Masters, a Survey and Guide*, by Mr. Horace Shipp, is a perfectly matter-of-fact little handbook, yet it told me that 'Giotto was the true humanist, and man in action interested him more than remote Deity or saints in glory'.[1] As we follow the grand succession of masters from that early fourteenth century until the middle of the sixteenth we find this transference of interest becoming ever bolder and more pronounced. The handbook sums it up by saying that 'Painting, which had taken two hundred and fifty years to come to earth from the golden Byzantine heavens, left the earth again in an ideal perfection of the human form, with the kingdom, the power and the glory of the world as its attributes'. The painters 'not only brought art from heaven to earth, but scaled heaven anew in the apotheosis of man'. 'The result was to remove the vortex of man's being from the future life to this.'[2]

Here, then, was a definite beginning of the revolt against other-worldliness, but only as concealed among the esoteric secrets of changing aesthetic styles. For any considerable revolt of an outspoken kind and in definite philosophical terms Europe had to wait until the late seventeenth and eighteenth centuries, when at last there appeared in England the important deistic or free-thinking movement, leading finally to

[1] p. 35.   [2] Ibid., pp. 76, 79, 77.

the *Aufklärung* in Germany, and in France to the writings of the *philosophes* and the ideas of the French Revolution.

The great philosopher of antiquity had defined wisdom or *philosophia* as 'a meditation upon death'; 'those who philosophize aright', he had said, 'study nothing but dying and being dead'.[1] But in the middle of the seventeenth century we find another philosopher, Spinoza, taking up these words and contradicting them. 'The free man', he writes, 'thinks of nothing less than of death; his wisdom is a meditation not upon death but upon life.'[2] The two contrasted sayings have often been quoted together as typifying the change that has taken place. Many more examples might be found, however. We might cite the pithy words of Thomas Fuller: 'To smell to a turf of fresh earth is wholesome for the body; no less are thoughts of mortality cordial to the soul.'[3] And we might place beside them some maxims of the eighteenth-century Vauvenargues: 'On ne peut juger de la vie par une plus fausse règle que la mort', and again, 'La pensée de la mort nous trompe, car elle nous fait oublier de vivre'.

Yet even in the eighteenth century the revolt manifested itself only within certain narrow limits. There can indeed be no doubt that the interest and attention of these rationalists had for the most part been shifted from the heavenly to the terrene stage. Yet to hardly one of them did it occur that they could dispense with the thought of heaven altogether. It is a very noteworthy circumstance that the doctrine of a future life was not only one of the few traditional Christian doctrines which they never dreamed of doubting, but was even one of

---

[1] Plato, *Phaedo*, 64.   [2] *Ethica*, iv. 67.

[3] The passage will be found in Charles Lamb's *Specimens from the Writings of Fuller*.

the central dogmas of their own dissenting creed. It is one of the five 'truly catholic truths' which the 'father of deism', Lord Herbert, held to be instinctive in every rational creature, and in this opinion the later writers, with hardly an exception, are found cordially concurring. The traditional Christian teaching about the future is indeed reduced to its barest possible terms, being not only stripped of all its vivid detail, but suffering also the loss of the most truly religious (not to say mystical) aspects of its significance. But that there *was* a future life in which rewards and punishments would be meted out for the virtues and vices of this present life was, in the eighteenth century, as firmly believed by the most extreme rationalists as by the most orthodox churchmen.[1] Their interest was indeed in the affairs of this present life, but they could not see how even these could be successfully conducted, if no reward were provided for obscure virtue and no punishment for secret sin. Moreover, it must be remembered that the number of men affected by such free-thought was still very small, and that the open profession of its tenets involved always a definite break with the Christian Church.

If these, then, are the original seeds of our current outlook, it will be realized at once how different is the final fruit. It is perhaps the least part of this difference that there are now many among us who deny the fact of immortality outright. More significant is the fact that the new hither-worldly temper has nowadays spread beyond the few bespectacled pundits to great masses of the people. And possibly most significant of all is its spread—or at the very least the weakening of the

[1] 'They dismantled heaven, somewhat prematurely it seems, since they retained their faith in the immortality of the soul.'—C. L. Becker, *The Heavenly City of the Eighteenth-Century Philosophers* (New Haven and London, 1932), p. 31.

opposite temper of other-worldliness—within the Christian Church itself. How remarkably has our preaching changed in this respect since the nineteenth century was young! How it has changed even within our own memory! I will not ask how often during the last twenty-five years you and I have listened to an old-style warning against the flames of hell. I will not even ask how many sermons have been preached in our hearing about a future day of reckoning when men shall reap according as they have sown. It will be enough to ask how many preachers, during these years, have dwelt on the joys of the heavenly rest with anything like the old ardent love and impatient longing, or have spoken of the world that now is as a place of sojourn and pilgrimage.

In saying all this I am not unaware that quite recently there have been many signs of a turning of the tide in a contrary direction. There can be little doubt that, if we have regard to the leaders of thought both within and without the churches, it is not in the years since the Great War, but rather in the years immediately preceding it, that the receding tide of Christian other-worldliness reached its lowest ebb. That great cataclysm undoubtedly came as a rude shock to many jerry-built philosophies of life, and to none more than to those which had founded exaggerated hopes on the promise of the present world. A very striking proportion of the philosophical and religious writings which have recently attracted the most widespread attention in the leading European languages —and certainly a majority of the books I have myself found most thought-provoking—have been in one way or another symptomatic of this reaction. (And to this reaction what I now write will no doubt be put down as belonging.) Nevertheless it cannot be claimed that its influence has as yet been in any way decisive. One reason for this is that it has frequently made its appearance in far too extreme a form, making no real allowance for the elements of truth that were contained in the previous movement. It is hardly thinkable that our new age should ever return to just the old way of thinking about future rewards and punishments; yet some of our recent monitors come very near to making such a demand, and because they ask so much many refuse to give them any ear at all. There are those whom strong medicine would benefit, but who leave it untouched because they know it to be over-strong. Another important circumstance is that the force of the reaction seems to have varied directly with the extent to which the shock of the War was actually felt. Thus it has, up to the present, been least powerful in America and most powerful in Germany. Finally, we must remember that even when among the leaders of thought a movement seems almost to have accomplished itself, the rank and file of us may still be lingering a long way behind; and with the rank and file the great body of our youth, because, as Mr. T. S. Eliot has recently reminded us, 'youth is from one point of view merely a symptom of the results of what the middle-aged have been thinking and saying'.[1] Moreover, our individual souls are so complex, and the multitude of our thoughts within us so great, that it may well happen that in respect of one part of us we are on the crest of the new wave while in respect of another part we are still splashing uncertainly in the trough of the last one. Every way, then, it will be richly worth our while to think what reply we can make to the young man who tells us that he is not interested in a life after death.

[1] *Thoughts after Lambeth* (1931), p. 8.

CHAPTER II

THE PROPER CLAIMS OF EARTH

I

THE first part of our reply must be to acknowledge the important elements of truth for which the protest stands and the measure of right feeling that lies behind it. I can remember how, as a youth, I used to rebel against certain verses and phrases in the hymns we sang about the Christian hope. Much of this rebellion was, I am now sure, due to my own unwisdom and inexperience, and to this aspect of the matter I shall presently be forced to recur; but something of it was due also to an instinctive perception of truth which I am as little willing to surrender now as I was then. One familiar hymn had it that

> Here in the body pent
> Absent from Him I roam,
> Yet nightly pitch my moving tent
> A day's march nearer home.

But I remember protesting that the word 'pent' was a slander on the body, which was much more and better than a prison, and that the words 'absent from Him' were a slander on this present life, in which the presence of God might in very real measure be enjoyed. I still do not think that I was entirely wrong in these protestations, and it is my sincere hope that none of the disillusionments and repentances of more advanced age will ever make me disloyal to these generous

17

intuitions of boyhood. There was another hymn which began:

> I'm but a stranger here,
> Heaven is my home;
> Earth is a desert drear,
> Heaven is my home.

And again I felt that something noble and beautiful was being defamed. Earth a dreary desert—yes, I know better now than I did then how often and for how many people it can be just that. But I am as sure now as I was then that this is not the whole of the truth about it. It is also a garden of delights. It is also a field for heroes. And if no view of it can be true which forgets its gall and its weariness, neither can any be true which forgets its laughter and its glory.

The writer of a good American novel makes the youthful hero, whose name is Wait-Still-on-the-Lord Lowe, speak as follows:

'And when the fire-red sun came up, the mist streaked out and then rolled up in round bundles out of the hollows, and the smell of the earth was good. And Waits stood up and looked upon his home-place, and said: "Being a man is bound to dwell in one corner of the earth, this is most surely the likeliest. Even had I the run of the stars, I'd come full circle to this place where I started. Preachers all time talk about a better land—but great for ever! what better place could a person crave but this! Truly my home-place is a desirous place to be in!" '[1]

I think we must allow, then, that our Christian other-worldliness, before it can successfully be defended against the modern attack, must first be purged of certain elements that

---

[1] Maristan Chapman, *The Happy Mountain*, p. 107.

have very frequently been associated with it in the past. It is indeed not difficult to show that some of the elements in question are foreign intruders which form no part of the proper and native substance of the Christian gospel. The doctrine that the body is a prison in which we are pent is not Christian but pagan; it came not from Palestine but from Greece, and not from the old Greece of Homer and the Olympic gods but from the later Orphic cults. Σῶμα σῆμα, 'the body a tomb'—such was the celebrated pun in which the Orphic teaching was summed up. In a later chapter we shall have to notice very carefully how the Orphic worshipper looked upon his bodily frame as the great hindrance to the enjoyment of God's presence and of eternal life, so that the longing for release from the body was at the very centre of his hope of immortality. This conception had long and potent influence in Western thought, which it reached mainly through the Platonists. 'Plotinus'—so runs the first sentence of Porphyry's contemporary *Life* of the great Neoplatonist—'seemed ashamed of being in the body.' And at times this conception became so intimately fused with the Christian rule of faith and life that the effort to think them apart may appear to some an ungrateful task. But the true and original Christian doctrine undoubtedly was that the body is not a tomb but a temple. 'What? Know ye not that your body is the temple of the Holy Ghost?'[1]—it was to a Greek address that St. Paul dispatched these warning words. Likewise also the original Christian hope was emphatically not a hope of release from embodiment as such, but rather a hope of the revivification of the whole man, soul and body, unto life eternal. The ascetic

[1] 1 Cor. vi. 19.

doctrine that the body and the things of the body were as such evil could never really flourish unchecked among those who believed in the resurrection of the body to everlasting glory.

In the letters written by St. Paul to the Christian churches in Greece we have the opportunity of observing just how much the Greek and Christian views have in common and just where they diverge, and also of studying the tension between the two. To this also we shall be recurring in a later chapter, so that all we need do at present is to set down the broad outline of the case. There is no doubt that St. Paul longs very ardently for release from such bodily conditions as are at present familiar to us. 'I know', he exclaims in his Second Letter to the church at Corinth, 'that while I am at home in the body I am absent from my home with the Lord, having to depend on faith in Him rather than on seeing Him.'[1] It was here, very evidently, that the author of one of the hymns I quoted found his line, 'Absent from Him I roam'. The word (τὸ σκῆνος) by which St. Paul designates his body in the context of this passage literally means tent or booth. It was originally an Orphic term, being connected with the representation of human life as a fair (πανήγυρις)[2]; but by St. Paul's time it was a familiar enough way of referring to the body, so that it is doubtful how much Greek influence we should here find to be present in his thought. He may indeed seem to resemble the Orphics in his keen sense of the disabilities imposed on him by his bodily weaknesses and imperfections and in his longing to be rid of them. In the previous chapter he has just been telling the Corinthians that his 'outer

[1] 2 Cor. v. 6–7.
[2] See J. Burnet, *Greek Philosophy, Thales to Plato*, p. 200 n.

man' is all but worn out and that this 'affliction of the present moment' has made him look forward all the more keenly to the 'surpassing and eternal weight of glory' which awaits him beyond the veil. Yet how natural such a sentiment is after all, and how often have we ourselves seen our own contemporaries moved to it by experiences of suffering and weakness similar to the Apostle's! But where St. Paul definitely parts company with the Orphic teaching is in the pains he always takes to make it clear that it is only from the present conditions of bodily existence that he seeks release and not from embodiment of every kind. 'All flesh is not the same flesh', he had explained to this same Greek church in his former letter; 'but there is one flesh of men, and another flesh of beasts, and another flesh of birds, and another of fishes. . . . So also is the resurrection of the dead. . . . If there is an animate body, there is also a spiritual body.'[1] And now we find him arguing that his longing is not really a longing to be done with the earthly body—such as dwellers in the Greek atmosphere of Corinth might be too ready to suppose it—but rather a longing to be blessed with a heavenly one. 'I groan within this tent of mine, being heavily burdened; not that I long to put this tent off, but to put on the other over it, so that my mortality may be swallowed up in life.'[2] And then he concludes by reminding himself and his readers that though in this life he must be content with faith rather than vision, yet

[1] 1 Cor. xv. 39–44.
[2] 2 Cor. v. 4. Cf. H. A. A. Kennedy, *St. Paul's Conceptions of the Last Things*, p. 270: 'But then, perhaps struck by the conception of the future life which is most familiar to his friends at Corinth, he goes on to affirm: "It is not merely to get rid of the carnal, material body we long; it is not for a condition of spiritual nakedness, a disembodied existence of the spirit: our hope, our glory is in the new spiritual organism which we look forward to possessing." '

he can serve God in this life as truly as in the next; that it is on his service here that his destiny there depends; and that accordingly his *governing* desire must be, not for a change of state, but for grace to do God's will in whatever state God wills him to be. 'Wherefore I make it my ambition, whether continuing in the body or leaving it, to be well-pleasing to Him; for we must all appear without disguise before Christ's judgement-seat, that every one may receive according to what he has done with his body, whether good or bad.'[1] Again and again in the course of his other correspondence we find the Apostle coming back to this same position as the practical issue of his argument. Thus in the Epistle to the Philippians: 'My earnest desire and hope is that I may never have cause for shame, but that, now as always, Christ may be glorified in my body through my utter boldness of speech, either by my life or by my death. For with me to live is Christ and to die is gain. But if I am to live on in the flesh, that means fruitful work for me, so that I cannot tell which to choose. I am in a dilemma; my strong desire being to depart and be with Christ, for that is best by far; but for you it is more necessary that I should still remain in the flesh. Of that I am convinced, and so I know that I shall remain and go on serving you all, promoting your progress and your joy in the faith.'[2] And again in Romans: 'If we live, we live unto the Lord; and if we die, we die unto the Lord: whether therefore we live or die, we are the Lord's.'[3]

With such a conclusion we can indeed have no quarrel. The Apostle here provides us with as wise and temperate a rule for the settlement of the relative claims of time and

[1] 2 Cor. v. 9–10.   [2] Phil. i. 20–5.   [3] Rom. xiv. 8.

eternity as we are ever likely to possess. For, however tragic may be his sense of the present life and however keen may be his desire for the more glorious fulfilment of the next, yet in the end he stands firm on the principle that our immediate business can only be to serve and glorify God *where we now are*, throwing our whole heart and energy into the manning of the station to which it has now pleased Him, for however short or long a time, to appoint us. Such surely is the principle which must be set up as a limit to all one-sided other-worldlinesses. If our hope of a fuller life beyond is to be recognized as a fine and manly thing, it must never lead us to be unjust to the values and the demands of the life that now is. It must never lessen our interest in the present life, or make us feel it to be less worth living, or tempt us to hurry through with it. It must never have the effect of taking our minds off our present tasks, so that they shall be done less thoroughly and well; rather should it lead to their *more* thorough and conscientious performance. And lastly, it must never tempt us to think even for a moment that what particular thing we do does not greatly matter, that our life in time is not worth improving, or our lot bettering, or our health mending, or this whole earthly order of things worth patching up and bringing nearer to heart's desire.

But can we now claim that St. Paul, and can we claim that the Christian saints who came after him, really succeeded in avoiding such an attitude of mind? The modern rebellion against Christian other-worldliness is intimately associated with the feeling that in fact they did not so succeed—and with the fear that none will ever do so who share their other-worldly hope.

The indictment is twofold. First, it is charged that the glories of heaven have always blinded the eyes of those that envisioned them to the more intimate glories of earth. Second, it is charged that those whose real hopes are in eternity have always been lacking in zeal for progress in time. The former of these results is often loosely labelled 'puritanism' and the latter 'quietism'. I think there are few of us to-day who have not some degree of sympathy with the motive of this indictment and some feeling also that it is partly justified.

II

The former charge is delicately represented in the gentle rebuke administered by the dying Thoreau to the friend who sought to turn his mind to the things of eternity: 'One world at a time, brother; one world at a time!' That is to say, Thoreau found the interests of the present life to possess a quite autonomous and independent value of their own. This, as we have seen, is the true humanistic temper, and it is a temper by which no modern man is entirely unaffected. We are all children of the Renaissance to this extent at least, that however conscious we may be of the errors and limitations of post-Renaissance humanism, none of us is really willing to return to the *status quo ante*. The 'ages of faith', however glorious their achievements, suffered from a certain narrowness of outlook which we are anxious to avoid for our modern selves. Even in the New Testament documents, and in the lives of the New Testament saints, we miss something which we have learned to treasure very dearly—the conscious love of nature, the delight in art, the pursuit of learning, the scientific spirit. As we travel down the Christian centuries, we find many of these things being given larger place in response to inspiration coming from Greek and Roman sources. But never until after the Renaissance are they given such place as really satisfies us; so that with the dawning of the modern era we are conscious of a real liberation of spirit. Which of us would now be prepared to stand with anything like entire sympathy beside Savonarola as he makes holocaust of 'the vanities' on the Piazza della Signoria in Florence?

The outlook to which Savonarola was anxious to have Italy revert is well expressed by the fourteenth-century Henry Suso when he writes that: 'As much as one small drop counts in the vast depths of the ocean, just so much can all that this world is able to afford, contribute to the fulfilment of thy desires.'[1] The life of earth was of importance only as a preparation for eternity, and the only interest and occupation of eternity was the worship of God. Art and science, therefore, except as they had occasional instrumental value in leading men's thoughts to higher things, were merely *toys*—innocent diversions from the one appallingly serious business of life. There is a verse in one of Isaac Watts's well-known hymns which runs:

> See how we grovel here below
> Fond of these earthly toys.
> Our souls, how heavily they go,
> To reach eternal joys.

Now it is precisely to this characterization of his earthly pre-occupations as toys that the modern man so strenuously objects. Michelangelo will not have it that his sculptures are toys, nor Raphael his canvases, nor Ghiberti his brasses. Keats will not have it that his poems are toys, nor Gibbon his

[1] *Little Book of Eternal Wisdom*, Part I, ch. xi.

histories, nor Ibsen his plays. Darwin will not have it that his biology is a toy, nor Tylor his anthropology, nor Einstein his physics. The scientist *knows* that he does well to be seriously engrossed in his specimens, and the historian in his facts, and the artist in his forms and colours. Nor, on the other hand, can our demand be satisfied by merely allowing some degree of instrumental value to these secular preoccupations. Keats will not have it that his poetry is of serious importance, or Darwin his science, only in so far as these can be made directly ancillary to moral and religious ends. 'Not to delight in any created thing but for Thy sake'—such was the grace with which Thomas à Kempis besought God to anoint him; because, as he put it, 'all human glory, all temporal honour, all worldly highness, compared to Thine eternal glory is vanity and folly'.[1] And as to temporal honours and worldly highnesses this will be allowed to be true. But there are some things that lie *between* the pursuit of wealth and fame and power on the one hand and the worship of God on the other —there is the love of truth, there is the thirst for knowledge, there is the nature-lover's passion, there is the musician's rapture, there is the antiquary's zeal; and it is strongly felt that these middle things must in some real sense be allowed to be a law unto themselves. Science can never flourish while it remains the mere handmaid of religion; and certainly it never *did* flourish within Christendom until the Renaissance released it from its traditional ancillary position. The astronomer, the physicist, the geologist, the biologist, and the anthropologist must not always be looking aside to watch the moral effect of their results upon men's minds, still less look-

[1] Bk. iii. 40

ing over their shoulders to see what the priests will say to them. Similarly, the historian must be allowed to pursue his inquiries to their proper end without stopping at every point to ask whether his results are spiritually edifying, still less whether they are in conformity with sacred writ—as was prior to the Renaissance too much the fashion. And as for the artist —shall we say that his motto must now be 'art for art's sake'? Some will say so unhesitatingly, and the rest will at least agree that it must not be 'art with a moral' or 'sacred art' alone.

To this general protest I believe it is quite impossible to deny an important measure of validity. The liberation of science, of history, and of the arts from their too complete and servile subordination to the ends of an other-worldly religion has indeed been carried nowadays to anarchical extremes, thereby giving rise to even more disastrous errors of an opposite kind; and with these errors we must deal faithfully towards the conclusion of our study. But that some liberation was required we must surely be ready to acknowledge; and it is with this acknowledgement alone that we are now concerned. Let it be granted, then, that our Christian other-worldliness cannot be defended against the humanist attack until, by a more successful integration of secular and religious interests than has often characterized it in the past, it has ceased to allow the greater glories of heaven to blind its eyes to the lesser glories of earth.

III

The second charge—that those whose hopes are in eternity must always be lacking in zeal for earthly progress and betterment—must be considered even more carefully. For it is something very precious to us moderns that is here being threatened. Not indeed to quite all of us: Mr. Norman Douglas's recently published autobiography[1] has been described as revealing 'a man tolerant of almost every failing in others but the desire to improve the world'.[2] But such defiance of the prevailing climate of opinion is comparatively rare. There can be no doubt that the idea of progress is the most representative concept of the whole modern era. It is an idea which has taken many forms, and at a later stage of our discussion we may have occasion to see how disastrously misleading some forms of it have turned out to be. But there is at least one form in which nearly all of us will allow that it has made a lasting contribution to the outlook of our race. We may perhaps distinguish four main forms which the idea has assumed—the *dogma* that progress is a natural law necessarily governing all historical change, the *opinion* that progress has as a matter of fact taken place, the *faith* that progress is possible, and the *resolve* that progress shall be made. The four forms of the idea are obviously not quite independent of each other—one cannot, for instance, resolve to progress unless one believes that progress is possible; but it is with the fourth form, the resolve to progress, that we are here primarily concerned.

Nothing else has been so characteristic of our modern period as the determination that this world in which we live shall be made a better place to live in; that we will be wiser than our fathers were and our children wiser than we; that knowledge shall, with every year that passes, 'grow from more to

[1] *Looking Back* (1933).
[2] *Times Literary Supplement* (London, 4 May 1933, p. 308).

more'; that our human control of our planetary environment shall gradually be increased; that each succeeding generation shall have the promise of a happier and freer existence than the generation going out; that 'old shapes of foul disease' shall more and more be conquered and life be made both happier and longer; and last, but very far from least, that we will better learn how to live with one another in peace and amity, in *liberté*, *égalité*, *fraternité*, 'with sweeter manners, purer laws', so that poverty and oppression and injustice and 'the feud of rich and poor' may at last for ever disappear. I have quoted these phrases from Lord Tennyson, and there has been nobody who was more typically the prophet of this new outlook than was he. There are other equally well-known words of his which might almost be written into its charter:

> Forward, forward let us range,
> Let the great world spin for ever down the ringing grooves of change.

> Through the shadow of the globe we sweep into the younger day:
> Better fifty years of Europe than a cycle of Cathay.[1]

And now what will be claimed by the apostles of modernity is that it was precisely the weakening of the old absorption in eternity that heralded the dawn of this new era of hope and of resolve.

I believe the claim to be capable of large justification. It cannot, I believe, be successfully denied that in those periods and among those groups in which the apocalyptic expectation of 'a new Jerusalem which cometh down out of heaven

---

[1] *Locksley Hall.* The other phrases are from *In Memoriam*, cvi.

from God' has been most impatient and all-engrossing, there has been less eagerness to complete the building of Jerusalem (according to the phrase of a much later amateur of apocalypse) 'in England's green and pleasant land'. It was not that a different opinion then prevailed as to what things were ultimately desirable; it was simply that the hope of attaining them was renounced for the present life, being postponed to the life to come. It was perfectly well understood that disease and squalor and poverty and oppression and class-distinctions could have no place in a perfect society, and they were accordingly allowed no place in the heavenly Jerusalem. At death all social distinctions disappeared, and in heaven every blessing of health and prosperity would be enjoyed. But it was generally understood also that what would be evils in the eternal order were a necessary part and parcel of our appointed lot during our brief earthly pilgrimage. And where men's minds were preoccupied not only with the brevity of each individual life but with the imminent collapse of human history as a whole, there seemed to be a further reason for letting things remain as they were. This may be illustrated even from the New Testament. In reading certain of its pages we undoubtedly have the feeling that such fervour for the redress of social wrong as we should naturally expect to be one outcome of our Lord's mission to the lost sheep of His native land, and of St. Paul's keen sense of human brotherhood in Christ, is suffering some real inhibition from the other belief that the whole earthly order of things is so very near its end as to be hardly worth troubling to set right. 'The time is short', and therefore 'every man should remain in the condition of life in which he was when he was called. If you were a slave when you were called, do not let that worry you; though if an opportunity of securing your freedom arises, you had better take advantage of it.'[1] These are the words of St. Paul, and there is in them a degree of complacency with existing social conditions which cannot, I am sure, be altogether explained apart from the influence of the apocalyptic expectation. From the history of a slightly later period many more examples might be given, but one will suffice. The second-century author of the *Second Epistle of Clement* writes as follows:

'This age and the future are two enemies. . . . We cannot therefore be friends of the two, but must bid farewell to the one and hold companionship with the other. Let us consider that it is better to hate the things which are here, because they are mean and for a short time and perishable, and to love the things which are there, for they are good and imperishable.'[2]

Since when has this attitude of complacency towards existing earthly conditions begun to yield to another temper of an opposite kind? The answer, it must be allowed, stands out clearly enough. It is since the close of what are commonly known as 'the ages of faith', and in close causal connexion with the fact of their coming to an end, that there has for the first time appeared throughout Christendom a determined movement for the reorganization of our earthly society according to the principles of Christian brotherhood. It was as the old preoccupation with eternity began to disappear and the traditional eschatological picture—that vast triptych of hell, purgatory, and paradise—to lose its power over the imagina-

---

[1] 1 Cor. vii. 29, 20-1.
[2] § 6. Lightfoot's translation.

tion, that the cry for social reform was first clearly heard in the land. We praise the great thirteenth century and we do so rightly, but we cannot afford to forget the darker side of its life. In his book on *The Universities of Europe in the Middle Ages* the late Dean Rashdall suggested that 'from an evening tour to some of the worst dens and alleys of Seven Dials and the Ratcliffe Highway, before the institution [in London] of the Metropolitan Police, there might have been gathered some faint conception of what life in a medieval university town must have been like, say at the end of the thirteenth century.' But soon after the Renaissance a change began to manifest itself. 'It is in fact,' writes M. Bergson in his last book, 'since the fifteenth or sixteenth century that men have seemed to aspire after an enlargement of the material conditions of life.'[1] And with the intervening centuries this aspiration has grown rapidly both in intensity and in range. The desire for political freedom, the movement towards the emancipation of the disinherited classes, the abolition of slavery, the advent of universal education, the gradual emancipation of womanhood and, as one born out of due season, the movement to make an end of war—these are all typical products of our modern period and are definitely associated with the modern shifting of the imagination from the eternal to the

[1] The passage is perhaps worth quoting in full: 'Par le fait, c'est à partir du quinzième ou du seizième siècle que les hommes semblent aspirer à un élargissement de la vie matérielle. Pendant tout le moyen âge un idéal d'ascétisme avait prédominé. Inutile de rappeler les exagérations auxquelles il avait conduit; déjà il y avait eu frénésie: On dira que cet ascétisme fut le fait d'un petit nombre, et l'on aura raison. Mais de même que le mysticisme, privilège de quelques-uns, fut vulgarisé par la religion, ainsi l'ascétisme concentré, qui fut sans doute exceptionnel, se dilua pour le commun des hommes en une indifférence générale aux conditions de l'existence quotidienne.'—*Les deux sources de la morale et de la religion* (1932), p. 322 f.

temporal prospect. Poverty was once a grace; it has now become a disgrace—a disgrace not to the poor themselves but to the social order which excludes them from that earthly portion which is the proper right of all.

> The Lady Poverty was fair;
> But she has lost her looks of late . . .
>
> . . . Oh, is this she
> Whom Francis met, whose step was free,
> Who with Obedience carolled hymns,
> In Umbria walked with Chastity?[1]

Once the under-privileged were taught that, so far as this present life was concerned, they must acquiesce in their condition, and that their reward would be in heaven; whereas now we are earnestly endeavouring to rouse them from such acquiescence and are teaching them to work for an amelioration of their lot on earth.

A fact which those of us who are churchmen should never allow ourselves to forget is that the French Revolution, which is now almost generally regarded as having, in the sum, brought great benefit to mankind and as being a highly significant landmark in the history of modern social progress, was accompanied by as black and bitter and furious a hatred of the Christian Church (Voltaire's name for which was 'The Infamy') as has ever appeared in the world. The same National Convention which proclaimed the liberty, equality, and brotherhood of man also formally abolished the Christian religion, including the Christian calendar and the Christian day of rest—though indeed it was not long before the deist

[1] Alice Meynell.

Robespierre issued a decree which brought back into acknowledgement the existence of a Supreme Being and the immortality of the soul.

It was, however, in the socialist teaching of Karl Marx that
this line of revolt seemed finally to culminate. And the
Marxian teaching has now, after two generations of merely
academic development, been given legislative effect in Soviet
Russia. What we have here to deal with is the dogmatic and
excited persuasion that a more equitable social order can never
be introduced until all other-worldly gospels have ceased to
sway men's minds. So long as men's treasure is in heaven, so
long, it is taught, will they continue to be indifferent towards
earthly wrongs. So long as the concept of a better world re-
tains its theological meaning, so long will men fail to learn
its sociological meaning. Thus has the peace which is from
above become suspect in our time.

Many centuries before the beginning of the Christian era
the view had been put forward by certain Greek Sophists that
religion was an invention of the ruling classes with a view to
the deception and consequent subjugation of the people.
In the eighteenth century this theory had been resuscitated
by the English free-thinkers and attained considerable popularity within their ranks. Since the beginning of the nineteenth century it has generally been regarded as discredited,
it being realized that if there was any deception in the matter,
it must have been self-deception; if the rulers deceived the
people, that was only because they had first deceived themselves—so that there could be no question of deliberate invention. The Marxians have sometimes attempted to revive
this theory in all its eighteenth-century crudity, but on other

occasions they have rested content with the milder doctrine that religion is a consolatory self-deception practised by the people themselves in order to compensate for the wretchedness of their earthly lot. The Soviet Union seems to have accepted as the official symbol of its attitude the well-known words of Marx himself: 'Religion is the opium of the people.'[1] In one of Marx's letters dating from 1843 we have a somewhat fuller statement:

'The struggle against religion is . . . indirectly the struggle against that world whose spiritual aroma religion is. . . . The abolition of religion as the *illusory* happiness of the people is the demand for its *real* happiness. The demand to surrender illusions about its conditions is a demand to surrender the conditions which *need* illusions.'[2]

Marx's collaborator Engels adds something to this conception when he writes:

'Religion is nothing but the fantastic reflection in the heads of men of those earthly powers which rule over their daily life, a reflection in which earthly powers take on the form of unearthly ones.'[3]

And this is how Lenin puts it:

'Religion is one of the forms of spiritual oppression. . . . The helplessness of the exploited classes in their struggle with the exploiters just as inevitably generates faith in a better life beyond the grave as the helplessness of the savage in his struggle with nature produces faith in gods, devils, miracles, &c. To him who works and is poor all his life religion teaches passivity and patience in earthly life, consoling him with the hope of a heavenly

---

[1] *Zur Kritik der Hegelschen Rechtsphilosophie*, in Marx's *Nachlass*, vol. i, p. 385.
[2] Quoted and translated by S. Hook in *Journal of Philosophy*, vol. xxv, p. 115.
[3] *Anti-Dühring*, ad fin.

reward. To those who live on the labour of others religion teaches benevolence in earthly life, offering them a very cheap justification for all their exploiting existence and selling tickets to heavenly happiness at a reduced price.'[1]

If such statements are at their weakest when they are made to rest upon some hasty and hopelessly unhistorical guess as to the origin and intrinsic nature of religion, they must be taken much more seriously when they confine themselves to the charge that religion, no matter how it came into being, has in fact commonly tended to foster a wrong attitude of mind towards earthly affairs. It will perhaps be worth while to quote some words written by the English Marxian, Ernest Belfort Bax, as early as 1886. With the coming of Christianity into the Graeco-Roman world, he tells us, 'religion is henceforth separated from life, the *religious* sphere of *another* world is set over against the *irreligious* sphere of *this* world. Earth is drained of its ideal to feed Heaven.' And now:

'We daily see around us the result of sixteen hundred years of "otherworldliness" on character and conduct. Men and women upon whom the mere greed for gain palls are driven to the one ideal resource their education has given them or they can comprehend—the hope of a glorified immortality for themselves. Those only who know from bitter experience the smile of honest contempt with which such people greet the idea of the sacrifice of personal or class privileges, or anything else for a social object, can appreciate the depth to which the canker has eaten into their souls. Yet it would be unjust to say that these people are bad. They are religious and antisocial, just as there are many others irreligious and antisocial. In what sense Socialism is not religious will now be clear. It utterly despises the "other world" with all

[1] Quoted by William H. Chamberlin, *Soviet Russia: a Living Record and a History* (1930), p. 306.

its stage properties—that is, the present objects of religion. In what sense it is not irreligious will be also, I think, tolerably clear. It brings back religion from heaven to earth, which, as we have sought to show, was its original sphere. It looks beyond the present moment or the present individual life, though not, indeed, to another world, but to another and a higher social life in this world.'[1]

Such declarations as these ought, I am sure, to be very seriously pondered. The attitude to religion which they re-reveal, and which is so largely common to the French and Russian Revolutions, is indeed a tragically misguided one, and I hope that before the end of our study the essential weakness of it will have been made abundantly clear. But if we dismiss it contemptuously from our minds as being altogether beneath our notice we shall be making a grievous mistake. For there is something of truth contained in it and something of great importance which we may all learn from it. One day we may come to rejoice at the airing it is now receiving, while continuing to regret that it was aired in so extreme and even grotesque a form. It is not an entirely bad thing that Voltaire and Marx and Lenin have spoken as they did. They have opened our eyes to one dangerous aberration to which high spiritual religion has at many times been prone. They have shown us very clearly how its preoccupation with the eternal prospect has tended to issue in a regrettable acquiescence in preventable earthly evils. And my hope and belief is that from the present trial in which their words are involving it the Christian Church will emerge stronger and wiser than it has ever been before.

[1] *The Religion of Socialism* (1st ed., 1886; 7th ed., 1908), p. 51 f.

IV

Yet let us not be traitorous to the past by admitting too much. There are, more particularly, four points which require to be made in order to give balance to our discussion.

First, we must remind ourselves that it is only towards *exterior* evils that Christianity can possibly be held to have ever fostered a complacent attitude. The doctrine that this life is but a prelude to a life everlasting, while it may have done something to prevent men from mending the outward conditions of life, never had the smallest tendency to prevent them from *mending their own ways* but rather—and that most notoriously—tended in an exactly opposite direction. It has always been the Christian teaching that upon the use we make of our life here our destiny hereafter will depend, and it is clear that the result of such teaching must be to make men give not less but far more heed to their earthly walk and conversation. It was the testimony of a first-century writer that 'every man that hath this hope in Him purifieth himself'.[1] And hundreds of years earlier Plato had made Socrates say: 'I, then, Callicles, being persuaded of the truth of these doctrines, consider by what means I can present my soul to the Judge in the healthiest condition.'[2] The practical precept in which every New Testament expression of the apocalyptic expectation finally issues is not 'Dally on!'—that was left to the unbelieving Omar Khayyam—but 'Wake up!' 'The day of the Lord so cometh as a thief in the night'; 'wherefore', says St. Paul, 'let us not sleep like other men but be wakeful and sober.'[3] The critical importance of the present life was in-

[1] 1 John iii. 3. [2] *Gorgias*, 526 D. [3] 1 Thess. v. 1, 6.

deed the very fulcrum of the old evangelical appeal. 'Behold, now is the accepted time; behold, now is the day of salvation.' 'The night cometh, when no man can work.' Such are the texts which have served for centuries of other-worldly preaching. 'If thou seek rest in this life', we read in the *Imitation*, 'how wilt thou then attain to the rest everlasting?'[1] And it would be seriously unfair to find any *selfishness* in such a temper—as if it had been only in the salvation of *their own* souls that the Christian saints were interested. Whatever charge may be brought against the religion of our fathers, it can hardly be the lack of evangelic missionary zeal. The contrast with which we are concerned is not really a contrast between oneself and one's fellows, but a contrast between the things of the body and the things of the soul; and the best Christians were those who, being as little concerned for their own bodily comfort as they were for their neighbours', were also as much concerned about their neighbours' souls as they were about their own. It is unfortunately true that there were often many outwardly pious people who valued bodily comfort for themselves but were complacent towards its absence from the lives of others; but such an outlook must be laid to the account of a still unconquered worldliness rather than to that of the other-worldliness of the Christian religion. And as for St. Paul, it is surely clear enough that his persuasion of the imminence of eternity and his preoccupation with its interests led him not to any kind of bemused inaction but to as restless and campaigning a career as the whole of history has to show.

Second, we must keep it steadily in mind that while the

[1] Bk. iii. 35.

D

Christians of the early ages acquiesced far too readily in a political and social and economic order of things that involved the continued existence of poverty and oppression, yet the extent of the sympathy and succour which they were ready to extend to the poor and oppressed themselves is such as can call forth nothing but wonder and praise. Our Lord's own mission was inspired by no more unmistakable motive than by compassion for the poor, and in general for 'the lost sheep', the dispossessed fringe, of the society He knew, as well as for all who suffered from bodily weakness or disease. 'I was an hungered, and ye gave me meat: I was thirsty, and ye gave me drink: I was a stranger, and ye took me in; naked, and ye clothed me: I was sick, and ye visited me: I was in prison, and ye came unto me.' Anybody who is in doubt as to how far these words were actually taken as the charter of the Christian religion during its early days need only read the long chapter on 'The Gospel of Love and Charity' in Adolf von Harnack's *Expansion of Christianity*. The contrast here again is not between selfishness and unselfishness or between indifference and tender concern, but between reliance upon 'love and charity' on the one hand and reliance upon legislation on the other. Where we differ from our forefathers is certainly not in having kinder hearts, but in believing it possible to remodel the secular social order by the growth of Christian influence, and in holding it worth while thus to compel people to do by law what they are not yet Christians enough to do freely. No doubt behind this difference there lies the deeper difference of two contrasted philosophies such as are brought out by a recent writer when he says: 'Individual virtue . . . has not made too successful a hand at bringing about good conditions; so why shouldn't good conditions have a shot at bringing about individual virtue?'[1] It is a question, clearly, not of the relation of self to others but of the relation of the inward to the outward.

Nevertheless—and this is our third point—we must not speak as if the contrast with which we are here concerned were a contrast simply between the Christian philosophy of life and a new philosophy of life that is not Christian. The case is more complex than that. It is true that, in contrast to the characteristically Christian hope of reforming society by first reforming its individual members, the dream of being able to reform individuals by first reforming the social order to which they belong is characteristically Platonic. Yet the particular direction which we are nowadays desirous that our social reforms should take is most assuredly not Platonic but Christian. The form of the idea is Greek, but its filling is Christian. The reformer's head is Western, but his heart is Eastern. In this sense, then, our modern zeal for the abolition of poverty and oppression goes back as truly for its original inspiration to the redemptive passion that stirred the heart of Jesus as does the long earlier history of Christian charity towards the individual poor and oppressed. It may have been left to the modern period to agitate for the abolition of slavery as an institution, of pauperism as something that need always be with us, and of war as an acknowledged means of international settlement; but nobody can hold it an accident that such agitation, when it did come, made its first appearance within the borders of Christendom. Even here we are but

[1] The sentiment is put into the mouth of 'a young revolutionary' by Mr. Day Lewis in his contribution to *New Country*, edited by Michael Roberts (London, 1933).

following out the logic of the New Testament message, though (having taken the hint from the *Republic* and the *Laws*) we are following it to a conclusion which the New Testament writers never themselves drew. It is a fact well worth pondering that it was in an atmosphere of the most intense concentration upon the life everlasting that those very ideals of earthly brotherhood, which we have of late discovered to be patient of this further application, found their first clear and impassioned expression.

But a fourth point must be made, and another piece of history alluded to. We must on no account allow ourselves to suppose that the philosophy of acquiescence in outward ills first came into the world with the emergence of the immortal hope and that, before this hope began to be entertained, the ruling philosophy was one of rebellion. In the outlook of all the early human civilizations the two notes of resignation and rebellion are found balancing one another; but the former always seems to pull the greater weight, and in most of the great pagan systems of belief its dominance comes to be unquestioned. All the great religions of the Far East—of India and of China—are religions enjoining submission. And, in spite of the noble day-dreams of a Plato, the same thing is true of Greece and Rome. The most popular of the philosophies current in the classical world before the rise of Christianity was Stoicism, and in this system the doctrine of acquiescence in outward ills was pushed to its farthest possible one-sided limit and made to be the essence of all wisdom in the conduct of life. Over against all these systems Christianity appears as a religion of zealous action, and almost of rebellion. A notable recent book dealing with the teaching and life of our Lord was entitled not *The Faith That Acquiesces* but *The Faith That Rebels*.[1] I am indeed far from meaning to suggest that Christianity has no counsel of acquiescence; I am anxious only to make it clear that nowhere else is the counsel of acquiescence held in such constant tension with the opposite counsel of rebellion. The modern doctrine of progress is, of course, nowhere to be found in the ancient or medieval world. Never before the Renaissance and hardly before the eighteenth century, and nowhere outside of such countries as have been influenced by the European thought of this latest period, has the belief existed that the life of man on this planet either in the ordinary nature of things is, or by any effort of ours can be made to be, a forward march to an ideal goal. The large majority of our race have probably been unaware of any change from one age to another and have accordingly supposed that history remains always on the same dead level; but where knowledge has gone farther than this—extending, for example, to the rise and fall of civilizations—the view most commonly hit upon has been some form of the cyclical theory of an endless series of advances and declines, history being not so much a march as a wheel. 'And when we ask', writes Mr. Edwyn Bevan, 'what idea of the world-process was held by the thinkers and teachers of Graeco-Roman society, we find that they all thought of it as, in one way or another, a vain recurrence leading nowhere.'[2] Where then did the idea of the time-process as a forward movement leading to an ideal consummation first arise? The answer has been given us by Mr. Bevan and the late Archbishop

[1] By Principal D. S. Cairns, 1928.
[2] *The Hope of a World to Come underlying Judaism and Christianity* (1930), p. 28.

Söderblom, and deserves our very careful notice. The idea in question has arisen only twice in the history of human thought prior to our own modern period, namely in the two 'prophetic' religions of Zoroastrianism and Hebraism. Nowhere, except where the influence of one of these two religions has reached, has the hope ever been entertained that the future will bring us better than the past has brought, or that history is leading onwards to something supremely good. The Hebrew hope passed, of course, into Christianity, and we are justified in saying that among the complex causes which went to secure the ultimate victory of Christianity in the Graeco-Roman world none was more important than the fact that—the words are again Mr. Bevan's—'a view of the time-process which gave it interest and meaning had a wonderful attraction for men who had never thought of it as leading anywhere'.[1] The doctrine which thus came into the world was indeed far from being the modern doctrine of progress; for the consummation hoped for was to be brought about not by slow stages and by human initiative, but suddenly and cataclysmically by the supernatural power of God; and meanwhile the process of earthly history, though indeed containing manifestations which bore significant relation to the consummation, was not conceived as gradually approximating to it in quality but even, very commonly, as more and more deteriorating. Yet it is significant that the only philosophy of history known to the world which resembles the modern gospel of progress in making the time-process lead anywhere at all and in looking forward with hope to better days to come is the other-worldly

[1] *The Hope of a World to Come underlying Judaism and Christianity*, p. 36. Cf. the same writer's *Hellenism and Christianity* (1921), pp. 186 ff.

apocalyptic of the Persian and Hebrew-Christian tradition. For thus it appears that in the Christian hope of eternal life the gospel of progress finds, not its arch-enemy, but the nearest approach to an ally to which it can point anywhere in the history of earlier thought. 'And', as remarks another eminent scholar, Professor Burkitt of Cambridge, 'those who cling to the belief that human history is not altogether meaningless and that it marches, however slowly and haltingly, to a definite goal ought to regard the ideas enshrined in books like Enoch [and, we might add, in the New Testament books] with sympathy.'[1]

As has been indicated, the authentic Christian view is undoubtedly one which leaves room both for the mood of submission and for the mood of reforming zeal, holding the two in constant tension one against the other and neither minimizing nor on the other hand exaggerating man's power to alter and improve his own earthly lot. In this way other-worldliness and hither-worldliness—*Jenseitigkeit* and *Diesseitigkeit*, as the Germans call them—are made to join hands with each other and keep each other from excess, until we have, in the wise words of Friedrich von Hügel, 'a sufficient other-worldliness without fanaticism, and a sufficient this-worldliness without philistinism'.[2] 'The sons of God,' says à Kempis, 'standing upon the things that are present, do contemplate those things which are eternal. They look on transitory things with the left eye, and with the right do

---

[1] *Jewish and Christian Apocalypses* (1914), p. 33.
[2] *Eternal Life*, p. 255. I have adopted the word 'hither-worldliness' as being the neatest opposite to 'other-worldliness'. I think it is justified, because the dictionaries allow 'hither' to be not only an adverb meaning 'towards this place', but also an adjective meaning 'situated on this side'.

behold the things of heaven.'[1] In our own day the tendency, assuredly, is to destroy this balance by placing all our reliance upon the earthly prospect, and it is against this tendency that I shall be arguing in what follows. But it has appeared among us in express protest against an opposite error on the part of many past generations of Christians and has gained greatly in plausibility from this fact. Our argument in this chapter has been that the Christian doctrine of the heavenly prospect cannot successfully be defended until the partial justice of this protest has been recognized and the necessary adjustments made accordingly.

[1] Bk. iii. 38.

Chapter III

APPROACH TO THE ETERNAL PROSPECT

I

WE have done our best to bring out the measure of true and right insight that may often lie concealed behind a young man's protest that he is not interested in the prospect of eternal life. We have shown what age may here learn from youth. Let us now ask whether youth has not something also to learn from age. In so doing we need not in any way embroil ourselves in the general and secular dispute between youth and age—*jeunesse folâtre et vieillesse revêche*. To do that would, in these days, be to run the risk of burning one's fingers pretty badly! The question I have in mind is not whether in general the old are wiser than the young, or second thoughts better than first, but only whether in this particular matter of eternal life there is not a special reason why the findings of youth should not be too much trusted.

I think there is such a reason. Youth, in the very nature of things, cannot reasonably be expected to have the same interest in eternal life which is natural to maturer age. The facts and experiences from which this interest arises are not yet before it in anything like their fullness. The discovery of the shortness of our earthly term has not yet been made. When we are young, our present life seems itself to be eternal. They did indeed tell me in my small-boyhood that 'The days of our years are threescore years and ten; and if by reason of strength they be fourscore years, yet is their strength labour and sorrow; for it is soon cut off, and we fly away'. But the news moved me not at all, because threescore years and ten then seemed to me to be, for all practical purposes, only another way of saying eternity; it was an 'astronomical figure'. I know better now. In this one thing at least my riper age is wiser than my youth. I understand better now than I did then what can and what cannot be looked for within our allotted span. I can well remember the things that long ago I planned to do 'some day'—all the foreign lands I wanted to visit, and then, a little later, all the literatures I wanted to read, the languages I wanted to acquire, the historical investigations I wanted leisurely to pursue. I think there is a sense in which I still want to do these things, only it is with a desire strangely chastened by the knowledge that most of them must remain undone. How often it is with us, as with a friend of mine who, though naturally a slow reader, had in his student days amassed a large library, hoping gradually to read it all and much more besides, but who recently confessed to me how sometimes now, in middle age, a voice seems to speak to him from the topmost, dustiest shelves and say, 'Thou fool!'

Here, then, is a sound reason why, if a young man finds that the prospect of eternal life does not seem necessary to his peace of mind, he should beware of attaching too much importance to the fact. If, after he has doubled his present age, his finding should still remain unchanged, it must then indeed be taken more gravely. But on this matter I will not listen too long to brave-and-twenty. The psychiatrists and the priests would, I think, be in agreement that it is in the early or middle forties that the majority of men first learn to take the true measure of our human term of life and to look death squarely in the face. This is the true *âge dangereux*. It is now that most men begin really to *know*, for the first time, how much of their lifelong ambition is ever going to be realized. Until now they have always assumed that it would all be realized 'some day', in spite of past and present postponements; but now the truth breaks on them bleakly, so that in a pathetically large number of cases there ensues a period of the gravest interior crisis. But whether this spiritual climacteric comes early or late, surely we must all agree that when a man has passed through it, and has retained or rediscovered his peace of mind, his feelings in the matter of eternal life take on a certain added weight and interest.

But the realization of the brevity of our own lives is by no means the only realization that comes with maturer age. Besides the brevity of life there is its bitterness while it lasts, and of this also youth is often blessedly ignorant. Such was the reflection stirred in the mind of Thomas Gray by the distant prospect of the towers of Eton College:

> Alas! regardless of their doom
> The little victims play!

The things that make later life bitter for us are too many to be counted here, but looming large among them is the fact that the lives of those we love are as brief and uncertain as our own and often terminate before them. Now it seems to me very clear that until one has entered deeply into this experience of having loved and lost there is lacking from one's total experience one of the most important data on which to ground a judgement concerning the desirability of immortality. Certainly it is not impossible that one should enter deeply into this experience through the mere power of imaginative sympathy long before one is called to pass through it for oneself; this possibility is indeed one of the facts of human nature which was long ago built into the foundations of the Christian religion. Yet when the blow strikes at ourselves directly and the Reaper for the first time invades our own charmed circle, how many of us can claim that we were prepared for all this depth of woe? If I were to say that 'I knew a man in Christ above fourteen years ago' who still looks back on the morning after the little circle of his nursery days had first been broken as having shed a quite new light for him upon the question of the immortal hope, how many of my readers would have to confess that they also knew such a man! It is noteworthy that even so austere a philosopher as the late F. H. Bradley, who prefaces his few pages on immortality with the remark that 'this is a topic on which for several reasons I would rather keep silence', confesses that this 'appeal to the affections', this 'desire to meet once more those whom we have loved', is 'the only appeal as to the future life which to me individually is not hollow'.[1]

We are thus led to put to the man who protests that he is not interested in immortality what I think will turn out to be a very pertinent question. We must ask him *whose* immortality he is not interested in. Perhaps he will say that it is of course his own immortality he has in mind, and perhaps we are all of us apt to think primarily of ourselves when we are discussing this question in an academic way. But I wonder whether this is not only another of the many places

---

[1] *Appearance and Reality*, 2nd ed., pp. 501, 509. Bradley goes on to say that this appeal 'can hardly be turned into a proof'.

in our lives where to think of ourselves is to do wrong, and where the beginning of wisdom is to look away from ourselves and think rather of others. Indeed it might be said that in trying to attain to clarity of mind on any question it is a sound principle to keep oneself, one's own case, and (if we may borrow the familiar phrase of the astronomers) one's own 'personal equation' as much out of the matter as one can. If we have in our mind's eye a particular case, let it not be our own. For when we poor mortals think of ourselves, we are prone to all sorts of distorting sins and errors. How many glaringly obvious duties, for example, about whose claim on the attention of my neighbours I cannot be in any doubt whatever, immediately become obscured in a cloud of casuistical hesitations when I refer them to myself! And now in arguing this matter of immortality the same thing seems to be true. If in trying to think the matter out I have in mind only my own immortality, it becomes difficult to know whether the desire for it would be a strength or a weakness in me, whether to hold my soul immortal would be sinful self-conceit or to hold it mortal sinful self-disdain. To hit the golden mean between these opposites, uniting a self-assertion that is not proud with a self-effacement that is not base, has been the achievement of a very few—perhaps of Socrates, perhaps only of Jesus Christ; but for most of us it is a cruelly searching test. Mr. Chesterton has indeed provided us with what looks like a formula: 'One can hardly think too little of one's self. One can hardly think too much of one's soul.'[1] How admirably sound is this distinction, and how difficult to apply to one's own case! For it is just to the *intro*spective

[1] *Orthodoxy*, p. 172.

glance that the point where 'soul' ends and mere 'self' begins appears so difficult to discern. And all the advice the original propounder of the doctrine of the mean can give us is to 'lean over backwards' in a direction contrary to that to which we are naturally prone, following the principle by which we straighten pieces of wood that are warped.[1]

Let me then, when I ask myself whether or not it is well that death should be the end of all and the soul perish with the body, have in mind not my own soul and my own death but the soul and death of another. And let this other be the other who is most precious to me. Some will think of a parent, of a dear brother or sister, of a husband or wife; and that is well, for love begins at home. But it may serve others better to look still farther away from the centre of their own private happiness and think rather of a beloved leader, a father in God, the friend whose friendship has been sweetest to them, or the hero they have most learnt to revere. In either case let each have in mind *the most precious soul he knows*.

Now so long as I kept thinking of myself and looking at my own soul, it may indeed have seemed to me that there was not very much in me or about me that was worth conserving, and that my complete and final annihilation would be no great loss to the world. In one way, no doubt, we are all prone to value ourselves too highly, but in another way many of us are weary enough of our own company long before we have lived out our threescore years and ten. 'The banality of human amusements', I read recently in a novel, 'is the most cogent argument against the immortality of the soul.'[2] But now we see that the critical question is not whether we are

[1] Aristotle, *Eth. Nic.* 1109 B.   [2] John Presland, *Escape-Me-Never*, p. 101.

weary of our own company, but whether there *is* a company of which we are not weary. Perhaps in certain moods I can contemplate my own death and say, 'I do not care whether that is the end of me or not; the thing does not interest me.' But surely in *no* mood can I contemplate the death of the most precious soul I know, the death of him whom I most love and reverence, and say, 'I do not care whether that is the end of *him* or not; the thing does not interest me.' The former might be mistaken for humility; the latter could never be taken for anything but what it is, namely, treason. The man who can see his beloved die, believing that it is for ever, and say, 'I don't care', is a traitor to his beloved and to all that their love has brought them. *He has no right not to care.*

What matters, after all, is not whether I want eternal life but whether I ought to want it, not the fitful ebb and flow of things desired but the unchanging sum of things properly desirable. The question I must put is not whether I am such as to be content with the belief that my beloved's life is extinguished for ever like a candle's flame, but whether that belief is such that I have any right to be content with it. To a question so stated there is only one answer that can be given. No man who was not a cad could stand by his beloved's death-bed and say (or think) that he was not interested in immortality. Try only to picture him, saying not merely, 'For all I know' (which an honest man might well be forced to say), but, 'For all I know *or care*, this is the end of you, my dear!'

Moreover, this insight carries farther than might at first sight appear. For it now becomes plain to me not only that I must care about my beloved's immortality, but that I must care about my own too. Here, as so often, it is through the outgoing of my heart to others that I first learn to understand what lies within its own secret citadel. Within me there is indeed much that I would willingly see extinguished, and so I was tempted to think that if *all* should be extinguished the loss were no great disaster. But now I am led to ask whether there is not something in me that goes beyond myself; something that concerns another, and another whom I love. So the contemplation of my beloved's immortality is found to involve the contemplation of my own. If I have ever loved and been loved—and who is so poor as to say he has not?— then the right to contemplate my own extinction with equanimity is a luxury I must forgo; and not the only luxury I must forgo for that same love's sake. What we ought to feel about the hope of immortality may here be very simply tested by what we actually do feel about the sadness of death. Let a good man be warned by his doctors that he has not long to live, and where do his first thoughts fly? I do not believe it is ever to his own case or to the much-canvassed *conatus perseverare in esse suo* or to the last agonies he may so soon have to endure. No, I think it is sometimes to the work that he will leave unfinished; but even more commonly it is to the loved ones whom he must leave behind—to the difference it will make to them and the sadness it will bring to them. In either case his thought is very much the same, since he is thinking not of how his death will affect himself but of how it will affect others. And it is through this care for others that he comes to care about himself. If there had been nobody who needed him, if there had been nobody who loved him, he could have faced death without any sadness. But as things are, *he has no right not to be sad.*

Thus what the self-analysis of the soul and the introspective survey of

all
The terrors, pains, and early miseries,
Regrets, vexations, lassitudes interfused
Within my mind[1]

was unable to accomplish, my bond of love to another has accomplished for me. I am caught up into my beloved's immortality—to the extent at least of now knowing clearly that the immortality which I desire for him I must desire also for myself. And it is worth observing also that it is much more his love for me than my love for him that has taught me this lesson.

I do not see, then, how it is possible to escape the conclusion that eternal life is something which it is the duty of all of us to desire for ourselves and for those we love and honour. To be complacent about the prospect of extinction spells baseness and disloyalty. Not to wish that eternal life were available is wicked. But now, has this undoubted fact any light to throw on the question whether or not eternal life *is* available? Loyal love must cry out for continuance and fulfilment, but must its cry be heard and answered? Have we any reason to believe that the just and necessary demands of love will be satisfied?

Clearly we have no such reason if love be merely an incident of our animal organization and part of what Bishop Butler called 'the particular constitution of human nature'. What is merely human and temporal can, *vi terminorum*, have no claims upon the universal and eternal order. We can say

---

[1] Wordsworth, *The Prelude*, Book I, lines 345 ff.

only, with Nietzsche's Zarathustra, *Doch alle Lust will Ewigkeit*; and leave the matter there. But if we have any kind of feeling that in the loyal love of soul for soul we are touching something that is more than merely animal or creaturely, then the situation is obviously changed. If it be true that love, instead of being an accidental animal impulse thrown up with countless other such accidents in the march of evolution, is the universe's own ultimate principle of coherence, so that when we love one another the universal pattern is as it were shining through within us, then plainly what love finds desirable has some relevance to what is real. So far, accordingly, as we become aware of this further depth of meaning within our human loves will the desire for eternal life be turned into something like the beginning of a conviction of its reality.

And yet this movement of the mind is not likely to complete itself and become firmly established—it is not likely, perhaps, to go much farther than appears in a scene in one of Mr. Hugh Walpole's novels in which one says to another, 'There is a kind of sniff of immortality about our love for one another'[1]—until and unless our capacities of loving are still further developed and the deep meaning of love still more deeply understood. It is not enough to realize that when we love one another a Universal Lover is dwelling within us; we must go on to love this Universal Lover for His own sake. Thus are we led into a still more secret citadel of the soul—the 'ultimate heart's occult abode' of which Francis Thompson speaks. Just as formerly we were led by love beyond ourselves to one another and thus were made for the first time to understand ourselves, so now are we led beyond one another

[1] *Hans Frost*, p. 341.

to One who is Eternal and are made to understand ourselves more deeply yet.

> The sweetest wife on sweetest marriage-day,—
> Their souls at grapple in mid-way,
> Sweet to her sweet may say:
>
> 'I take you to my inmost heart, my true!'
> Ah, fool! but there is one heart you
> Shall never take him to!
>
> The hold that falls not when the town is got,
> The heart's heart, whose immured plot
> Hath keys yourself keeps not! . . .
>
> Its keys are at the cincture hung of God;
> Its gates are trepidant to His nod;
> By Him its floors are trod.[1]

In this way we are brought face to face with the question whether, when we look into this most secret place of our souls and are lifted above the love of our fellow-creatures to the love of God and to the knowledge of His love for us, the sense of the desirability of eternal life does not pass over into a sure and certain conviction of its reality. In the discovery of the love of God is not the assurance of immortality enclosed?

II

Now there is no doubt that it is by means of such a line of reflection as has here been suggested that the Christian assurance of immortality actually came into the world. In putting the question which has just been stated we have at last arrived

[1] Francis Thompson, *A Fallen Yew*.

at the point from which the New Testament thinking about eternal life begins. And until we have arrived at this point we are not really in a position to understand what the New Testament has to say.

Since men first began to reflect at all, they have been led along the way of self-analysis to dreams of some kind of survival. But the Christian hope of eternal life is something very different from these and has sprung from an entirely different source. The preparation for it was in Greece and Israel, but, as all the world knows, the consummation of it is inseparably linked with the name of Jesus Christ. When we ask how it was that the early Christians succeeded in attaining to that triumphant faith in an eternal world which has ever since been the inspiration of the Church they founded and of so much of the spiritual life of the West, we can only answer that it was *not* by the contemplation of their own souls or by the thought of their own death, but by the contemplation of Another who had died before their eyes, that Other whom they most loved and found most precious, even Jesus Christ. He it is 'who hath abolished death, and hath brought life and immortality to light'.[1] 'Thou art the King of Glory, O Christ', says the *Te Deum*, '. . . When Thou hadst overcome the sharpness of death, Thou didst open the Kingdom of Heaven to all believers.' And if from the *Te Deum* we take a long leap to so unlikely a person as David Hume, we shall find him beginning an essay (never to be published while he lived) *Of the Immortality of the Soul* with the words: 'By the mere light of reason it seems difficult to prove the Immortality of the Soul. . . . It is the gospel, and the gospel alone,

[1] 2 Tim. i. 10.

that has brought life and immortality to light.'[1] Behind such a beginning, considering that it dates from the eighteenth century, there is an admirably shrewd insight—an insight, moreover, which may easily be disengaged from Hume's unquestioning utilization of the eighteenth-century distinction between reason and revelation. It is not really important whether or not Hume wrote the words with his tongue in his cheek: what is important is the true historical and psychological generalization which they contain. Christ's followers did not argue from a general resurrection to the Resurrection of their Lord; rather was the Resurrection of their Lord the earnest of their own. He whom they loved had risen and they were caught up into His immortality. To live with Him (συνζῆν αὐτῷ)—that was the essence of their hope. The Christians of the first generation, having as yet no New Testament at their disposal, had nothing to quote to one another for their mutual fortification but a few 'trusty words', as they were called—πιστοὶ λόγοι—which had gradually crystallized into epigrammatic form. Several of these are quoted in the New Testament and other early Christian literature, but none so frequently as that which ran: 'If we have died with Him, we shall also live with Him', or, in the fuller form to which St. Paul expands it: 'If we have grown into Him by a death like His, we shall grow into Him by a resurrection like His.'[2]

Yet if their relationship to Jesus had been thought of by them as a merely human bond, their hope of continued life with Him must always have remained at the level of mere desire. It was only because they found in this relationship

---

[1] See Green and Grose's edition of the *Essays*, vol. ii, p. 399.
[2] See 2 Tim. ii. 11; Rom. vi. 5 and 8; Rom. viii. 17; Col. iii. 1.

a deeper and diviner meaning that their hope passed into triumphant and assured conviction. They believed that in the love that filled the heart of Christ and sent Him to His death they had come upon the clue to the infinite mystery. They believed that here the universal pattern was shining through. They could not think of the love of Christ as a merely human thing: they were absolutely certain that *God was in it*. 'Love is of God', they said, 'and every one that loveth is born of God, and knoweth God.... God is love, and he that dwelleth in love dwelleth in God, and God in him.'[1] And again, 'Herein is love, not that we loved God, but that He loved us, and sent His Son to be the propitiation for our sins.'[2] And it was because they knew that God was in the love of Christ that they knew it would last for ever. Behind the love of Christ they could discern the love of God, and in that discernment was the pledge of its eternity. Eternal life was thus from the beginning what some modern writer has called 'a function of the friendship of God'. Nowhere are the grounds and the quality of the Christian hope more clearly expressed than in the magnificent peroration of the eighth chapter of Romans:

'Who shall separate us from the love of Christ? shall tribulation, or distress, or persecution, or famine, or nakedness, or peril, or sword? . . . Nay, in all these things we are more than conquerors through Him that loved us. For I am persuaded that neither death, nor life, nor angels, nor principalities, nor powers, nor things present, nor things to come, nor height, nor depth, nor any other creature, shall be able to separate us from the love of God, which is in Christ Jesus our Lord.'

[1] 1 John iv. 7, 16.   [2] 1 John iv. 10.

Three centuries after that Athanasius wrote:

'For as, when a tyrant has been utterly vanquished by a true emperor, and is bound hand and foot, all who pass by jeer at him, smiting and abusing him, no longer fearing his rage and cruelty, because of the victorious emperor; so also death, having been conquered and branded as infamous by the Saviour on the Cross, and bound hand and foot, all in Christ who pass through trample on it, and as witnesses to Christ deride death, scoffing at it, and saying the words written against it above: "Where, Death, is thy victory? where, Hades, thy sting?" '[1]

If, in our consideration of this great subject, we are looking not only to life and life's radiant morning but to death and death's infinite sadness, if we are looking not only to our own death but to the death of another, if this other be one to whom we are bound in tenderest love, and if through and behind and above this human love we are able in some measure to discern the eternal love of God, whom now we begin to love for His own sake alone, then we are at least standing where our Lord's disciples stood and may hope to see something of what they saw. This is that exalted station of the spirit, of which the Pisgah of ancient story is but a type and a shadow, and from which alone we who have wandered in the wilderness may obtain a first prospect of the Promised Land.

[1] *De Incarnatione Verbi Dei*, xxvii, Bindley's translation.

61

Chapter IV

A TALE—AND SOME COMMENTS

I

BEFORE we attempt the further and more detailed understanding of the Christian hope, it is necessary that we should first set it in its proper context against the background of the long history of human ideas. The present chapter will be devoted to this task.

At the outset some well-known lines of Tennyson are almost sure to occur to us:

> Since our dying race began,
> Ever, ever, and for ever was the leading light of man.
> Those that in barbarian burials kill'd the slave, and slew the wife,
> Felt within themselves the sacred passion of the second life.[1]

How far is this statement historically accurate?

It is certainly true that, no matter how far back we penetrate into the history of our kind, we are unable to reach a period from which all belief in survival is absent. The manner in which the cave-man of Palaeolithic times is now known to have buried his dead makes it quite clear that he believed in a continued existence beyond the grave. No other animal but man inters or entombs his dead at all. 'The gorilla, the chimpanzee, the orang-outang, and their kind', writes Miguel de Unamuno, 'must look upon man as a feeble and infirm animal whose strange custom it is to store up his dead.' But as for man himself, 'stone was used for sepulchres before it was used for houses'[2]. It is probable that the very idea of

[1] *Locksley Hall, Sixty Years After.*
[2] *The Tragic Sense of Life*, Eng. tr., pp. 20, 41.

burial is eschatological in origin, but in any case all known burial (except among the sporadic unbelievers of our modern West) is ceremonial in nature, and the ceremonies attaching to it testify most eloquently to the belief that death is not the final end of being; as, for example, when prehistoric man places food and drink, weapons and ornaments, beside the carefully postured body in every grave he digs.

Nevertheless to speak, as Tennyson does, of 'ever, ever, and for ever' in this connexion is to go far beyond the warrant of the facts. That death was not the end was taken for granted, but that there was *no* end was not a thought which primitive man could possibly have formed or understood. Not only must we leave prehistoric times far behind us but we must travel a long way down into the history of remembered civilizations before we meet with anything like the conception of true endlessness, much less of true eternity. Even more important, however, is the fact that the primitive belief in the continued existence of the dead never had anything of the character of a 'sacred passion' or of 'the leading light of man'. It was apparently looked upon, and is still looked upon by the many savage races still surviving on our globe, very much as we should now look upon a scientific theory of whose truth we have no doubt. We have to do, that is to say, not with a cherished hope such as might be attended by great religious fervour and exaltation, but with a simple fact of no very definite emotional colouring. It is worth while to quote the words in which Sir James Frazer summarizes the results of his inquiry into primitive eschatology:

'It is impossible not to be struck by the strength, and perhaps we may say the universality, of the natural belief in immortality among the savage races of mankind. With them a life after death is not a matter of speculation and conjecture, of hope and fear; it is a practical certainty which the individual as little dreams of doubting as he doubts the reality of his conscious existence. He assumes it without inquiry and acts upon it without hesitation, as if it were one of the best-ascertained truths within the limits of human experience.'[1]

The fact of survival essentially belongs, then, not to the savage's religion but to his lay philosophy of things—as we should say, to his natural science. That brilliant practitioner in the dissociation of ideas, Remy de Gourmont, thought that 'there have been few discoveries more important for the history of human beliefs' than this one, which he believed to have been first made nearly forty years ago by a French writer called Marillier—the discovery that, as he puts it, 'the idea of immortality was at first a purely scientific conception', in the formation of which 'the idea of justice has had not the slightest share'.[2]

It is of course true that in many different parts of the world belief in survival has afterwards come to be associated with religion in one very important way—those who have passed beyond the grave have come to be regarded as divine and have been made the object of religious worship. But this associa-

---

[1] *Belief in Immortality and the Worship of the Dead*, vol. i, p. 468. The only exception to the universality of belief in survival to which, as I remember, Sir James draws our attention is that the natives of the Tonga or Friendly Islands think that only the souls of noblemen survive. 'This aristocratic view', he adds slyly, 'is not likely to find favour in our democratic age' (vol. i, p. 33).

[2] See the essay on 'Glory and the Idea of Immortality' in his *Le Chemin de velours*. The essay is translated in the volume of selections called *Decadence* (London, 1922); see p. 44. I regret not having been able to see Marillier's own book, *La Survivance de l'âme et l'idée de justice chez les peuples non-civilisés* (Paris, 1894).

tion is, in a sense, an accidental one. Certain anthropologists of the last century, chief among whom was Herbert Spencer, did indeed incline to regard the cult of ancestors as the earliest form of religion and hence to make religion itself a fruit of the belief in survival, but this view has now been generally abandoned. Ancestor-worship, it is now held, is neither genuinely primitive nor did it ever become universal.[1] The origin of the impulse of worship must be sought elsewhere. The fact of survival, taken by itself, seems to have no sacred associations whatsoever for the savage mind.[2]

Above all, survival is never made the object of anything that can properly be called religious *hope*. Among a number of peoples, it is true, the picture of the ghostly world is subject to a certain kind of idealization; so that Tennyson is not without justification when he writes that 'Indian warriors dream of ampler hunting-grounds beyond the night'. The Gilbert Islanders believed .

'that as soon as a person dies, his soul or shade ascends into the air and is carried about by the winds whithersoever they may chance to blow. At last it is supposed to arrive at a sort of elysium, called Kainakiki, where the spirits pass their time in feasting, dancing, and whatever occupations were most agreeable to them in their bodily existence. This elysium is placed by some in the island of Tarawa.'[3]

---

[1] For references see my *Interpretation of Religion*, pp. 167–70.

[2] A recent investigator, James Thayer Addison, sums up his results as follows: 'The rudimentary beliefs about the after-life which we have been reviewing have little connection with religion. In ancestor-worship, of course, the spirits themselves are the object of worship.... In general, however, the religions appropriate to this lower level of thought do not concern themselves with the life after death.' (*Life beyond Death in the Beliefs of Mankind* (Boston and New York, 1932), p. 103.)

[3] J. G. Frazer, op. cit., vol. iii, p. 48 f.

Or again, several of the native tribes of Queensland in south-eastern Australia believed that 'the souls of the dead go up into the sky':

'The Buandik thought that everything in skyland was better than on earth; a fat kangaroo, for example, was compared to a kangaroo of heaven where, of course, the animals might be expected to abound. The Kulin imagined that the spirits of the dead ascended to heaven by the bright rays of the setting sun.'[1]

Another writer tells us that 'the tribes of New Guinea, rendered anaemic by hunger, dream of eating unlimited sago throughout eternity'.[2] On the other hand, there is nearly always an underlying consciousness of the disabilities attaching to this future state. It is a ghostly existence in a world of shadows, an existence which seldom succeeds in completely shaking off its association in the minds of the people with the darkness and dampness of the grave. But for the most part what primitive man expects to find in the next world is simply a continuation of his present everyday existence. Very typical is the belief of the Kai tribe of Papuans in German New Guinea, as it appears in Sir James Frazer's account:

'Life in the other world goes on just like life in this one. Houses are built exactly like houses on earth, and there as here pigs swarm in the streets. Fields are tilled and crops are got in; ghostly men marry ghostly women, who give birth to ghostly children. The same old round of love and hate, of quarrelling and fighting, of battle, murder and sudden death goes on in the shadowy realm below ground just as in the more solid world above ground.'[3]

---

[1] J. G. Frazer, op. cit., vol. i, p. 138 f.
[2] Quoted by Remy de Gourmont, op. cit., p. 45.
[3] J. G. Frazer, op. cit., vol. i, p. 286 f.

Here, obviously, we are very far away from any thought of a 'better world' or heavenly consummation such as could make our earthly life seem by comparison to be only a 'weary pilgrimage'. It is also to be noted that where primitive peoples believe in any differentiation between more and less privileged states of being after death, the differentiation is not given any moral or religious significance. This came out in the quotation from Remy de Gourmont, and it has been insisted on by many other writers. One writes that 'just as the simplest type of after-world is a ghostly duplication of the present life, so the simplest notion of distinctions is to extend beyond the grave the same differences that we see here. . . . The rich are still rich and the poor poor.'[1]

Another question is as to exactly *what* in a man is considered by primitive peoples to survive death. Speaking generally, we may say that what survives is his 'shadow', his 'shade', his 'double', his 'ghost'. Bergson puts it cleverly when he says that the primitive conception of that which survives consists simply of 'the visual image of the body dissociated from the tactile image'.[2] At first, perhaps, there is a 'pre-animistic' stage in which the whole man is conceived of as continuing to exist in some shadowy way. Then, with the maturing of the animistic view proper, the 'shade' becomes a 'soul' essentially distinct from the body. But even then there is room for difference of opinion as to whether death results in a complete separation of body and soul, so that the future life of the soul is an entirely discarnate one. Moreover, there are a great many tribes scattered throughout the world or known to us

[1] J. T. Addison, op. cit., p. 85.
[2] *Les Deux Sources de la morae e et de la religion*, p 139

from history who have hit upon the notion of the *reincarnation* of souls in other human bodies or in the bodies of animals. To take only one example, 'the Hopi of Arizona used to make a road from the grave of a little child towards its old home so that its soul might live again in the next baby born to the family'.[1] But with these varieties of conception[2] we need not concern ourselves. Once again they represent differences in the prevailing lay philosophy of things rather than in religious insight or feeling itself.

II

We may now leave savage races behind us and pass onwards to the great peoples who have supplied the sources of our Western culture. Speaking of Israel, Greece, and Rome, Professor Pringle-Pattison has written that 'To these three nations we owe nearly all the elements of our European civilization; yet in none of them, during the longest and most brilliant period of their history, did popular or traditional belief about the soul advance beyond the stage of primitive animism'.[3] But the truth is, I think, even stranger than this. What we discover is not merely the absence of any advance but actually a kind of retrogression. It seems to have been a genuine case of *reculer pour mieux sauter*.

First as regards Greece. There is every reason to suppose that in early times the Greeks followed much the same view as other primitive peoples, and in fact such a view seems to have survived in some degree among the common people to

[1] J. T. Addison, op. cit., p. 74.
[2] For a good summary see *Encycl. of Religion and Ethics*, under 'Soul (Primitive)'.
[3] *The Idea of Immortality*, p. 14.

the end. But the great literature of classical Greece stands in the main, and in spite of many vestigial traces of the older way of thinking, for a distinctly changed conception. Man, according to Homer, possesses besides his familiar bodily selfhood a *psyche* which, so far, is very much the ordinary soul or ghost or double of a fully developed animistic doctrine. During earthly life this soul exists all unsuspected within our familiar selfhood, but at death, when our familiar selfhood perishes, the soul escapes to Erebus, the abode of King Hades, and there continues to live its own life. It is when we ask what this life is that we receive so surprising an answer. It is an existence barely worthy of the name. The shades of the dead are represented as unconscious, or at most as half-conscious. They are without wit or memory; incapable alike of action and of passion; feebly floating about as they emit their feeble complaints. The picture of Erebus itself is one of unrelieved dankness, dreariness, and gloom. It is a true underworld, such as men might imagine to exist in the dark and damp bottom of a grave. There is, of course, also an overworld, but that is not for the souls of men, being the abode of the gods only. And far away 'beyond the Western wave' there are the Elysian Fields (Homer) or Islands of the Blest (Hesiod and Pindar), but these are only for a few demigods and heroes who have been translated thither without going down to death at all or having their souls separated from their bodies. But Hades alone is the destiny of all who die. Clearly it is far from being a destiny in which anybody could rejoice. When, in the oft-quoted lines of the eleventh book of the *Odyssey*, Odysseus tries to comfort the dead Achilles by suggesting that he who was so mighty a man on earth may still 'have great power among the dead', Achilles answers, 'Don't speak to me of death! I would sooner be a hireling servant of the most penurious man alive than the ruler over all the kingdoms of the dead.'[1]

Such a picture of the future is plainly further than ever from having any religious significance. The absence of hope, which we noted among uncivilized races, now gives place to a positive shrinking. In the realm of the shades there is nothing fine and noble and no opportunity for dealings with the gods. Erwin Rohde, whose book still remains after forty years the most authoritative treatment of the subject, writes as follows:

'The Homeric picture of the shadow-life of the disembodied soul is the work of resignation, not of hope. Hope would never have beguiled itself with the anticipation of a state of things which neither afforded men the chance of further activity after death, nor, on the other hand, gave them rest from the toil of life; one which promised them only a restless, purposeless fluttering to and fro, an existence, indeed, but without any of the content that might have made it worthy of the name of life.'[2]

Nor can we find it surprising that with the acceptance of such a view the worship of the dead by the living (which we found in the case of uncivilized races to be the main respect in which belief in survival had made association with religion) virtually disappeared from the Greek scene. Less than ever, then, would a Greek have been likely to regard the fact of life in Hades with any kind of 'sacred passion'. As a matter of fact, what happened was that he ceased to give any serious thought to it at all. It seemed to have no practical bearings, so why should he trouble about it? And gradually, of course, such

[1] Lines 484 ff. [2] *Psyche* (1893), Eng. tr. (1925) from the 8th edition, p. 55.

inattention to the belief led to its disappearance from his mind. There is little doubt that by the Periclean age men's conceptions of the future state were even vaguer and dimmer than they had been in the age when Homer sang.

When we pass from Greece to Rome, we find that the case is only slightly different. There is the same general conception of the shades (*manes*) as continuing after death to dwell in a dim and gloomy underworld. The original Roman conception no doubt was that each shade haunted its own grave. At a later time these individual graves came to be fused into a single underworld. Yet the Romans continued always, to a much greater degree than the Greeks, to associate the ghosts of the dead with the places of their burial. Moreover, the worship of the dead, which had so little place in Greek religion, played a most significant part in the piety of Rome. The dead were regarded as divine beings; they were the *di inferi*, and were held to exercise an important influence on the fortunes of the living, while on the other hand there were many ways in which the living might benefit the dead. It follows from all this that the tendency to deny effective conscious life to the shades never went as far among the Romans as it did among the Greeks. Nevertheless for Roman as for Greek the underworld was a dismal sunless region; and life in it, far from being a glorious consummation, was an impoverished and enfeebled continuation of our life above ground. There was nothing either exhilarating or consolatory about the prospect of it, but rather much that was depressing. A good illustration is the interchange of letters between Cicero and his lawyer friend Sulpicius on the occasion of the greatest grief of his life—the sudden death in childbirth of his dear daughter Tullia at the age of thirty-one. Both writers are seeking eagerly for suggestions of solace, but to neither does it even occur to mention the fact that Tullia is not really dead at all, because her ghost still lives. The most striking suggestion is made by Sulpicius and is of a very different kind:

'I must pass on to you a reflection that has consoled me; perhaps it will succeed in lessening your grief. On my return from Asia, as I was sailing from Aegina towards Megara, I began to look at the country surrounding me. Megara was in front of me, Aegina behind, the Piraeus on the right, Corinth on the left. Formerly these were very flourishing cities; now they are but scattered ruins. At this sight I said to myself: How dare we, poor mortals that we are, complain of the death of our friends, whose life nature has made so short, when a single glance is enough to show us the mere corpses of so many great cities lying around us?'[1]

It was nearly two centuries after this that the emperor Hadrian, as he looked forward to his death, wrote the famous versicle in which he asked his little soul, which had these many years been the companion and guest of his body, whither it was now about to depart, 'pallid and rigid and naked' and with all its accustomed jesting at an end:

> Animula vagula blandula
> hospes comesque corporis,
> quae nunc abibis in loca
> pallidula rigida nudula;
> nec, ut soles, dabis iocos?

In classical Rome, then, as in classical Greece, the old eschatology had lost the greater part of its vividness and of its importance. But in Latin literature there is perhaps a greater

[1] *Ad fam.* iv. 5; see Gaston Boissier, *Cicero and His Friends*, Eng. tr., p. 102 f.

tendency for such indifference to pass into actual incredulity. This was because between the golden age of Greece and that of Rome the various sceptical movements in philosophy had made their appearance.

The case of Israel is again, in its general features, remarkably similar. All the evidence goes to show that the Israelites of pre-Mosaic times, like the Greeks of pre-Homeric times and like the Romans before they began to be influenced by Greek thought, shared in the common eschatology of primitive man as it is revealed in a book like Sir James Frazer's. When a man dies, his corpse gives way to corruption, but his *nephesh* or soul continues to live in the grave or (this being probably a later stage of the conception) in the united graveplace known as Sheol, the Hebrew Erebus. Life in Sheol is dim and shadowy, yet the souls or shades (*rephaim*) are conceived as possessing a real measure of conscious and active life, with free movement and memory and interest in the earthly fortunes of their descendants as well as some power to influence these fortunes. Moreover, as in so many other places, the worship of the dead by the living is commonly practised. But with the advent of Mosaic religion exactly the same thing happens to Sheol which in Greece, in approximately the same centuries, is happening to Erebus. It now becomes a place of nothing but the most dismal associations, 'a land of darkness', of 'disorder', and of 'dust', for which there is no commoner name than 'the pit'. And 'those that go down to the pit' are now conceived of as having no proper conscious life at all, lacking both memory of the past and knowledge of the happenings of the present; so that Sheol is further 'a land of silence', of 'forgetfulness', and of 'destruction' or

73

'annihilation'. 'They still believed', writes R. H. Charles in what is still the best single book on the subject, 'that the soul subsisted after death, though it did not exist';[1] and the distinction may serve. Moreover, as in Greece, the worship of the souls of the dead is found rapidly dying out. Of the dismal prospect awaiting him after death Job speaks thus:

> My days are few! let me alone awhile,
>> that I may have life bright with a brief smile,
> before I leave it to return no more,
>> before I pass to darkness and to gloom,
> to a land dark as midnight, utter chaos,
>> with no light but the shades of death.[2]

In the book of Isaiah the following verses are addressed to the King of Babylon:

> The underworld is astir to greet you,
>> astir to meet you,
> rousing all the ghosts for you
>> that on earth were chieftains,
> moving monarchs of the world from their thrones
>> to hail you, one and all of them, to cry to you,
> 'So you are weak now as we are?
>> so you fare as we fare?
> Your pomp has passed down to the world below,
>> you and your peals of music?
> Maggots are spread under you,
>> around your coverlet. . . .
> How low and limp you lie,
>> Who once swayed all the nations.'[3]

---

[1] *A Critical History of the Doctrine of a Future Life in Israel, Judaism and Christianity* (1st ed., 1899; 2nd ed.—to which my references apply—1913), p. 43.
[2] Job x. 21–2. This and the other immediately following passages from the Old Testament are quoted as in Dr. Moffatt's translation.
[3] Isaiah xiv. 9–12.

Moreover, it is very important to realize that the inhabitants of Sheol were cut off from all relations with Jehovah, the God of Israel; so that to 'go down to the pit', as the souls of all men must do, is not to go to God but to say farewell to Him. Here are a few of the relevant passages from the Old Testament:

Hear my prayer, O thou Eternal, listen to my cry,
    answer thou my tears;
for I am but a guest of thine,
    a passing waif, as all my fathers were.
Avert thy frown, that I may be at ease,
    ere I depart and be no more.[1]

Daily I call to thee, O thou Eternal,
    I stretch my hands to thee.
Canst thou work wonders for the dead?
    Can ghosts arise to praise thee?
Can thy love be recounted in the grave,
    thy faithfulness within the world below?
Can thy wonders be known in the darkness,
    thy saving help in the land of oblivion?[2]

For death-land cannot thank thee,
    death cannot sing thy praise,
and those who pass down to the pit
    have no hope of thy love;
'tis living men who praise thee, as I praise thee to-day—
    the father telling to his sons how true thou art.[3]

The dead cannot praise the Eternal,
    nor any who sink to the silent land;
but we bless the Eternal now and evermore.[4]

These passages are entirely typical of the view that prevails

[1] Psalm xxxix. 12–13.   [2] Psalm lxxxviii. 9–12.
[3] Isaiah xxxviii. 18–19.   [4] Psalm cxv. 17–18.

throughout all but the whole of the Old Testament literature. Here again, then, the survival of one's ghost is taken to be an indubitable fact, but it is a fact of no religious significance whatsoever, and one which stands not for the consummation but for the death of hope.

What then is the nature of the change we have to record when we set the orthodox eschatology of Greece, Rome, and Israel against the picture offered us by Sir James Frazer of the eschatology of primitive peoples? The answer is sufficiently clear. There is no emergence of any new and higher idea. All that there is of eschatology is still on the same animistic level. But it is gradually fading out. Animistic belief is less vivid than it used to be. Ghosts are less important. Their continued existence is of so shadowy a kind as to be of no significance either to themselves or to those above ground. And as it grows more shadowy, so also it grows more gloomy. Whereas formerly the prospect of an after-life was, on the whole, without definite emotional colouring one way or the other, its associations are now almost always of a dismal and depressing kind. There is no longer any thought of 'ampler hunting-grounds beyond the night'.

III

If, therefore, we look back over the whole ground which we have thus hurriedly traversed, we see at once that all the belief in survival which has thus far come under our notice is of one piece and points to a single source. And what its source was has likewise been made clear to us. It came, if I may be allowed for the sake of vividness so to express it, *not from the priests but from the psychologists*. It was in no sense a product of ethical idealism or of religious faith and aspiration, but was merely a corollary of the ordinary lay psychology of the time and place. This is what Charles means when he argues that it was 'not the outcome of revelation'[1] and goes on to say that in the case of Israel 'no revelation was furnished ... for many centuries'[2] after the period with which we have been dealing. Whenever primitive man reflects upon the life he is now living in his mortal body, the result is an analysis which implies some kind of survival. According to a pre-animistic psychology such as Dr. Marett and others call 'animatistic' it is the whole self which survives; but with the arrival of animism proper there is distinguished within the ordinary selfhood a second self or ghost which, being released from the corpse at death, goes on to live a life of its own. If you had met an ancient Israelite or Greek, or if you met now an Australian blackfellow or a Melanesian savage, and challenged his belief in the reality of ghosts, he would not appeal to any considerations of a religious nature but would seek rather to initiate you into the principles of a true psychology, and in support of them would bring forward a large body of what seemed to him quite convincing evidence. Sir James Frazer does indeed speak, both in the title and throughout the text of his invaluable work, of this belief in ghosts as belief in *immortality*. But he does so only, as he says, 'for the sake of brevity', and he admits that 'the term is not strictly correct, since it seems to imply eternal duration'.[3] We might add that it is incorrect for another reason also— since it seems to imply some kind of 'consummation devoutly

[1] Op. cit., p. 19.   [2] Ibid., p. 50.   [3] Op. cit., vol. i, p. 25.

to be wished'. And even less is the use of a word like immortality justifiable in the case of the later civilizations. To believe that after one's death one's ghost will for a time continue to haunt one's grave, or that combined grave which is the underworld, is certainly not to believe in immortal life. Neither the Greeks nor the Romans, nor again the Israelites, would have understood such a usage at all. To all these, within the period of which we have spoken, the gods were alone 'the immortals'. To be immortal meant not to die, to go on living in the body; and this the gods do, for their bodies are incorruptible. But obviously it is the lot of all *men* to see corruption and they are therefore 'mortals'. And there was as yet no emergence of the idea that a man's *real selfhood* could survive death, still less that his body could rise again. But that one's real selfhood should die meant precisely that one was not immortal, and the fact that one's ghost continued to haunt a dim underworld was not considered to disturb this conclusion. If, for example, you had suggested to a Greek of the classical period that he was immortal, he would have thought you meant that, instead of dying, he would be caught up by the gods and wafted to the Elysian Fields, there to consort with Tiresias, Rhadamanthus, and similar heroes; but knowing that he was not, like them, of semi-divine origin, he would have protested that he could not hope to share their semi-divine destiny. And he might quote to you such words as those of the poet Pindar: 'We must seek from the gods such things as befit our mortal minds (θνηταῖς φρασίν), knowing what lies before us and to what portion we were born. Seek not, my soul, immortal life (βίον ἀθάνατον), but explore such resources as are practicable.'[1]

---

[1] *Pythia* iii, lines 59 ff.

Similarly, if you had suggested to a Hebrew that he was immortal, his mind would at once have flown to the cases of Enoch and Elijah who were 'caught up' to the abode of Jehovah without tasting death; and he too would have protested that a plain man like himself could lay no claim to so exceptional a destiny.

What we have so far to do with, then, is a psychological conclusion, based on self-analysis and backed by supposed empirical evidence, to the effect that, whether we like it or no, our ghosts will continue to live some kind of life after our earthly life is over. But it will be realized at once that the attempt to reach this conclusion in this way is by no means a thing of the far-distant past, but has enjoyed a considerable popularity down to our own time. It is plain that the majority of the proofs of survival which the philosophers have offered us are of just this type, proceeding from the same kind of premiss and reaching the same kind of conclusion. What they set out to do is to offer such an analysis of the soul as will make it clear that it cannot be altogether destructible, but must in some manner continue in existence.

The first parents of all philosophic proofs of survival after death, like the first parents of all philosophic proofs of the existence of God, are to be found in the dialogues of Plato. Just as it is in the *Laws* that we first read of an ἀπόδειξις ὡς εἰσὶν θεοί or demonstration that there are gods, so it is in the *Phaedo* that we first read of an ἀπόδειξις ὅτι ἐστὶ ψυχὴ ἀθάνατόν τε καὶ ἀνώλεθρον or demonstration that soul is immortal and indestructible. It will be noticed that Plato here employs the term 'immortal' in a way in which, as we have said, earlier Greek writers would not have employed it. This is because an element of an entirely new kind has come into his thinking, an element which makes him think of the soul's after-life in a quite new and revolutionary way. To this element in Plato's thought we shall presently be attempting to do justice, but what we have meanwhile to note is that although Plato's own interest in the after-life is of an entirely new kind and springs from a source that is now definitely religious, yet (with one exception to which we shall presently advert) the arguments which he brings forward in support of it seem to bear little relation to any specifically religious insight, being rather of the kind that we should associate with the older or animistic approach to the matter. The same is true of the proofs which Plato offers in the *Laws* for the existence of God. We should nowadays feel that the discovery of God's reality is a fruit of religious experience and of that alone, but Plato set the fashion, which was destined to prevail in European philosophy for more than two thousand years, of seeking to establish a conclusion which was itself the fruit of religious insight without appealing to such insight at all, but only to the conclusions of an independent scientific inquiry. What he undertakes in the *Phaedo* is essentially a psychological analysis of the nature of the soul, and here too he set a fashion that was to have a long history.

The philosophy of Plato may from one point of view be described as a defence of animism—a defence, that is to say, of the doctrine that all natural processes are ultimately due to the agency of souls. In the *Phaedo* three lines are suggested along which it is possible to argue for the immortality of such souls. The first sets out from the characteristic Platonic contention that all learning is really recollection. When Socrates taught, he did not seem to be putting anything into his pupil's mind, but rather drawing something out of it, something which the pupil had once known and had forgotten. This indicates that the present is not the first life which the pupil's soul has enjoyed; and if it is not the first, why then should it be the last? The second argument is as follows: There are three orders of existence, namely, in Plato's language, bodies, souls, and forms; or, in modern philosophical parlance, the realm of matter, the realm of mind, and the realm of essence (or of universals). Matter is composite, variable, and perishable: 'change and decay in all around I see'. Forms or universals, on the other hand, are simple, invariable, and eternal. Are souls, which have connexion with both matter and universals, perishable like the former or eternal like the latter? Clearly, argues Plato, their real affinity is with the universals; for, like them, they are invisible and non-composite. And what is non-composite is, of course, indispersible and indissoluble. The soul therefore shares in the eternity of the ideal objects of its contemplation. The third argument is that since the very essence of the soul is to be alive (ψυχή being just another word for the principle of life), it is impossible without contradiction to think of the soul as dying. In the later *Phaedrus* Plato returns to the subject and seems now to place his reliance on a single central argument. Souls, he now sees clearly, are self-moved movers. They are the sources of all natural processes. And from this it follows at once that they are indestructible, because there is nothing outside themselves that could initiate the process of their destruction. The passage is worth quoting:

'All soul is immortal, for that is immortal which remains ever in motion; but that which besides moving other things is moved by them, in ceasing to move, ceases also to live. Therefore only that which is self-moving never fails itself and never ceases to move, but is the source and beginning of the motion of all other things. Now a beginning is unbegotten, for that which is begotten has a beginning; but a beginning has no beginning, for if a beginning were begotten by something else, it would not be a beginning. But that which is unbegotten must also be indestructible; for if a beginning should perish, it could neither itself have beginning out of anything else nor anything else have beginning out of it; since all things must have a beginning. Hence the beginning of motion is in that which moves itself; and this can neither be destroyed nor brought into being; for in that case the whole heaven and all the bringing of things into being would collapse and come to a standstill and never again be moved or come into being. Since then that which moves itself must be immortal, he who claims that self-motion is the very essence of soul will not be put to shame. For every body moved from without is soul-less, but that which is moved of itself from within has a soul, this being involved in the very nature of soul. But if we are right in saying that soul is thus self-moving, then soul must be unbegotten and immortal. Let this suffice concerning the soul's immortality.'[1]

It is clear, then, that the reasons Plato suggests for believing in the continued existence of the soul correspond very closely to the reasons which had, from the Old Stone Age onwards, led men to believe in it. It would of course be absurd to attribute to Plato the whole mental outlook which Tylor characterized as animism, yet it is clear that he not only accepts but builds the whole structure of his philosophy upon what is

---

[1] *Phaedrus*, 245–6. The *Republic*, it may be added, has also a more or less distinctive argument of its own.

actually the first principle of the animistic psychological analysis—that souls are the ultimate agents in all processes of whatever kind. To think of Plato as a defender of animism will not be so incongruous when we remember that Tylor himself declared that animism 'embodies the very essence of spiritualistic, as opposed to materialistic, philosophy',[1] and that a leading psychologist of our own time gave to one of his widely read books the sub-title *A History and a Defence of Animism*.[2] Moreover, we must not forget that Plato never championed any belief more hotly than he did the animistic belief that the heavenly bodies have souls. It is, then, to the self-analysis of animistic psychology that Plato appeals in support of his doctrine of the future of the soul. And yet, as we have already indicated and as we shall presently have to bring out more clearly, the doctrine he thus supports by animistic arguments is not itself the animistic doctrine at all, but something new and different. It is not at all the old belief in the dim 'subsistence' of one's ghost after oneself is dead, but a new belief (the provenance of which we shall presently have to explore) in a glorious destiny awaiting that part of one which is one's most real self. The fact that Plato uses for this most real self the same term (*psyche*) which had originally been used only to denote one's shadowy second self or ghost is indeed confusing, but it must not be allowed to obscure our perception of the facts.

No one who passes from the reading of earlier Greek literature like the Homeric poems to the reading of the *Phaedo* can fail to be aware of the new way in which the soul is now spoken

---

[1] *Primitive Culture*, vol. i, p. 415.
[2] William McDougall, *Body and Mind, A History and a Defence of Animism*, 1911.

of. The facts of the changed usage were carefully set down as long ago as 1893 by Erwin Rohde, but it is to the paper on 'The Socratic Doctrine of the Soul' which the late John Burnet read to the British Academy in January 1916 that we owe the clear perception that the Socrates of the Platonic dialogues was himself mainly responsible for the change.[1] The word now bears the definitely ethical and religious connotation which it has ever since retained in Christian usage. 'For the sake of the soul!' (τῆς ψυχῆς ἕνεκα) is now proposed as the ideal signature of all a good man's actions. 'I do nothing', said Socrates in his last defence, 'but go about persuading you all, both young and old, not to care about the body or money, but to care first and foremost about the soul and how it can be made most good.'[2] So much so, indeed, that according to Aristophanes his disciples came to be nicknamed 'the Souls' (ψυχαί).[3] Equally new and surprising is it to find the survival of the soul after death spoken of as *immortality* and as *a thing to be rejoiced in and looked forward to with eager anticipation*. 'Nay, if this be true', said Socrates to his judges, after having told them what he believed about the future life, '*let me die again and again.*'[4] What had, from time immemorial, been regarded as a colourless psychological fact is now become a treasured religious conviction. That the hope of immortality is very dear to Plato's heart and is closely linked with his most sacred aspirations is clear to us every time he pronounces the word *athanasia*. The very fall of the vowels is

---

[1] *Proceedings of the British Academy*, vii (1915–16), pp. 235 ff.; reprinted separately in 1916 and now included in the posthumous *Essays and Addresses* (1929). See also Burnet's article 'Soul (Greek)' in the *Encycl. of Religion and Ethics* and the introduction to his edition of the *Phaedo* (1911), pp. xlviii–lv.

[2] *Apol.* 30.   [3] *Clouds*, 94.   [4] *Apol.* 41.

charged with intensity. Yet when he goes about to prove that such immortality is available to us, the grounds of hope which he brings forward are, in the main, not any new grounds of a religious kind but the ancient animistic ones. And so two questions are likely to arise in the reader's mind: first, whether the old grounds are sufficient to support the new conclusion—whether an animistic analysis of the soul can ever lead to more than animism's own shadowy and cheerless prospect; and second, whether Plato's cherished new belief had not, in actual fact, been derived from sources of a very different kind, sources of which very little mention is made. Perhaps if Plato had told us why it had come to seem so *important* to him to believe in immortality, he would have brought us farther on the way to believing it than he does by all his parade of supposedly scientific proofs. Indirectly he does tell us this, as we shall see in our next chapter.

It was, however, indicated above that one of the arguments used by Plato is capable of being interpreted as carrying beyond the animistic self-analysis into the region of direct religious experience. This is when he argues that the soul must share in the eternity of the ideal objects of its contemplation. We shall have occasion at a later point to dwell on the historical influence of this most characteristic Platonic conception; and justice will then be done to its religious implications. But it must be said that these implications are obscured by the form in which the argument is presented in the *Phaedo*.

Meanwhile the habit of thought started by the *Phaedo* was destined to have a long history. As Jeremy Taylor declared in his sermon at the funeral of Sir George Dalston, 'Men cast out every line, and turned every stone, and tried every argument: and sometimes proved it well, and when they did not, yet they believed strongly; and *they were sure of the thing, when they were not sure of the argument.*[1] Thinker after thinker from Plato's time down to our own have striven afresh to prove the essential indestructibility of the soul by appeal to considerations of a psychological or psycho-physiological kind. They have investigated both the soul's structure and its function, and have particularly followed Plato in studying the relation of the soul to the body and in arguing the question of the relative priority of mind and matter. During these twenty and more centuries the scientific understanding of things has made splendid and spectacular advances, and there are few of these advances that have not been swiftly related, in one way or another, to the question of the soul's immortality. What is the event? What has really been contributed? What should we now feel that science—and more particularly Plato's science of psycho-physics—has really to tell us concerning this matter?

IV

There are a few among us who depart so far from Plato as to opine that natural science not only is not able to prove the soul's continuance, but actually is able to prove its annihilation;[2] or at least they would hold that there is much good evidence pointing to annihilation and none at all pointing to continuance. The modern understanding of the relation of the mind to the bodily organism, they would tell us, has

[1] Coleridge comments on this passage in his *Aids to Reflection*, 'Aphorisms on Spiritual Religion,' xxiii.

[2] This seems to be Unamuno's view in *The Tragic Sense of Life*, though he adds the not very satisfactory qualification that science can only prove this 'within its limits, which are the limits of rationality'.

effectively destroyed the whole animistic outlook on which our forebears, from the cave-man onwards, founded their expectation of an after-life. Mind and body are now known to be so intimately involved in one another as to make it all but certain that when the body dies, the mind also ceases to exist.

This opinion, however, seems to me far from well founded. I do not deny that *some* of the things we know about mind, and about the observed relation of mind to matter, would, if they were *all* that we knew, point in the direction of such a conclusion. There is, for instance, the apparent fact that, whatever may be true of other orders of precedence which Plato may have had in mind, at least in the order of temporal evolution in the created world soul is not older than body, but body older than soul. Mind seems, as we say, to have 'evolved' or 'emerged' out of a prior state of things that was not itself mental but purely bodily. It looks, therefore, as if mind came into being as the effect of a certain conjunction of organic conditions; making it natural to suppose that when this conjunction is disturbed and all its constituents destroyed by the death of the organism, mind also should cease to be. To this we can add many other observed facts concerning the dependence of mind on body and the obliterating effect exercised upon our mental activity by many partial and temporary disturbances of the bodily condition. When the brain sickens, the mind sickens also; why then, when the brain dies, should not the mind die too? Nor is it only on the perfect preservation of the brain that the mind now seems to modern science to be thus dependent, but on the perfect preservation also of a large part of the nervous system and of the sympathetic glands. When the endocrine glands sicken, the mind sickens also; why then, when they utterly decay, should not the mind disappear with them? And again, if you give a man a certain amount of alcohol, you will affect his body and affect also his mind; why then, if you give him more alcohol and utterly destroy his body, should you not at the same time destroy his mind?

If such facts as these were all we knew about the nature of mind and its relation to the body, then indeed the scientific evidence would be strongly on the side of annihilation. But every reader will be aware that the above facts have been carefully selected. For one thing, nothing has yet been said of the surprising extent to which the mind appears, again from empirical observation, to be independent of its brother the body. The body may be all but utterly wasted and destroyed by disease, and yet the mind may rise triumphant above such weakness and be as brave and firm and clear as it was before. Again, no mention has yet been made of mind as a cause or agent, but only as an effect or patient. Yet the influence of mind on body is at least as authentic and as striking an empirical fact as the influence of body on mind. If one of the sensational developments of recent psycho-physical research has been the science of endocrinology with its revelation of the surprising extent to which the mental condition can be damaged, and again repaired, by inducing variations in certain glandular secretions, the other sensational development has been the science of psychiatry with its revelation of the no less surprising extent to which variations in one's state of mind may damage or repair the bodily condition. Indeed it may be said that at the present time no responsible medical authority is prepared to set a limit to the power which mind has over body both in the causation and in the cure of disease. Thus if on the one hand more and more mental disorders are being traced to bodily deficiencies, on the other hand more and more bodily disorders are being traced to mental 'complexes'. If my mental distress is ascribed to the condition of my liver or of my thyroid gland, my bodily distress is just as likely to be ascribed to some load that I am carrying on my conscience. Now it is on the basis of the first of these two sets of facts that the 'materialistic' or 'organic' view of mind was built up, and it is difficult to see how it can possibly be made consonant with the second set. One might also mention certain other aspects of mental activity, such as the phenomena of hypnotism, of trance, of dual personality, of telepathy, and of psychometry which, though nobody is yet in a position to dogmatize about them, tend nevertheless to put any over-simplified scheme of psycho-physics out of court. I must myself confess to a strong initial incredulity concerning some of these phenomena, and even to a certain secret *hope* that there may turn out to be much less in them than appears, but even I have been astonished at the unwillingness of some of my naturalistically minded friends to examine them with even a semblance of fairness. One is bound to think also of M. Bergson's *Matière et mémoire* with its brilliantly argued contention that the facts of memory can be explained only on the hypothesis that the major part of psychic activity is independent of the body, our souls being like cones with only their apexes inserted into matter—a contention to which he returns in his latest work, as leading, he says, 'to the possibility and even probability of a survival of the soul, because we have observed and as it were touched with our finger, from here below, something of its independence in relation to the body'.[1] Moreover, we have not yet said anything about the *inside* knowledge of our own minds which is available to us through introspection. When we do include such knowledge, we are led to such a comprehension of the nature of mental process as makes it difficult to see what can even be meant by the glib statement (from which we set out) that mind has 'evolved out of' matter. What can it mean to say that the philosophy of Plato or the art of Phidias or the religion of Christ evolved out of, or was an effect produced by, the movement of certain atoms of carbon, nitrogen, phosphorus, and the rest? What can it even mean to say that the movement of atoms produced at last (in the brains of Leucippus and Democritus) the idea of the atom? Or if we discard the language of cause and effect in favour of the conception of 'emergence' and content ourselves with affirming that first there was matter only, and afterwards matter plus mind, then we are left with the alternative of believing that something (whether suddenly or gradually) emerged for no reason out of nothing; unless we fall back on the Platonic conviction that, although in the history of this planet bodies may have existed prior to souls, yet prior to these bodies there must have existed, beyond this planet, a Supreme Soul.[2]

[1] *Les Deux Sources*, p. 283. In an essay on 'The Mind and the Brain' contributed to *Immortality* (ed. Streeter, 1917), Dr. J. A. Hadfield brings forward evidence of a scientific kind which 'will encourage us in the belief that in the course of evolution the mind shows an ever-increasing tendency to free itself from physical control and, breaking loose from its bonds, to assert its independence and live a life undetermined except by the laws of its own nature' (p. 21).

[2] For a brilliant exposure of the meaningless way in which the word 'evolution' is often bandied about by popular and hasty thinkers, see H. W. B. Joseph's Spencer Lecture on *The Concept of Evolution* (Oxford, 1924).

It is, then, a suspicious circumstance that those writers who give such account of the relation of soul to body as makes it absurd to suppose that the soul should survive bodily death, should be resting their case upon a carefully selected set of facts and should be tending to suppress another set of facts which must be regarded as at least equally pertinent and enlightening. The *main* facts of the dependence of mind on body were as much in Plato's mind as they can be in ours. The materialistic view of the universe and also the naturalistic or epiphenomenal view of mind were as rampant in the Athens of his day as they have been lately in our modern West. In the *Phaedo* he finds himself faced with the view that the soul is no more than an attunement or harmony (ἁρμονία) of certain bodily conditions and can no more survive the disappearance of these conditions than the tune can survive the breaking up of the lyre. 'If the soul is only a harmony dependent on the proper admixture of bodily elements', Simmias is made to say, 'it follows clearly that when the body (like the lyre) is either slackened or tightened out of due proportion by sickness or other mishap, then the soul, however divine it may be, like other harmonies in music and other works of art, must at once perish, though the bodily remains may continue in existence for a long time until they are cremated or become decomposed.'[1] Plato, then, was fully aware of the case that could be made for such a view of mind, but he was also aware of another set of facts that seemed to him to put this view entirely out of court.

Empirically speaking, the materialistic view that mind is a function of the body is no better grounded than the idealistic

[1] *Phaedo*, 86.

view that body is a function of the mind. There is no better warrant for regarding man as a thinking organism than for regarding him as an embodied soul.

Furthermore, we must bear it in mind that even if the dependence of the soul on the body were much more complete and one-sided than an impartial opinion can ever hold it to be, the possibility of survival would still be by no means ruled out. For though Plato and his philosophic disciples evidently looked forward to an immortality of an entirely disembodied kind, yet in so doing they have been almost alone among believers in a future life. The ancient distinction was not really between *body* and *mind*. It is only in Plato and Aristotle that the mind lives bodiless after the body dies. The ancient distinction, universal among primitive folk as among Hebrews, Greeks, and Romans, is between the *ordinary* self and the shadowy *second* self, the soul or double. The ordinary self was the 'full-blooded' self; but the soul, though 'bloodless', was certainly not conceived as being bereft of all bodily organization. And, as we shall presently see, the Christian view has from the beginning been emphatically not that of a totally disembodied immortality, but rather of the bestowal upon us by God, after the death of our present bodies, of 'new and glorious' bodies that shall be the vehicles of a far higher life of the soul than we are now able to enjoy. But what possible or thinkable evidence can science bring forward to show that we shall *not*, by the power of God, be endued with such glorified bodies when we pass beyond the veil?

There is thus no foundation for the view that science is in possession of evidence pointing to the extinction of the soul at death. It is even difficult to imagine how science could *ever* hope to attain such negative evidence. I believe all fair-minded men will agree that if some genuine positive evidence of survival were to emerge, such as would compel the belief of all, there is not a single empirically known fact about mind that would appear to be definitely contradicted; though it may be that most men would then prefer on scientific grounds, as most men in the past have preferred on religious grounds, to contemplate the provision of some new form of embodiment rather than the possibility of an entirely disembodied life of the soul.

But—and here we pass to the second half of our inquiry—is any such genuine positive evidence really available? If science has nothing to bring forward in favour of dissolution, has it anything to bring forward in favour of continuance? It must be admitted that most of the scientific proofs that have been offered are strangely unconvincing. I think that in our school-days most of us found the proofs of the *Phaedo* strangely unconvincing. *Something* in the dialogue impressed us tremendously. I am myself not ashamed to remember how more than one evening I wept over the preparation of that Greek lesson. But what impressed me, I think, was not the evidence Plato brought forward, but the firmness and eagerness of his own belief. It should be noted that the question we are now raising is not that of the general success of the animistic analysis of the self, or of the relative justification of the general animistic outlook as over against the materialistic one. We may well hold the animist to be right in his fundamental contention that a true understanding of the psycho-physical relation must lead to the belief that the ultimate

93

origination of all processes is due to soul—or that, as Plato put it, soul is the ἀρχὴ κινήσεως ἁπάσης. But the question we are raising is whether, even if this were established, it would follow that the soul would live on after death. It is here, I think, that our real doubts lie. To us the least convincing part of primitive man's animistic outlook is what we should call his belief in ghosts. And I know of no later proof grounded in this way on the analysis of the soul and its psycho-physical relations for which I should care to claim much persuasive power.[1]

Yet there is a reason, already hinted at, why it would be unprofitable to concern ourselves too closely with the balancing of probabilities on this point of evidence. For the real source of our dissatisfaction with the scientific (as with its lineal precursor, the animistic) line of argument is not that its proof fails of conviction, but that its conclusion fails of interest. Even were we able to regard its logic as altogether impeccable, could we really rejoice in the prospect that were thus opened out to us? Of what use to us is mere continuance? Do we want merely to go on living for ever, without regard to the kind of life we are to live, or on the presumption that our life hereafter will be no more than a repetition of this present 'petty pace'? Surely there is nothing in such a prospect that religion has ever taught us to glory in, or even that Plato prized. It appears then that even if our efforts to establish a presumption in favour of the soul's indestructibility by means of an analysis of the psycho-physical relationship should be more successful in the future than they have been

[1] 'The Platonic conception of the soul has not advanced our knowledge of the soul a single step, in spite of two thousand years of meditation upon it.' Bergson, *Les Deux Sources*, p. 282.

in the past, we should not thereby be brought any nearer to the essential Christian hope. The interest of religion is not primarily in the indestructibility of the finite but in the fellowship of the Infinite, and it is only so far as the latter is contained in the former that it is interested in the former at all. What possible feeling, we may ask, except one of *horror* could the saints of the Christian Church have had towards the conclusion of such a contemporary philosopher as the late J. M. E. McTaggart, who thought that he could conclusively prove the immortality of the soul—but from premises which led with equal rigour to the non-existence of God, thus offering the prospect of a Godless eternity? 'One might indeed say', writes his biographer, 'that he had a positive dislike for the conception of God'; and he quotes McTaggart himself as saying in a letter to a friend: 'I know very few people who believe as vividly in heaven as I do. . . . But it can't be nice to believe in God. . . . I have no room left in my life for God.'[1] But to speak of *heaven* without *God* is to depart entirely from the accepted meaning of the term. What McTaggart did, if he did anything, was to prove the existence of hell and the non-existence of heaven (though I have been disappointed to find this nowhere clearly pointed out by his critics). Hell, according to the definition (majestic in phrase if awful in intent) of the Westminster Confession of Faith, means 'everlasting destruction from the presence of the Lord and from the glory of His power'.[2]

Francis Bacon's celebrated judgement on the limits of scientific evidence regarding all such matters was that 'it

[1] *J. M. E. McTaggart*, by G. Lowes Dickinson (1931), p. 87.
[2] ch. xxxiii. 2.

sufficeth to convince atheism, but not to inform religion'.[1] If we are clear about our concurrence in the latter half of this dictum, it matters much less how we feel about the former.

The same considerations appear to apply to another type of evidence concerning which we have not yet said anything. If you ask a savage in almost any part of the world how he knows that the soul continues to live after death, his answer is twofold. He first gives you a little lesson in psychology, explaining how the soul's continuance is implied in its essential nature. With this part of his answer we have already dealt. But next he gives you a little lesson in necromancy, offering you direct sensible evidence of continuance, and relating to you a number of (as he thinks) well-authenticated experiences that he has had with ghosts. It is about this second part of his answer that a word must now be said.

It is an answer, as is well known, that is given us not only by savages but by a surprising number of people in our own very emancipated West, including not a few scientists of real note. There are many who believe that by the pursuit of what has come to be called 'psychical research' they have already succeeded in establishing the soul's continuance, and there are many more who, though not yet claiming to have attained certainty, continue eagerly to hope that they may one day do so. We have Shelley's confession in the *Hymn to Intellectual Beauty*:

> While yet a boy I sought for ghosts, and sped
> Through many a listening chamber, cave and ruin,
> And starlight wood, with fearful steps pursuing
> Hopes of high talk with the departed dead.

[1] *Of the Advancement of Learning*, book ii.

An enormous mass of evidence has been collected in the *Proceedings of the Society for Psychical Research* and elsewhere, but it is notoriously difficult both to evaluate and to interpret. The extent of the fraud that has been practised in this field is admittedly very great, so that there are many who doubt whether any authentic phenomena at all have been brought to light; while even those who admit the existence of the phenomena often think themselves able to suggest a simpler explanation of them than that of supposing them to be communications from the realm of the dead.

Here again, however, it is fortunately not necessary that we should force ourselves to reach a premature conclusion on a matter so difficult, because even if the 'spiritualists' should turn out to be right, the result would have little real bearing on the standing of our Christian hope. It would not even suffice 'to convince atheism', let alone 'to inform religion'. To some savages the existence of ghosts has indeed religious associations, because they are ancestor-worshippers and regard the ghosts as divine; but to those who hold no such belief, what is there about mere continuance, taken by itself, that could excite religious interest? It has been pointed out[1] that in such a work as the late F. W. H. Myers's two bulky volumes on *Human Personality and Its Survival of Bodily Death* no reference is made to the reality of God at all. But again we must remind ourselves that the traditional Christian name for such endless existence without God is not eternal life but *eternal death*. 'I had rather choose', writes à Kempis, 'to be a pilgrim on earth with Thee than without Thee to possess heaven. Where Thou art, there is heaven: and where

[1] By A. E. Taylor, *The Faith of a Moralist*, vol. i, p. 255.

Thou art not, there is death and hell.'[1] And Whittier has it in his hymn that

> To turn aside from Thee is hell,
> To walk with Thee is heaven!

It must be said, then, of animism's proffered sensible evidence, as of its proffered deductive demonstration, that it can yield at most animism's dismal conclusion—the prospect, not of fruition and of glory, but only of dreary continuance. If we suppose a man who is entirely out of sympathy with the Christian outlook to be convinced by psychical research of the continued existence of the soul, we shall realize at once that he would not thereby be brought any nearer to sharing the essential Christian hope. He would indeed now be believing, in common with Christians, that there is some kind of further life beyond the veil, but there would be no available bridge whereby he could pass from this belief, which is itself not religious at all, to anything that could be regarded as the true essence of a religious view of destiny. The Christian outlook on the future is not to be approached by way of any secular proof of the existence of *some* kind of future, but only by a deepening of our Christian outlook on the present. If the promise of *fruition* does not come to us from our experience of the *quest*, it is difficult to see how we can reach it by any more royal road. This appears to be as true of our interest in the heavenly security of those whom we have loved and lost, as it is of our own longing for the heavenly vision of God and for the enjoyment of His presence; but instead of saying this in my own words I shall take leave to transcribe what seem to me to be some very wise words from another pen.

[1] Book iii. 59.

The demand for such assurance of the fate of our loved ones as psychical research may conceivably be able to give us is, according to Dean Sperry of Harvard,

'in some measure a confession that life itself, with long years of friendship and affection, has not yielded that assurance as a kind of inner certainty which needs no further proof. There is something belated in this quest for comfort, as it were a tacit confession that the years of human communion had not granted the conviction which they should have granted. I would prefer not to try to overtake, by plucking at the mystery, the failure of my own experience as friend and kinsman. And in the case of those whom I think I did come to know well and to love well, I would prefer to leave the matter there, with the sure memories and persuasions which experience yielded. Personally I should be very loath to seek at the hands of a medium in trance messages from my own dear dead. I should feel that somehow I was faithless to that which they gave me and were to me in life. . . . This may be an idiosyncrasy. I record it for what it is worth.'[1]

The Archbishop of York goes farther yet, holding it

'positively undesirable that there should be experimental proof of our survival of death—at least of such survival in the case of those who have had no spiritual faith on earth. . . . It might or might not encourage the belief that God exists; it would certainly, as I think, make very much harder the essential business of faith which is the transference of the centre of interest and concern from self to God. If such knowledge comes, it must be accepted. . . . But I confess I hope that such research will continue to issue in such dubious results as are all that I can trace to it up to date.'[2]

[1] In the composite volume on *Christianity and Modern Thought* (Yale University Press, 1924), p. 130 f.
[2] W. Temple, *The Idea of Immortality in Religion and Ethics*, being the Drew Lecture for 1931, p. 9 f.

CHAPTER V

THE SEQUEL OF THE TALE

I

IN the last chapter we were concerned with that belief in the continued existence of one's ghost after death which is a fruit of the animistic interpretation of experience and which appears to be universal among mankind from prehistoric times onwards, though tending to fade out among certain more highly civilized peoples. In the present chapter we shall be concerned with the Christian doctrine of eternal life. And our first business must be to make it clear that the latter is no mere development of the former, but that there is between the two something like a clean 'break'.

This does not mean, however, that there was no historical preparation at all for the Christian hope. Had there not been such a *praeparatio evangelica*, it is unlikely that the evangel, when it came, would have found any to understand it, much less to receive it. Preparations and adumbrations are to be found in the religions of India and of ancient Persia. Persian thought on the matter was in many respects paralleled by the thought of Judaism, which it must to some extent have influenced; but the Jews were finally to go beyond anything the Persians had contemplated. And beside this later thought of the Jews there stands the later thought of the Greeks. The 'break' of which I have spoken is not, then, if we speak strictly, to be placed between the final developments in Greece or Judaea and the teaching of the Christian Church, but rather between the outlook which Greece and Judaea had shared for thousands of years with all the other peoples of the earth and the very different outlook which, within certain limited circles, each seems to have developed during the centuries immediately preceding the advent of Christianity. This 'break' has been commented on by most of the best recent writers on the subject, but it is from Professor Webb that I have borrowed the word. It does, he writes, appear

'to be the fact that neither the Jewish hope of immortality which Christianity took up into itself (both Jesus himself and St. Paul ranging themselves with the Pharisees and against the Sadducees in this matter), nor the Platonic affirmation of the deathlessness of the human soul, were refined interpretations, still less mere survivals, of the beliefs associated with primitive animism all the world over. They represent a new departure, and they presuppose a break with those earlier notions. . . .

'There is in both cases a notable break intervening between the prevalence of these older faiths and the higher creeds which were to take their place.'[1]

II

Let us look first at what happened in the classical world. We have already noted how with the advance of Greek and Roman culture the reality of the underworld, instead of becoming more vivid and more sharply defined, tended rather to grow dimmer and more uncertain, until at last it was altogether lost hold of by many of the most thoughtful and inquiring minds. 'The Athenians of the Periclean age', wrote the late Professor Burnet, 'had no definite views about the soul at all.'[2] The Roman educated man of the age of Cicero,

---

[1] *Divine Personality and Human Life*, pp. 261, 257.
[2] In the article on 'Soul (Greek)' in the *Encycl. of Religion and Ethics*, vol. xi, p. 740.

writes Professor Warde Fowler, had 'lapsed into a condition of mind mainly indifferent but partly sceptical about the soul. . . .'[1] Since the age of Cicero such scepticism has immensely increased. But it has not yet quite won the day. There are some among us still who give some degree of credence to all the old beliefs—who still suspect it may be true that the ghosts of dead men continue to exist, that their existence is of a very shadowy, ineffective, dreary, and mournful kind, but otherwise not unlike our present everyday life, that they continue to visit their old haunts though perhaps also having 'a place of their own', and that it is highly advisable, if no longer perhaps to propitiate them with offerings, at least to refrain from offending them by careless word or deed.

It is clear that, as Rohde says, such a conception 'did not contain within itself the seeds of further development'.[2] The new creed, when it came, sprang from an entirely different source. The novelty of its first emergence is well brought out in the often quoted episode towards the end of the *Republic* in which Socrates is made to put to Glaucon the sudden question whether, since threescore years and ten are but a fragment of eternity, *immortal beings* should regard it in too serious a light. Glaucon, who represents cultivated Athenian youth at its best, interrupts with '*What* was that you said?' 'Have you not then discovered', rejoins Socrates, 'that our souls are immortal and never perish?' At which Glaucon can only stare in astonishment (ἐμβλέψας καὶ θαυμάσας) and reply, 'I can't say I have, by Zeus! Can you say you have?'[3]

---

[1] In the article on 'Soul (Roman)' in the *Encycl. of Religion and Ethics*, vol. xi, p. 748. [2] *Psyche*, Eng. tr., p. 253. [3] *Republic*, 608 D.

Where and how, then, did the new creed arise? The answer is clear. It was born of *a new kind of religious experience*—'a second order of religion', as Rohde calls it, 'which, though little remarked by the religion of the people and by orthodox believers, gained a footing in isolated sects and influenced certain philosophical schools'.[1] The reference is, of course, to the mystery cults.

Even in the Eleusinian mysteries which were native to Greece and of ancient establishment we may find a certain foreshadowing of the new outlook. For among the promises made to those who participated was one which had never before fallen on Greek ears, namely, that of a privileged fate after death and of an existence in the realm of Hades that was really worthy of the name of life. And it is instructive to realize by which of the existing categories of thought this promise succeeded in expressing itself. It had, as we have seen, been part of the teaching of the poets that, though all men now living must die and go down to Erebus, there to live the sad life of ghosts, yet long ago a few earth-dwellers such as Menelaus, Rhadamanthus, Penelope, and Telemachus, who were specially favoured of the gods or were of semi-divine descent, had not died and gone down to Erebus at all, but had been translated alive (soul and body unseparate) to what Homer calls the Elysian Fields and Hesiod the Islands of the Blest—those 'ends of the world where dwells auburn-haired Rhadamanthus, and where life is most easy for men. There neither snow is nor wintry weather nor any rain; and Oceanus sends forth only the gently-blowing breezes of the west wind, that men may be refreshed.'[2] It is plain, as Rohde says, that

---

[1] Op. cit., p. 254. [2] *Odyssey*, iv. 562 ff.

such fanciful poetic pictures really sprang from a suppressed aspiration on the part of the living after a better and more joyful destiny beyond the grave. Suppressed it certainly was, for such translation was always regarded as being strictly miraculous and exceptional and entirely a thing of the far distant past. The Islands of the Blest receive 'no additions from the life of to-day. . . . The circle of the fortunate . . . is now closed, just as the circle of epic story is complete also. Such miracles no longer happen.'[1] In the post-Homeric literature, indeed, we find increasing reference to another class of fortunates who enjoy a privileged destiny and whose number is not necessarily regarded as closed, namely, the Heroes. The Heroes were once men. They died like other men and their souls went down to the realm of Hades, but after death they were elevated to heroic rank, so that now they are enjoying an altogether higher type of existence than other ghosts, and, like the gods and those who have been translated to Elysium, they will live on for ever. Yet elevation to the rank of a hero was still regarded as a marvel beyond the common and familiar order of nature, and every instance of it was 'a fresh and special miracle'.[2]

Now what the Eleusinian mysteries did was to hold out some prospect of this kind to the ordinary man. Future bliss is no longer a poet's fancy. No longer is it reserved for the miraculously translated demigods and the miraculously elevated heroes of long ago. It is offered freely to all who desire it. 'It was these promises of a blessed immortality that for centuries drew so many worshippers to the Eleusinian festival. Nowhere else could such promises be obtained with such

[1] Rohde, op. cit., p. 78.   [2] Ibid., p. 138.

distinctness and assurance.'[1] The condition imposed was that one should take part in the festival, piously worshipping Demeter and her attendant circle of deities after due initiation and purification. Here then we have, in its true and original historical *locus*, the doctrine of conditional immortality, though not in the sense of the modern doctrine which requires the complete *extinction* of those not thus immortalized. The Eleusinian teaching was that while for other men there is only dreary continuance, there is for the initiated a prospect of something that is really worthy of the name of life. 'The continued conscious existence of the soul after its separation from the body was not a doctrine but a presupposition of Eleusis', Rohde writes. 'The advantage obtained by the initiated at Eleusis was that a livelier and fuller *content* was given to the bare existence of the disembodied soul. . . . Not *that* the soul, relieved of the presence of the body, will live hereafter, but *how* it will live, was what Eleusis taught men.'[2]

Yet it is doubtful, after all, whether we do right in applying such a term as immortality to the privileged life in Hades which Demeter promised to her worshippers, for it is not until we come to the cult of Dionysus that we find promise of a blessedness that deserves so noble a name. 'The worship of Dionysus,' says Rohde, 'must have sown the first seed of belief in an immortal life of the soul.'[3] Dionysus was not a native Greek deity but was introduced from Thrace, and the promises which he made to men were of an entirely new kind, being utterly opposed to the most fundamental of native

[1] Ibid., p. 223.
[2] Ibid., p. 225.
[3] Ibid., p. 255.

Greek religious ideas. Any talk of *immortality* in connexion with *man* was to the Greek ear both nonsense and blasphemy, for it was just in regard to this matter of death and deathlessness that the great and unbridgeable gulf between gods and men was most clearly defined. But now from the mountainous wilds of Thrace there comes the remarkable rumour that a method has after all been found by which the gulf may be bridged—a new kind of religious relationship in which man may be 'possessed of God', God 'entering into man' until he becomes ἔνθεος, he in God and God in him. It was believed that in the wild fever and frenzy of these ritual dances on the mountain-tops the soul 'stood apart' from the body in temporary liberation (λύσις). The Greek for 'standing apart' is ἔκστασις, and so came into being our word 'ecstasy', just as our word 'enthusiasm' is derived from ἔνθεος. The soul, when liberated, united with the god and became one with him. In this way, then, the hope naturally sprang into being that when, at death, the souls of the worshippers were completely and finally liberated from their bodies, they would be wholly united with the god for evermore, so sharing his own immortal nature. It is very impressive to discover how, contrary as all this was to every native prejudice, it finally found so eager a response in the Hellenic mind. Here at last we have the Greeks contemplating the immortality of man. And it is quite clear that the triumph of such a conception was due, not to any process of detached philosophic reflection, but to the direct findings of a new religious experience. 'No mere intellectual arguments', says Rohde, 'could give such powerful support to a spiritualization of this kind as the personal experience itself which, even in this life, supplied a foretaste of what the individual was one day to enjoy as his own for ever.'[1] It was in the very act of religious communion that 'the sense of its own divinity' and therefore of 'its eternity' was 'blindingly revealed' to the soul.[2] For indeed it is clear, as Rohde is careful to insist, that the emphasis is primarily on the quality of this new life of communion, and only secondarily on its continuance. 'The new belief ... was that a highly exalted state of feeling could raise man above the normal level of his limited, everyday consciousness, and could elevate him to heights of vision and knowledge unlimited; that, further, to the human soul it was not denied, in very truth and not in vain fancy, to live for a moment the life of divinity.'[3] Had he not, in his union with the god, tasted a higher *kind* of life, he would have been no more deeply concerned with life's effective continuance than other Greeks had been. But in this higher kind of life there seemed to be latently contained the seeds both of a desire for its continuance and of a promise that the desire should be fulfilled. That is to say, those very Greeks who (except for subterranean longings that came to the surface only in poetic fancy) showed themselves so indifferent to a continuance of their ordinary existence now found themselves ardently desiring the continuance of the life lived in union with deity; and moreover found themselves firmly persuaded that a life thus united with an immortal being must share in his immortality.

The next step is taken with the formation of the so-called Orphic sects. These were private religious associations which began to appear in the Greek states and colonies in the second

---

[1] Rohde, op. cit., p. 265.   [2] Ibid., p. 264.
[3] Ibid., p. 291.

half of the sixth century before Christ. Their purpose was the worship of Dionysus, but what specially characterizes them is the peculiar mingling of a strong intellectual interest with this devotional one. A generation previously Greek science and philosophy had together been born in the Ionian colonies, and now the great Pythagoras was carrying on this tradition in the colonies of Southern Italy. In the thought of Pythagoras the scientific tradition on the one hand and the Dionysiac religion on the other seem to be fused into a single whole. How far Pythagoras was the founder of Orphism and how far he was influenced by Orphic sects already existing it is now very difficult to say; but it is certain that the Pythagorean fusion of interests is reflected to a large extent in the Orphic movement as a whole.

What the Orphics did was to provide the worship of Dionysus with an elaborate doctrinal system. This they professed to accomplish by rendering explicit that which was latently present in the ecstatic experience itself. The soul of man, they argued, could not thus unite with the God unless it were divine in its own original nature. Indeed, the immortal quality of life which the worshipper enjoys is directly felt by him to be no mere adventitious privilege, but his proper birthright. Seeing, then, that the soul of man is not now normally one with Dionysus or participant in his divinity, it must somehow have *fallen*—and here, so far as Greece is concerned, is the beginning of the Doctrine of the Fall. But wherein did the Fall consist? The answer is given clearly. Seeing that reunion with the god has been found to be possible only when the soul 'stands apart' from the body in a state of 'liberation', it follows that the original separation can only have come about through the soul being imprisoned within the body. The Orphics, like the Hebrews, told a myth about the Fall. The god Dionysus, they explained, had in his form as a bull been overcome by the wily stratagems of the Titans, the powers of evil, and his body had been torn to shreds and eaten by his murderers. Zeus then destroyed the Titans with a thunderbolt, and out of their ashes the human race was born. But the meaning of the myth was transparent enough, for it was explained that each human soul was one of the pieces into which Dionysus had been torn, and that just as the Dionysiac element in man was represented by the soul, so the Titanic element in him was represented by the body. 'The body a tomb' was the familiar cliché concerning which we have already had occasion to speak in an earlier chapter.

It is only the few *Mystae* who in the experience of ecstasy have attained to the *unio mystica* (as the Latin expression finally went) that can now hope for a restoration of their souls to immortal divine life. Nevertheless the realization that, before the Fall, all souls were naturally divine and immortal had the effect of leading the Orphics to a much livelier belief in the reality of the life that awaits even the uninitiated beyond the grave. A ghostly continuance for everybody was, of course, taken for granted by all—though in many quarters it was gradually paling into the position of a vestigial belief, or was even subjected to active incredulity. But now the Orphics had recourse to the idea of the transmigration of souls and their reincarnation in one body after another, in order that by this means they might give more reality to the future life of all. This, as we saw in the last chapter, is an idea common to a considerable number of primitive peoples, but there is no evidence of its having ever appeared in Greece until the Orphics introduced it. Very probably they borrowed it from Dionysus' own original home in the mountains of Thrace—though we cannot be sure. At all events their teaching now was that since the Fall all souls have become involved in the Wheel of Birth (κύκλος or τροχός τῆς γενέσεως —in Latin, *rota generationis*). Those who have not attained to the mystic experience will for ever remain involved in this circle of successive births and deaths, and the bodies in which they will from time to time be incarnated will depend on their behaviour within the previous bodies. But the mystic experience offers a way of 'escape' and of 'salvation' from this doom. Not indeed immediately; for even the purest soul must pass through a number of rebirths in which the sins of the past are duly expiated. But they will be rebirths into future lives of ever-increasing happiness; and then, at last, the truly purified soul will be withdrawn from the cycle of birth and death altogether, and, leaving earth as well as Hades for ever behind it, will become one with immortal God throughout an eternity of unbroken blessedness. What must carefully be noted is that survival by reincarnation is here regarded as being essentially a *doom*, and that even the purified soul's migration to ever happier embodiments is regarded as no more than an alleviation of this doom, the final redemption consisting in release from mortality's whole 'trival round' and from embodiment of every kind.

Here, then, in the Dionysiac and Orphic teaching are born together into the Western World two apparently new and closely related ideas—the idea of the body as a hindrance rather than a help to the life of the soul and the idea of a blessed immortality devoid of all embodiment. Here is the *fons et origo* of all Western mysticism, of all Western asceticism, of all Western monasticism, and of the doctrine of the immortality of the discarnate soul. That all these should have developed from the wild and manic orgies of the Bacchanalian festival—such as are described in idealized form in Euripides' *Bacchae*—may appear not a little perplexing to us. But this is the kind of perplexity to which evolutionary history is constantly giving rise in our minds; and you and I must take history as we find it.

It is in the dialogues of Plato that these conceptions are given their final elaboration. Yet we have already seen how between Orphism and Platonism another forward step has been taken for which we must, following Professor Burnet, suppose Socrates to have been responsible. This is the identification of the soul with the 'normal consciousness' of a man, with the seat of knowledge and of character; so that when a man's soul enjoys immortality, it is not merely his ghost that is thus immortal but his most real self. This final adjustment of belief seems but the natural and fitting culmination of the earlier development, and for the rest it is quite plain that what Plato says about the soul's destiny has its roots in Orphic religion. Nowhere indeed is the Orphic eschatology worked out more impressively than in the Platonic myths. What now appears to us to be Plato's great mistake is that when we ask him for the *grounds* of this great faith of his in the future of the soul, he leads us not into that region of communion with God wherein his own faith had been born, but into the region of disinterested scientific speculation. Instead of showing us how by union with God we may attain to the experience of immortal life and then arguing from this experience to the immortal origin of the souls that are capable of it, he rests his case on his ability to prove that all souls are as such indestructible. It is noteworthy that even Rohde, though he recognizes no teaching to be a true doctrine of immortality which does not extend in this way to the inherent indestructibility of all souls, and though for the rest his interest in the matter is a purely historical one, recognizes this procedure of Plato's to be seriously mistaken. The process, he writes, by which Plato arrived at his belief 'is not to be found in the "proofs" by which he attempts in the *Phaedo* to establish the truth of the soul's immortality in which he himself already believed. Those proofs in reality do not prove what they are intended to prove...; they cannot therefore be the reasons that led the philosopher to hold his conviction. He has in fact borrowed this article of his faith from the creeds which already contained it. He himself scarcely conceals the fact. As authority for the main outlines of the soul's history as given by himself he refers almost apologetically, and as though excusing himself for not providing a philosophical proof, to the *theologi* and priests of the mysteries.'[1] If then it be not presumption to say so, what Plato should have done in the *Phaedo* and elsewhere was to offer us a keenly analytic and critical description of that Orphic experience of oneness with God in which his own desire for eternal life and his firm persuasion of its reality had their common root. Perhaps, as has been said, the argument in the *Phaedo* about the soul sharing in the eternity of the ideas it contemplates may, on

---

[1] Op. cit., p. 468 f. I do not speak of the criticism passed by Plato on other aspects of the Orphic mythology.

a sympathetic reading, be taken as not unconnected with the Orphic rapture.

In this Greek teaching it is possible to see a very real preparation for the Christian hope. It was a true light. But its rays did not long shine steadily, nor did they reach very far into the life of the people. In the Lyceum, in the Porch, in the Garden, we find them flickering or altogether extinguished. Among the Neoplatonists they leap once more, for a brief space, into vigorous being. Yet it is really with the carefully balanced uncertainty of a Marcus Aurelius that the history of pagan thought comes to an end. The rest of the story is Christian and concerns those who were begotten again unto a lively hope. It was, says Schweitzer, 'as the religion of immortality that Christianity was consecrated to take the place of the slowly dying civilization of the ancient world'.[1] And it will be remembered that the promise of the heavenly bliss is one of the 'five causes of the growth of Christianity' in the Roman Empire set out by Gibbon in his celebrated fifteenth chapter.

III

Leaving the Greeks now behind us, and before going on to the Jews, let us cast a glance, as it were in passing, at what had happened in India. This is of less importance for our present purpose because, unlike the developments in Greece and Israel, it forms no part of the direct ancestry of the Christian hope; but it is of no small interest as bringing to light the beginnings of a similar development in still another part of the world.

[1] *Von Reimarus zu Wrede* (1906), p. 252; Eng. trans., p. 254.

Judging by the accounts given by scholars on the basis of such evidence as is available, the ancient Indian ideas about the survival of souls corresponded very closely to those of other primitives. But the Indians apparently were not, any more than were the Greeks, among those numerous primitive peoples who believed in the reincarnation of souls in other bodies. In the Vedic hymns, India's oldest literature, there is no trace of such a doctrine. But in the Upanishads, the date of which cannot be later than the sixth century B.C., we find it firmly established in a form not unlike that introduced by the Orphics into Greece—so that the 'Wheel of Birth' is as much an Indian phrase as it is a Greek. Like Orphism the Brahminism of the Upanishads is a philosophical (or perhaps we should in both cases rather say 'theosophical') religion. And its central doctrine of a supreme divine soul called Brahma which is immanent in the world as its body has distinct points of resemblance to the Orphic doctrine of a divine soul called Dionysus whose broken-up fragments are imprisoned in our human bodies. Likewise its idea of reincarnation corresponds very closely to that of Orphism. In particular, the ethical conception of retribution is in both cases central, thus marking them off at once from all ideas of reincarnation current among primitive peoples. The nature of a man's successive incarnations is determined absolutely by the nature of his deeds in his previous lives. There is no arbitrary divine judgement in the matter, but, as in the teaching of Plato's Orphic myths, a man naturally finds his own level, 'like going to like'.[1] It is what we should now call a natural law—the Law of the Deed, the Law of *Karma* (which is Sanskrit for deed).

[1] The phrase is Plato's.

Once introduced, this doctrine of transmigration according to *karma* seems to have taken complete hold of the Indian mind, and it has ever since been regarded by every Indian religious sect and theosophical school (save only the materialistic Charvakas) as the axiomatic presupposition of all further reflection on the problems of the spirit. It forms the starting-point of Buddhism, Jainism, and Sikhism no less than of all the forms of Hinduism. And what we must note particularly is that it is always taken, as the Orphics took their parallel belief, to forebode nothing but *doom*. In early India the continuance of the soul was only vaguely conceived, but such conceptions as existed were not unpleasing ones. Men looked forward to a state of indolent and innocent, if somewhat colourless, happiness. Now, with the coming of the new teaching, the belief in continuance is immensely more vivid and influential, but instead of making men rejoice this plunges them into unrelieved gloom. The thought of an endless succession of lives is not a hope but a nightmare. And thus all Indian thought becomes fundamentally pessimistic. One writer says:

'The conception of "the round of rebirth" or "the wheel of existence" is everywhere taken for granted, and the atmosphere of spiritual depression which it engenders has saturated the fibre of the Hindu race. Depression has been the result because the cycle of rebirth is endless. If the Hindu could view his life as only a prelude to something higher and better, or even if he could see it as only a brief span before extinction, he might be less pessimistic about its character. He would not then regard suffering as the key-note of existence. But if all that he must endure in one life is to be repeated with variations through an infinite round of future lives (some better perhaps, but others no doubt worse) there arises a sense of utter futility—the meaningless futility of a squirrel in a cage or a beast of burden in a treadmill. The consolation that no state is permanent and that hope of rising higher may always be cherished is obliterated by the oppressive consciousness that there is no end.'[1]

The oppressive consciousness that there is no end—there you have the endless continuance of life made the object, not of joyous anticipation, but of the greatest possible dread.

But every religion must be a message of hope and salvation, and what all the Indian religions do is to offer, just as did Orphism, some way of escape from this endless continuance in the weary round. No religion which did not do this would have any *raison d'être* in India, at least as a separate cult. For the doctrine of *karma* is common to them all, a presupposition rather than an asserted dogma; and what differentiates one from the other is the particular method of *escape* from *karma* and reincarnation which each proposes.

Nevertheless all the methods betray a certain family likeness to one another. Release is found, in each case, in some new religious experience—usually, as with Orphism in Greece, in an experience of a mystical kind. (*a*) The earliest Indian way of salvation is that of the Vedanta theology as first expressed in the Upanishads. It consists in the mystical realization of the identity of the human soul with God. The soul of man is *atman*, and *atman* is Brahma, the one supreme reality; and whoever knows this to be true is by the knowledge delivered from the bondage of rebirth. One loses one's personality in the great Impersonal, and after that one cannot be born into any more bodies. (*b*) Somewhat later, and in

---

[1] J. T. Addison, *Life Beyond Death in the Beliefs of Mankind* (1932), p. 124.

opposition to such monism, arose the dualistic Sankhya system. According to this teaching human souls are not all united in one impersonal *atman*, but exist separately, each in its own right; but what gives them personality and consciousness is their association with the body or matter. Now between souls and matter there is an absolute duality; and he who becomes aware of this distinction of the soul from matter is thereby released from the bondage of matter and finally, instead of being born into further bodies, loses his personality and becomes quite unconscious. (*c*) Very similar is the way of escape proposed, at a still later period, by Gautama, the founder of Buddhism. As he sat under the Bo-tree the Great Illumination came to him. He saw in a flash that the cause of all human misery lay in the existence of desire, and in this enlightenment lay the beginning of the extinction of desire, which was therefore the way of salvation. It is desire for life and its sham delights that causes rebirth: it is the extinction of desire that frees from rebirth and leads to *nirvana*. But when Gautama was asked by his disciples whether *nirvana* meant total extinction or only complete unconsciousness, he refused to answer the question. (*d*) The doctrine of release in Jainism is very similar to that of Buddhism. Here again the extinction of desire leads to *nirvana*. (*e*) In many later Hindu cults release from the wheel of rebirth is sought rather by faith in some personal saviour-god than in union with the impersonal —by *bhakti* rather than by *yoga*; and some of these teach that the released soul is not absorbed in the god, but lives in a blissful union with him that falls short of identity. These later cults, however, are all post-Christian in origin.'[1]

[1] For good summary statements of the Indian doctrines see the essay on

In India, then, it is possible to trace a preparation for the Christian hope which, so far as it goes, has striking parallels with the Greek development. Here, as in Greece and in Israel, there is a certain *reculer pour mieux sauter*. The realization of the horror of endless continuance in the ordinary round of living gives rise to an intense longing for loss of consciousness and personality, and in many cases for a state of being that is virtually indistinguishable from total annihilation. Yet in the concurrent tendency to regard *nirvana*—or *moksha*, or whatever it may be called—as a state not of utter annihilation but of (unconscious) blissful union with the divine, we may surely find a foreshadowing, however dim, of a positive doctrine of eternal life.

IV

Returning from this excursion to the Far East, which has been in the nature of a digression, let us now cross the *mare magnum* from Greece to the land of the Hebrews and see what preparation for the Christian hope there was on this very different soil. Up to a point, as we have seen already, the two cases are remarkably similar. Greece and Israel are found emerging out of the common background of animistic ancestor-worship into a more advanced outlook for which the ghostly underworld comes to have less and less significance, so that what was once a vividly imagined scene of busy life now fades into the dim and dank retreat of inert and witless shadows. And then, between this remove and the emergence

'Immortality in Indian Thought', by Professor A. A. Macdonell, in *Immortality* (ed. Marchant); and the articles 'Soul (Hindu)', 'State of the Dead (Hindu)', and 'State of the Dead (Buddhist)' in the *Encycl. of Religion and Ethics*; and J. T. Addison, op. cit., ch. xvi, 'Retribution by Transmigration'.

of a further insight, there is, in the case of Israel as in that of Greece, what looks like a clean 'break'.

The part played in Greece by the rise of the Dionysiac worship was played in Israel by the prophetic and apocalyptic movements. But it is instructive to find that the prophetic religion, unlike the Dionysiac, actually set itself to destroy the preoccupation of the people with the underworld and its ghostly inhabitants, so that the gradual fading out of the picture was due, not to a growing incredulity such as we may imagine to have been the case with the Greeks, but to the definite opposition of the new prophetic influence. During the progress of the conflict between the older Semitic religion and the monotheistic worship of Jehovah which was first associated with the name of Moses and which the prophets now make it their business to proclaim in all its uncompromising purity, the latter, we are told, 'annihilates all existence in Sheol, since the nature of this existence was heathen and non-moral, and could in no sense form a basis on which to found an ethical and spiritual doctrine of the future life'.[1] We can thus trace in the history of Israelite religion 'a provisional stage'[2] in which the animistic belief in ghosts is being zealously opposed and in which the belief in the soul's eternal life with God has not yet emerged. It looks as if it *could* not have emerged until the other had gone.

Surely we cannot but feel that this prophetic zeal was fully justified; and that likewise the growing indifference of the Greeks and Romans to the whole conception of life's ghostly aftermath was fully justified. The latter were right

[1] R. H. Charles, *A Critical History of the Doctrine of a Future Life in Israel, Judaism and Christianity*, 2nd ed., p. 53.
[2] Ibid.

in refusing to be interested in the prospect of a continuance of the common humdrum of life. The former were right in regarding with dread the prospect of a life out of touch with God, such as the life in Sheol was universally held to be, and in preferring to think of it as an unconscious 'subsistence' barely distinguishable from non-existence. It would have been indeed dreadful to feel obliged to admit the reality of an unending life that must be unblessed by the peace which passeth understanding. If *either* there be no God with whom to commune, *or* any future life there may be is to be conceived otherwise than as a life of close communion with Him, then it is devoutly to be wished that immortality will never be proved. And so, as was said at an earlier point, we can do nothing but congratulate ourselves that no non-religious argument for immortality—such as those put forward by McTaggart or by the adherents of Psychical Research—seems to be really valid. I have often marvelled at the *naïveté* with which certain modern writers raise doubts about the desirability of an endless continuance of our present pilgrimage, as if in so doing they were arguing against the Christian hope. Actually, they are arguing in its favour; or at least they are raising a doubt which, historically speaking, had not only to be raised but to be pressed to the limit before the Christian hope could arise.

Indeed, I have often said to myself that, in a deep sense, there is something fundamentally right-minded in the tendency of so many of us moderns to turn away from the thought of immortality. We are humanists; we have no overmastering conviction of the reality of the Eternal Lover; our lives have never been transfigured by His intimate presence; and therefore it is right and fine that we should look upon continuance as *karma*—an undesirable burden. Not indeed that we can rest quite happily in the thought of extinction. Loyalty to our human friendships must, as we have seen, always tend to disturb such complacency. But even so, it must be admitted that the contemplation of an eternity of quite *untransfigured* human friendships puzzles our desire. 'Whose wife', we ask, 'shall she be of the seven?' And unless we are able to reply *something* to the effect that 'in the resurrection they neither marry, nor are given in marriage, but are as the angels of God in heaven',[1] a cessation of desire—*nirvana*—is perhaps the proper result. I have sometimes felt myself in closer spiritual sympathy with those Victorian men of letters who resolutely turned their backs on the prospect of continuance than with those other Victorians who were more preoccupied with the prospect of continuance than they were with the fellowship of God. Tennyson was, indeed, a firm believer in God's reality, yet his absorption in the life of inner communion with Him hardly appears in his poetry as commensurate with his absorption in the soul's immortality. The latter frequently outruns the former, and so far as it does so, the reader rightly feels it to lack substance and reality. The straining after 'the glory of going on, and still to be'[2] is a little greater than appears natural. Is mere going on so very glorious? Perhaps to reach one's goal and find fulfilment is more glorious still.

But now, returning to our tale, let us observe how the very force of prophetic religion which was destroying the doctrine of ghostly survival was planting in the people's

---

[1] Matt. xxii. 28, 30. [2] Tennyson, *Wages.*

hearts the seeds of a new conception out of which would one day arise the hope of a blessed immortality. The hope itself is indeed as absent from the prophetic writings as it was from the thought of earlier times. This does not mean, however, that in Israelite religion there was *no* element of hope, but only that the hope entertained by the Israelites was a hope for the nation and not for the individual. We might express the facts, then, by saying that throughout its golden age Israel indeed looked forward to a blessed immortality, but that the nation and not the individual was the unit of the immortality in which it put its trust. This was natural enough, seeing that the nation (or in some cases the tribe or the family) was regarded as the unit both of moral responsibility and of the religious relation to God. The approach to Jehovah was a corporate act, and therefore the promises He made were for a corporate immortality. We find God saying to Abraham:

'And I will make thee exceeding fruitful, and I will make nations of thee, and kings shall come out of thee. And I will establish my covenant between Me and thee and thy seed after thee in their generations for an everlasting covenant, to be a God unto thee, and to thy seed after thee. And I will give unto thee, and to thy seed after thee, the land wherein thou art a stranger, all the land of Canaan, for an everlasting possession; and I will be their God.'[1]

But Abraham himself 'gave up the ghost, and died . . . and was gathered to his people'[2]; and many centuries were to pass before One was found to argue that if God was really the God of Abraham the individual, then Abraham the indi-

[1] Gen. xvii. 6–8. [2] Gen. xxv. 8.

vidual must be still alive, since God could not be the God of the dead.

What caused the change? Why did certain Hebrews at last come to believe that not only the race but also the individual will live for ever? The answer is simple. It was not because they had more faith in God's power than their forefathers had had, or more hope in His love; it was simply that under the guidance of the prophets they had come to entertain a new estimate of the importance of the individual. They had come to believe in individual ethical responsibility and individual communion with God. They had come to feel (though here we are translating their feeling into our own modern terms) that in living personality some value resides which could not reside in a mere tradition, however noble and long-lived. And therefore it seemed to them that, if what is most precious is to survive, not only the tradition but the individuals who are the carriers of it must have everlasting life.

This conclusion, however, the prophets themselves never drew. For that Hebrew thought had to wait no less than another five hundred years, when at last, in the two centuries immediately preceding the advent of our Lord, the apocalyptic movement made its appearance. 'The belief in a blessed future life', writes Dr. Charles, 'springs not from prophecy but from apocalyptic. With this doctrine the Old Testament prophet *qua* prophet was not concerned. Not even a hint of it is to be found in Old Testament prophecy. On the other hand, the apocalyptist made it a fundamental postulate of his belief in God.'[1]

[1] Op. cit., p. 178.

One reason why the prophets failed themselves to see that individual immortality was implied in the individual relationship to God on which they laid so much stress, was that they were far too ready to persuade themselves that the proper claims of the individual were always satisfied, and his accounts with divine Justice fully and fairly settled, within the limits and conditions of this present life. And it is in connexion with a later writer's perplexities over this very prophetic assumption that the first uncertain movements of the Hebrew mind towards a doctrine of immortality make their appearance in the literature. This later writer is the unknown author of the Book of Job, and the passages in the fourteenth and nineteenth chapters are well known. There are also several psalms—the sixteenth and seventeenth, the forty-ninth, the seventy-third—in which expressions of the same sort occur in connexion with this same problem of being rewarded according to one's works. Yet few present-day scholars seem to believe that the definite thought of immortality is contained in any one of these passages. All we can say with confidence is that these fourth-century writers are trembling on the brink of its discovery.

It was in a somewhat wider context of thought that the discovery was finally made. It is well known that the prophets taught the people to interpret the promises of God as applying to a definite future era of national blessedness which was to be introduced by the 'Day of Jehovah', and which afterwards came to be known as the Kingdom of God or the Messianic Age. Until now it had been assumed that only those who survive until the Day of Jehovah dawns can hope to taste of its blessings. But the astonishing assertion that now begins to be made is that this glorious future which is in store for the nation must be shared also by those who, having lived in their time in fellowship with Jehovah, have meanwhile died and gone down to Sheol. This of course can only happen by their being raised again from the dead. So arises the idea of resurrection.

There are only two passages in the Old Testament in which anything like this is really contemplated. The first is in the little apocalypse now embedded in the Book of Isaiah (chapters 24 to 27) and which (so the experts think) can hardly be later than the third century. The important words are these:

> O thou Eternal, thy dead shall live again,
>   awaking from the dust
>   with songs of joy;
> for thy dew falls with light and life,
>   till dead spirits rise.[1]

For the second, which is in the Book of Daniel, we have to wait until well towards the middle of the second century. We may safely leave the words in their familiar Elizabethan form:

'And many of them that sleep in the dust of the earth shall awake, some to everlasting life, and some to shame and everlasting contempt. And they that be wise shall shine as the brightness of the firmament; and they that turn many to righteousness as the stars for ever and ever.'[2]

It is most important to notice that what is here contemplated is not a happier fate for the soul in the underworld, but a

---

[1] Isaiah xxvi. 19, Moffatt's translation.
[2] Daniel xii. 2–3.

return of the man in his integrity, body and soul together, to a renewed earth after a temporary banishment to the underworld. Clearly, then, the doctrine of eternal life in the Kingdom of God is as far as possible from being a development of the animistic doctrine of ghostly survival in Sheol. If the new teaching has a link with anything at all in earlier Israelite belief, it is with the stories of the *translation* of Enoch and Elijah, who, instead of dying like other men and suffering separation of body and soul, were received, body and soul together, into eternal life; and of this link, such as it is, the upholders of the new teaching were well aware, the names of Enoch and Elijah being constantly on their lips. The situation is thus closely parallel to what we found in Greece, where it was evident that the prospect of blessedness offered by the mystery-cults was much more closely linked with the conception of the Elysian Fields to which a few fortunates had long ago been translated than with that of the realm of Hades where are collected the ghosts of dead men. But in the case of Israel as in the case of Greece it was true that, until the time of which we are now speaking, this glorious blessing of eternal life with God was held to have been granted only to a very, very few men of long ago and to have demanded in each case 'a fresh and special miracle'.

Beginning, then, with this Book of Daniel and with the roughly contemporary Book of Enoch there appeared a growing body of apocalyptic literature in which the conception of the Age to Come was developed in considerable detail. In all this literature the doctrine of the 'revivification' of those already dead now held an accepted place. And there is another change which soon began to be made. The prophets had taken it for granted that the golden age of which they spoke was to be simply an epoch of earthly history, though one that would be introduced by a miraculous divine act and that would last for ever. The apocalyptic writers, however, had apparently come to feel that this conception was too materialistic; earth as we now know it (and not least the Judaea that had now fallen on such evil times) is wholly unfit for the manifestation of such glory as shall be revealed. The scene of God's Kingdom accordingly came to be thought of as the *heavens*, where God Himself was conceived to dwell. Yet this could not mean the present firmament, which, for that matter, was as material as the earth itself. Hence some of the writings of the first century B.C. prefer rather to contemplate the provision by divine power of 'a new earth *and* a new heaven' as the theatre of the Kingdom. The centre of the new earth would of course be a 'new Jerusalem'. But the conception which ultimately gained the day is that which appears in the Jewish Rabbinic literature (dating from the early Christian generations) and in our Christian Book of Revelation—namely, the conception of a *temporary* golden age on the present earth to be followed after a certain period (which finally came to be fixed as exactly a millennium) by eternal life in heaven.[1] Closely connected with this question was the other question as to the *form* in which the dead are to arise from Sheol. Would soul, spirit, *and body* rise, or only soul and spirit? And if the body also, would it be *the same body*, or in what

---

[1] Authorities seem to be by no means agreed as to the precise course taken by reflection on this problem. See Volz, *Jüdische Eschatologie von Daniel bis Akiba* (1903), pp. 369–81; R. H. Charles, op. cit., pp. 127 n., 179 ff., 248 f., 364, &c.; Edwyn Bevan, *The Hope of a World to Come*, pp. 51–3.

way, if any, would it be changed? The literature reflects considerable uncertainty of mind in the answering of these questions, but the view that ultimately won acceptance was that there would indeed be a resurrection of the body, but that the resurrected body would consist of 'garments of glory and of light', being made, as are the bodies of the angels, of 'the light and glory of God'. Josephus, in giving an account of the accepted (Pharisaic) doctrine in the second book of *The Jewish War*, says that the souls of the righteous are believed to 'pass into another body (μεταβαίνειν εἰς ἕτερον σῶμα)'[1]—a body, that is to say, of a different kind from the present one.

Now it is most important to realize that the hope which thus emerges is essentially twofold in character and that nevertheless both parts of it have their ultimate roots in a single experience—in the new depth given to life by the prophetic discovery of communion with God. From this experience there emerged, first, the hope of a future period in which this new depth of life would no longer be the lonely possession of a few individuals, but would permeate society and utterly transfigure it. Here, then, we have the looking forward to a new social order in which God's will shall reign supreme. But from the same experience there emerged, second, the hope that those individuals who now in loneliness possess this new depth of life should be raised from the dead to share in the blessings of a society in which, for the first time, they would really feel at home. Here we have the looking forward to a future consummation of the individual life. It is the precious contribution of Judaism that it should have

[1] Op. cit., book ii, ch. viii, *ad fin.*

welded so completely into one the corporate and the individual hope.

Yet, as we had occasion to note in an earlier chapter, this very combination had already appeared—perhaps indeed as much as four hundred years before—in one other religious tradition, namely the religion of ancient Persia. According to Zoroastrian teaching the souls of all men, three nights after the death of the body, pass over the Bridge of Separation, where all are judged; and the righteous ascend to the House of Song while the wicked descend to the House of the Lie. But three millenniums after the death of Zarathustra (being twelve after the creation of the world) a saviour will appear to bring about the end of the present age and the great Renewal of the World. At his call the souls of the dead will be reunited to their old bodies, which will now rise from their graves to assist at the stupendous spectacle of the final judgement or Great Separation. The Renewal of the World will be by means of a flood of molten metal, through which the righteous will pass and be made young again (adults to about forty years of age and children to about fifteen).[1] The question has accordingly been raised whether it was not from the Persians that the Jews originally borrowed their conception of a future era of national blessedness and their conviction that the dead would rise from their graves to take part in it. The period of Jewish captivity in Babylonia began in 597 B.C.; some sixty years later Cyrus

---

[1] Nathan Söderblom, *La Vie future d'après le mazdéisme* (Paris, 1901); also *The Zoroastrian Doctrine of a Future Life from Death to the Individual Judgement*, by J. D. C. Parry (New York, Columbia University Press, 1926)—a thesis which it is to be hoped the author will continue so as to include the General Judgement at the end of the world.

captured Babylon, and the Jews came under the rule of the Persians; so that from this time onwards the influence of Zoroastrian on Mosaic religion is an entirely open possibility. The best opinion seems, however, to be more and more pointing to an independent origin of these doctrines among the Jews themselves. It is difficult to escape the impression that they are the natural outgrowth of the prophetic teaching. The decision partly turns on the question whether the earliest passages in the prophetic writings in which the hope of a restoration appears can or cannot be given a post-Exilic dating. The great Wellhausen and his followers thought they could, but the weight of opinion now seems to be against such a possibility. It might still be true, however, that the doctrine of the revivification of the dead was purely Persian in origin; for of that, as we have seen, there is no trace until long after the Exile. Yet the roots of this doctrine also are so clearly manifest in the prophetic insistence upon the responsibility of the individual to God that we may well hesitate to believe that it was simply taken over from another religion. It is not, however, doubted by anybody that during the Persian period the *detail* of Israel's hope was to a greater or lesser extent filled in from Persian sources. Archbishop Söderblom probably devoted more time and thought to this inquiry than any one else has ever done, but perhaps he goes too far in his denial of Persian influence:

'Jewish eschatology took over from Zoroastrianism only some insignificant details, and certainly not its original inspiration. There is only one capital point where Judaism may have been subjected to a certain influence through contact with Zoroastrianism, namely its idea of resurrection. But even that idea has a Jewish origin and developed itself in an independent way, if not without being affected, at least without having been itself borrowed.'[1]

Finally, after the victory of Alexander the Great at Issus in 333 B.C. the Jews were transferred from Persian to Greek rule and came very markedly under the influence of Hellenic thought. We have seen how, long before this period, the Greeks had arrived at the conception of a blessed immortality for the individual. And thus arises the further question whether it was not from the *Greeks* that the Jews borrowed, not certainly the hope of the Kingdom of God, but the additional hope that the individuals who look forward to it are to have part in it when it comes, even if meanwhile they go down to death. Here again the true conclusion seems to be that whereas, as time went on, Jewish writers came to be increasingly influenced by the Platonic conception of the immortality of the soul, yet the original Judaistic conception of 'the revivification of dead bodies' had separate roots that were entirely its own. The Jews cannot, after all, have borrowed the first suggestion of individual consummation *both* from Persia *and* from Greece. Perhaps they borrowed it from neither.

It must not, however, be supposed that every member of the Jewish nation came at once to share this new hope of a golden age preceded by the resurrection of the just. It was championed by the Pharisees, who, in spite of the grave faults which were so ruthlessly exposed by Jesus, were (at least originally) in many ways the guardians of the prophetic religion; and 'by A.D. 20 it had become', in Dr. Montefiore's words, 'an accepted dogma of the Pharisaic and Rabbinic

---

[1] I have translated these sentences from op. cit., p. 320 f.

synagogue'.[1] But it was strenuously opposed by the Sadducees. These formed the conservative party among the Jews, standing for the older Israelite religion as contained in the Pentateuch. Later writers, they held, were to be accepted only as far as they were in harmony with the religion of Moses. For this reason they completely rejected the doctrine of the resurrection, together with the elaborately detailed eschatology and angelology and demonology that had grown up in the Persian and Greek periods. It was all too reminiscent, they thought, of that old and evil preoccupation with the dead which had been the root of the detested ancestor-worship and which the prophets had laboured so hard to destroy. 'For the Sadducees say that there is no resurrection, neither angel, nor spirit; but the Pharisees confess both.'[2] The Sadducee did not perhaps deny the existence of the underworld, but, like the prophets, he denied its importance; and he stoutly denied, what the prophets had never contemplated, that any one who once went down to it could ever rise from it again. In Dr. Charles's words, he 'took the provisional stage' represented by the prophetic teaching 'to be one of true and eternal significance'.[3] To some extent his position in Judaism was parallel to the position in Greece of those who, disliking the Orphic tendencies, preferred the older Olympic religion.

V

Jesus refused to follow the Pharisees in the importance they attached to the later casuistical elaboration of the Mosaic

[1] See *Hibbert Journal*, vol. xxx, no. 4 (July 1932), p. 568.
[2] Acts xxiii. 8; cf. Mark xii. 18.   [3] Op. cit., p. 53.

Law, and He bitterly attacked them for their pride, insincerity, and corruption, but in the matter of hope He sided with them against the Sadducees; and in this St. Paul and the whole Christian movement were to go with Him.

Historically speaking, it is out of the conception of the Kingdom of God that Christianity was born. Jesus made it the framework of all His thought from the very beginning of His ministry. 'Now after that John was put in prison, Jesus came into Galilee, preaching the gospel of the Kingdom of God, and saying, The time is fulfilled, and the Kingdom of God is at hand; repent ye, and believe the gospel.'[1] Though insisting that none but God knew the date of the Kingdom's inauguration, He yet besought His followers to regard it as an imminent and vitally important reality and to make the preparation of their hearts for it their first and greatest care. Moreover, towards the close of His ministry He gave increasing utterance to the conviction that He Himself had been appointed by God to play the part of that Messiah or Anointed One who had figured in some of the apocalypses of the preceding centuries as the inaugurator of the Kingdom.

It is well known that in the decades immediately preceding the Great War there was much excited discussion among New Testament scholars as to how the Kingdom of God was conceived by Jesus. Was it simply the name of a future epoch in the story of the world, or was it the name of a kind of life which might be enjoyed now or at any time? Perhaps the true answer is at last becoming clear to us. The Kingdom of God, as Jesus conceived it, stood essentially for a

[1] Mark i. 14–15.

particular kind of corporate life with God. It stood for a transfigured commonwealth. Most of His teaching concerns either the nature of the life of this commonwealth or the nature of the spiritual preparation we should make for entrance into it. The characteristic form of His discourse is 'The Kingdom of God is likened unto . . .'. The Kingdom, He believed, would one day be established by divine power; and for the coming of that day we wait in eager yet patient expectation. But even now we may enjoy some foretaste of its blessings. The fullness of the transfigured life can indeed only be enjoyed in the transfigured community, yet even now it is possible to some extent to envisage ourselves proleptically as members of that community. Some scholars, it is true, still find difficulty in supposing that Jesus spoke of the life of the Kingdom in both these ways—both as a future and as a present reality. Yet if the double conception is present, as most would admit it to be present, in both the Pauline and the Johannine literature, why need we exclude it from the Gospels? One fact which points very strongly to its presence is the impossibility of clearly separating Jesus' teaching about the kind of life which prepares for the Kingdom from the life of the Kingdom itself. Fundamentally the two are continuous. The present life is a preparation, but it is not that only: it is not quite bare of fruition.

It is, then, this eager looking forward to a divinely transfigured corporate life that is the background of the whole teaching of Jesus; and if that background be denied to it, little of the teaching can remain.

But Jesus sided with the Pharisees not only in their hope for the community, but also in their hope for the individual.

He firmly believed that the faithful dead would rise again from Sheol to have part in the Kingdom of God when it came. The most important passage may be quoted in full.

'And there come unto Him Sadducees, which say that there is no resurrection; and they asked Him, saying, Master, Moses wrote unto us, If a man's brother die, and leave a wife behind him, and leave no child, that his brother should take his wife, and raise up seed unto his brother. There were seven brethren: and the first took a wife, and dying left no seed; and the second took her, and died, leaving no seed behind him; and the third likewise; and the seven left no seed. Last of all the woman also died. In the resurrection whose wife shall she be of them? for the seven had her to wife.

'Jesus said unto them, Is it not for this cause that ye err, that ye know not the Scriptures, nor the power of God? For when they shall rise from the dead, they neither marry, nor are given in marriage; but are as angels in heaven. But as touching the dead, that they are raised; have ye not read in the book of Moses, in the place concerning the Bush, how God spake unto him, saying, I am the God of Abraham, and the God of Isaac, and the God of Jacob? He is not the God of the dead, but of the living: ye do greatly err.'[1]

The Sadducees' point was that we must adhere at all costs to the Mosaic Law and that this new-fangled notion of the resurrection of the dead is not only absent from the Mosaic Law (here they were undoubtedly right), but definitely conflicts with it and makes nonsense of some of its provisions. They took the example of so-called Levirate marriage—itself originally connected with ancestor-worship. If a woman marries more than once which man is going to be

[1] Mark xii. 18–27, R.V.; cf. Matt. xxii. 23–33 and Luke xx. 27–38.

her husband in the Kingdom of God? Jesus' answer is of the utmost significance. The objection, he points out, depends on the supposition that the life of the Kingdom is identical in kind with the life that now is, and a mere continuation of it; whereas the true way to think of it is as a new and higher type of life. He goes on to say that when men rise from the dead they shall be 'as the angels' who know no such thing as marriage. Here Jesus is following what we saw to have come to be the prevalent view—that in the future life we shall indeed have bodies, but *angelic* bodies 'made from the light and glory of God', and not the earthly ones we now possess. This teaching is found as early as the Book of Enoch,[1] and 'was current among the cultured Pharisees in the century immediately preceding the Christian era'[2]— Josephus, as we saw, putting it down as the Pharisaic doctrine that the souls of the righteous will 'pass into a body of another kind'. The Talmud attributes to a well-known Rabbinic teacher belonging to an early Christian century the saying that 'In the world to come there is no eating or drinking or marrying or envy or hate.'[3] To refuse to contemplate the possibility of such a new embodiment is, says Jesus, 'not to know the power of God'.

But He does not leave the matter there. He goes on to show that they do not know 'the Scriptures' either, because the essential presuppositions from which the doctrine of resurrection follows are present even in the religion of Moses and the Prophets. He reminds the Sadducees that

[1] 1 Enoch li. 4; lxii. 15 f.
[2] Charles, op. cit., p. 295.
[3] For reference see C. G. Montefiore, *The Synoptic Gospels*, 2nd ed., vol. i, p. 283.

they habitually spoke of God as the God of Abraham, Isaac, and Jacob, and He argues that if the phrase means anything at all, it implies the immortality of these patriarchs. If God had been merely the nation's God, then the immortality of the nation would be all we could properly hope for. But if God is the God of individuals, if individuals can enter into fellowship with Him, if individuals are precious in His sight, then our hope in God necessarily becomes a hope for the individual.

The argument is unanswerable; and is indeed the only unanswerable argument for immortality that has ever been given, or ever can be given. It cannot be evaded except by a denial of the premisses. If the individual can commune with God, then he must matter to God; and if he matters to God, he must share God's eternity. For if God really rules, He cannot be conceived as scrapping what is precious in His sight. It is in the conjunction with God that the promise of eternal life resides. This, in Dante's phrase, is *come l'uom s'eterna*.[1]

VI

When Jesus was challenged to say why He believed in resurrection, His mind naturally turned, not to His own case, but to the great heroes of His faith. Yet His persuasion reached most amply to His own case also; and, if we are to believe the oldest and most reliable of our authorities, it applied to it in a very special way. According to St. Mark Jesus taught His disciples to expect that He would 'suffer many things . . . and be killed . . . and rise again after three

---

[1] *Inferno*, canto xv. 1, 85.

days'[1]—presumably, then, in advance of the general resurrection, though that too would come within the lifetime of some of those to whom He was then speaking.[2]

Jesus did indeed suffer many things and was killed; and on the third day His followers were convinced that He had risen again and had appeared to them. In reading the accounts of these appearances we have, however, the impression that the disciples were very far from expecting them and were quite unprepared for them in their minds. This may mean no more than that their faith was not sufficient to make them confident that their Lord's remarkable prediction would actually be fulfilled; yet it is difficult to escape the conclusion that *either* the definiteness of the prediction *or* the unexpectedness of its fulfilment must be exaggerated in our records.

What is quite certain is that all the disciples believed their Lord to have risen and that their belief was built into the very foundations of the Christian Church. Among the Jews the doctrine of resurrection had never, up to this date, met with universal acceptance. It was a moot question; and the Sadducees who denied it continued to flourish in Jerusalem until the destruction of the Temple in A.D. 70. But there was never any Sadduceeism within Christianity. In the hope of a blessed immortality Christianity had been born and in that hope it continued to live.

Here, then, we reach the culmination of the historical development we have been tracing, and arrive again at the point where we found ourselves at the end of Chapter III. It was not, we there noted, by having regard to their own souls that the first Christians became persuaded of the reality

[1] Mark .iii. 31.   [2] Mark viii. 38.

of eternal life, but by having regard to their Master and Lord. The New Testament never argues from a general resurrection to the Resurrection of Christ. The argument is the other way about, the faith that Christ had risen being made the starting-point of the faith that His saints will rise with Him to newness of life.

'But now hath Christ been raised from the dead, the firstfruits of them that are asleep. For since by man came death, by man came also the resurrection of the dead. For as in Adam all die, so also in Christ shall all be made alive.'[1]

'God both raised the Lord, and will raise up us through His power.'[2]

'He which raised up the Lord Jesus shall raise up us also with Jesus.'[3]

'But if the Spirit of Him that raised up Jesus from the dead dwelleth in you, He that raised up Christ Jesus from the dead shall quicken also your mortal bodies through His Spirit that dwelleth in you.'[4]

We must, however, enter the warning that this is not to be understood as if the faith that Jesus was alive was the sole original root of the Christians' hope that they too would live eternally. Most of them as followers of the Pharisaic tradition, and some of them as followers of the Platonic tradition, had entertained that hope before they ever knew Jesus. St. Paul cannot, in the passages just quoted from the Corinthian letters, have meant to say that prior to his conversion he looked forward to no resurrection. We are told in the Acts of the Apostles that, when he was on trial before the Sanhedrin, he shrewdly pointed out how natural

[1] 1 Cor. xv. 20-2, R.V.   [2] 1 Cor. vi. 14, R.V.
[3] 2 Cor. iv. 14, R.V.   [4] Rom. viii. 11, R.V.

it was that a Pharisee like himself should be tried for believing in resurrection; and that again he took the same Pharisaic ground in arguing for the resurrection before Agrippa, saying, 'After the most straitest sect of our religion I lived a Pharisee. And now I stand and am judged for the hope of the promise made of God unto our fathers ... Why should it be thought a thing incredible with you that God should raise the dead?' Moreover, Jesus had Himself, during His own lifetime, taught His disciples that they could assure themselves of immortality by looking—He could not then say to Himself, but—to Abraham and Isaac and Jacob. The faith that *these* are alive, He had argued, is ground for hope that we too may live. But the simple fact is that the argument never seemed to carry full conviction until for these names men could substitute the name of Jesus. The hope had long been entertained, but only now had it become a sure and firm persuasion, putting an end to all doubt. Men who had found it not altogether impossible to continue thinking (as their fathers had done) of Abraham, Isaac, and Jacob as being long ago dead and done with, now found it quite impossible to think of Jesus as dead and done with. That the patriarchs were dear to God and must accordingly share in His eternity is a thought that arrests; but that Jesus Christ was dear to God and must share in His eternity is a thought that compels. And again, that the children of Israel are so one with the patriarchs that they too must be immortal is a thought that arrests; but that the saints are so one with Christ that they too must be immortal is a thought that compels. Such, surely, is St. Paul's meaning.[1]

[1] The Fifth Lateran Council (1512–17) formally condemned the doctrine that

There are other misunderstandings to be avoided. The matter is sometimes stated as if upon the prior ground of the appearances of the risen Jesus there rested, as upon so much empiric evidence, the disciples' faith that He had risen and was still alive—and so the whole Christian faith. Such a view, however, can hardly be sustained. The New Testament does not really teach that there is available for the truth of Christianity such empiric evidence as must confound all unbelief. Rather is faith 'the evidence of things not seen'.[1] 'Now when an object of hope is seen', argues St. Paul, 'there is no further need to hope. Who ever hopes for what he sees already? But if we hope for something that we do not see, we wait for it patiently.'[2] To say that the disciples' faith rested solely on the appearances is therefore to deny to them all faith properly so called and to charge them with the refusal to believe except on the evidence of the senses. If this be true of them, then they were not only less noble-minded than the disciples of Socrates whose faith in immortality rose triumphant from their master's death, but were less noble-minded also than their own Jewish fathers and mothers whose belief in resurrection had survived the disappearance of many a loved one beneath the sod. And that we cannot think to have been the case. That, then, is one reason why we must not say that the Church's faith in its ever-living Lord rests upon the fact that He was seen by His disciples after His death.

But there is another reason. For the faith which mani-

the Resurrection of Christ is the only available ground for belief in immortality, and that apart from Biblical revelation we should be compelled to believe in annihilation.

[1] Hebrews xi. 1.   [2] Rom. viii. 24–5, Moffatt's translation.

fested itself in the disciples' hearts was not really of such a kind as to be *capable* of any mere ocular demonstration. No conclusion of religious significance could be held to follow logically, and no spiritual conviction would be likely to follow psychologically, from the mere fact that a man who had died and been buried was seen walking the earth once again. If we are to believe St. Luke, this very point was made by Jesus Himself. In the story of Dives and Lazarus He makes Dives plead with Abraham that he should send Lazarus back to earth to inform his five brothers of the reality of eternal life and the solemnity of the final judgement. 'But Abraham saith, They have Moses and the prophets; let them hear them. And he said, Nay, father Abraham: but if one go to them from the dead, they will repent. And he said unto him, If they hear not Moses and the prophets, neither will they be persuaded, if one rise from the dead.'[1] This second half of the parable may or may not be authentic, but in either case it seems likely that it was applied by St. Luke to the case of the Resurrection of Jesus Himself. Its meaning for him seems to be that you cannot hope to bring faith to birth in men's souls, or to convince them of the truth of Christianity, by merely pointing to the fact of Jesus' return to earth. 'Originally', writes Dr. Montefiore, 'this part of the parable may have meant no more than it says. But to Luke the meaning was much more definite. Had the Jews hearkened to Moses and the Prophets, they would not have rejected Jesus. The resurrection of Jesus cannot convert them.'[2]

---

[1] Luke xvi. 29–31, R.V.
[2] *The Synoptic Gospels*, 2nd ed., vol. ii, p. 540

The point is surely well taken. Supposing a man devoid of religious faith were to read in his morning paper that a remarkable thing had happened in a neighbouring city—a citizen who had died and been buried had, after the lapse of some days, and in agreement with his alleged predictions, appeared to a number of his friends and been engaged by them in conversation; what would be his natural feeling about the report? To begin with, he would rightly be exceedingly sceptical about its accuracy and would feel that a phenomenon so contrary to all human experience should not be received as authentic without the most scrupulous inquiry and the most complete, indeed 'water-tight', attestation. But if he satisfied himself that such an inquiry had been made, and that the evidence was indeed quite unimpeachable, then he would be forced to allow that a phenomenon of extraordinary scientific interest had occurred: a man who had been certified as dead by the doctors and had spent three days in a vault had (as foretold by himself) returned to earth alive and had again companied with his friends for a brief period before disappearing once again from their midst. But would he conclude, further, that the risen man must have been remarkable in any other respect, or that his ideas on things in general must have been profoundly wise and right, or that all men would rise as he did, or that even he would live on for ever? Or again, would his mind be turned in any way towards belief in the reality of God or in the possibility of fellowship with Him whether in this life or in glory everlasting? Surely the answer to all these questions must be No.[1]

[1] 'Supposons', writes the eminent French scholar Maurice Goguel, 'que . . . l'on trouve un document qui établirait sans discussion possible, qu'au matin du troisième jour la tombe de Jésus a été trouvée vide. Supposons que l'évidence

It will not do, then, to say that later disciples must believe because the first disciples saw. Even though it is not given to us to see as they saw, yet it may be that something is open even to us which may without impropriety be called a vision of the Risen Lord.

Since we here touch on topics often regarded as controversial, I shall surround myself with a great cloud of witnesses, belonging to schools of thought widely different from one another, but all anxious, as I understand them, to warn us against the error of making the disciples' ocular vision of the resurrected body of Christ the sole and sufficient basis of the Church's faith in His (and our) continued life with God.

I mention first Principal Cairns of Aberdeen, who has recently made a careful attempt to distinguish the Bible's view of miracle not only from what he calls the 'Modernist', but also from what he calls the 'Traditional' theory of it. According to this last, he writes, the purpose of the miracles of Jesus was 'evidential'.

'They were meant to give convincing evidence that God was on the side of Christ. Many traditionalists would put it more simply still, and would say that they are direct expressions of our

de la démonstration s'impose à tous les historiens. Pensez-vous qu'elle suffirait pour les convertir à la foi chrétienne? Certainement non encore.' Furthermore, M. Goguel shows that the idea of a dead man coming back to life did not appear as strange in the first century as it does to-day (*Revue d'histoire et de philosophie religieuses*, juillet-octobre 1931, p. 335 f., 'Le caractère de la foi à la résurrection dans le christianisme primitif'). Cf. also the words of Professor Webb in his *Divine Personality and Human Life*, p. 269, 'And as to the *religious* doctrine of Immortality, it is before everything else a doctrine of values; and the discovery that, as a matter of fact, some or all persons survived what we call death would not in itself establish such a doctrine any more than the discovery that some persons had recovered from a disease commonly supposed incurable, or had prolonged their earthly existence beyond the age of one hundred and fifty years.'

Lord's Divinity, acts of creative power that could only be wrought by a divine Being. They are, in any case, meant to authenticate His teaching as divine. They are not parts of the message, but proofs of its truth. They are seals attached to the document, not parts of the document. They are the crier ringing his bell to call attention to his message. . . . So it was with the miracles of Jesus and, above all, with His Resurrection. The crier rang His bell so hard that the contemporaries could not choose but hear.'[1]

To this view Dr. Cairns objects that

it does not correspond to the New Testament idea of the miracles at all. It is a meaning imposed upon the New Testament by a supposed apologetic necessity.'

He goes on to point out that

the picture of Jesus as one who works divine wonders for the purpose of calling attention to His message is strangely out of harmony with the Synoptic pictures. Over and over again in these narratives He refuses to work just such signs as the Traditionalist theory declares the miracles to have been, and condemns the spirit which demanded them as that of "an evil and adulterous generation". . . . Spiritual truth is spiritually discerned by a child-like heart, not forced home upon dazzled senses and stunned minds by the blows of supernatural power.'

Yet he adds that

In some respects even more serious is the way in which the Traditional theory blunts the most remarkable feature of the Synoptic narratives, their steady reiteration of the close and vital relation between the works which Christ wrought and "faith".'[2]

[1] *The Faith that Rebels: A Re-examination of the Miracles of Jesus* (London, 1928), p. 25.
[2] Ibid., p. 28 f. I do not claim that either Dr. Cairns or any of the other scholars whom I quote would agree with all I say about the Resurrection; nor could I agree with all they say. I quote them only with reference to this particular point.

I mention next Albrecht Ritschl, who argued that, instea
of faith presupposing miracle, 'every miracle presuppose
faith',[1] so that to make the belief rest on the sign was t
reverse the natural order of going; and with him his pup
Wilhelm Herrmann, who always insisted that the doctrin
of the Resurrection of Christ was not a *Glaubensgrund* bu
a *Glaubensgedanke*—part of faith's content rather than of i
basis.

After the Ritschlians I mention their great adversary
Professor Karl Barth. Historically speaking, he tells us, th
fact of Christ's Resurrection is

'a fact as ambiguous as are all earthly facts. He might even hav
been stolen. He might never have been really dead at all. Th
Gospels themselves never make the least effort to conceal the fa
that the empty tomb was something *toto coelo* different fro
seeing the Risen One; and it is not to the credit of Christia
Theology that it should ever have occurred to any one hotly t
argue over this tomb in a critical or apologetic interest. . . . Th
Gospels themselves, showing greater wisdom than did the me
of a later time, draw no positive conclusions whatever from th
mere fact that such and such things were seen (*aus dem, was*
und so zu sehen war).'[2]

I pass now from Germany to France and translate this fro
M. Goguel:

'Faith in the Resurrection of Jesus was, for primitive Chri
tianity, a fact of a religious order. This is the fact which it is o
business to explain, and we cannot do it without bringing in
play considerations of a religious and psychological kind. Wha
ever may be one's estimate of the historical value of the Resurre
tion-narratives, and even if one accepts at least the earliest

[1] *Unterricht in der christlichen Religion*, 4. Auflage (1890), p. 15.
[2] *Die Auferstehung der Toten*, 2. Auflage (1926), p. 79.

them as corresponding to what really took place, they do not explain the faith in Christ's final triumph over death. The problem of the Resurrection is not only a problem of literary and historical criticism, it is also and above everything a problem of the history and psychology of religion. It brings us into the presence of facts of a spiritual kind which, to my view, cannot, in the last analysis, be explained in any other way than by the action of Jesus upon the souls of His disciples.'[1]

From America I cite President Coffin of the Union Theological Seminary.

'Some spiritual preparation and capacity are essential to the perception of the risen Lord. The resurrection is not an event in the physical world, as we ordinarily understand it.'[2]

Finally, I take the following from a discussion by the late Principal Denney of Glasgow of the 'three ways in which the testimony to the resurrection is morally qualified'.

'It is just because of its moral significance—because of its meaning and purpose in the relations of God and man—that the resurrection, as the apostles preached it, rises above what is called the purely historical; it makes a kind of appeal to men which a purely historical event, if we could realize such an abstraction, never makes; it is on our susceptibility to this appeal that our appreciation of the testimony to it depends, and yet the testimony itself, in the last resort, is historical testimony. There would be nothing to go upon whatever if there were not men who had seen the risen Jesus—here is the point of attachment with history; but what the testimony of these men shall amount to for us— what weight it shall have in our minds—whether we shall take it as simply as it is given, or feel ourselves obliged to attempt the reduction of it to something by which the equilibrium of our

[1] Loc. cit., p. 351. [2] *The Meaning of the Cross* (1931), p. 160 f.

world shall be maintained and disturbing revelations excluded—here is the point at which the moral elements in the case exert their legitimate influence.'

'It is of extreme interest to notice how Paul adds to the direct historical testimony for the resurrection an indirect spiritual evidence which in its place is of the highest value. To put it broadly, Christian experience in all its forms implies the resurrection.'

'The resurrection is not attested in the gospels by outside witnesses who had inquired into it as the Psychical Research Society inquires into ghost stories; it is attested—in the only way in which it can be attested at all—by people who are within the circle of realities to which it belongs. . . .'[1]

Is it true that the Risen Christ was visible only to the eye of faith? Or was His return to earth an ordinary 'public' matter of fact, of the same substance as other earthly events? And again—the question is very nearly the same—was He seen in His earthly body of flesh and blood and bones, or as clothed in the 'angelic' body of the light and glory of God which He Himself had followed the Pharisees in believing would be ours in the life eternal? The different reports read differently in this regard. The story of the empty tomb makes the Resurrection of Jesus an event of 'public' history and notoriety, and perhaps implies that the earthly 'corruptible' body rose. And St. Luke's story of Jesus eating broiled fish, and asking his disciples to touch Him so that they might

[1] *Jesus and the Gospel* (1908), pp. 128, 133, 157. I have often thought that we may very simply test our understanding of the Resurrection of Christ by putting to ourselves the following question: 'Do we wish that there had been at the time something more corresponding to an impartial scientific inquiry, and that there were better attestation to the Resurrection on the part of disinterested outside observers; or do we realize that such attestation would be quite helpless to prove the thing that Christians really believe, and that only the testimony of those *within* the faith (which is precisely what we have) could here be of any avail?'

see that He was no mere spirit (πνεῦμα), but had 'flesh and bones' (together with the story in the Fourth Gospel of Doubting Thomas putting his finger on the stigmata), goes farther and seems to point to the corruptible body not yet having put on incorruption. But most of the reports read rather as if the Risen Jesus had appeared in a glorified body that was subject neither to the physical needs nor to the spatial limitations of earthly existence. He could appear suddenly in a room the doors of which were closed, and again He could appear in two places far distant from one another at almost the same time. He appeared to two of the disciples, according to one account, 'in another form (ἐν ἑτέρᾳ μορφῇ)'.[1] And it is in this way that our earliest account of the appearances reads, namely, that given by St. Paul in the First Epistle to the Corinthians in A.D. 55 or 56 or 57.

'For I delivered unto you first of all that which also I received, how that Christ died for our sins according to the scriptures; and that He was buried; and that He hath been raised on the third day according to the scriptures; and that He appeared to Cephas; then to the twelve; then He appeared to above five hundred brethren at once, of whom the greater part remain until now, but some are fallen asleep; then He appeared to James; then to all the apostles; and last of all, as unto one born out of due time, He appeared to me also.'[2]

Not only does St. Paul make no mention of the empty tomb or of the eating of the fish, but the question may be raised whether he does not hold a view of the nature of the resurrection body which would exclude the possibility of

---

[1] Mark xvi. 12. Cf. C. H. Robinson, *Studies in the Resurrection of Christ* (1909), 71 f.
[2] 1 Cor. xv. 3–8, R.V.

these incidents. At a later point in the same chapter he lays it down that 'flesh and blood cannot inherit the Kingdom of God' and that 'the dead shall be raised incorruptible, and we shall be changed'.[1] Whether this would involve for St. Paul the disappearance from the tomb of the earthly body so as to leave no remainder is not entirely clear, but it seems certain that it would rule out the possibility of eating and drinking. The latter point is allowed by Dr. Denney:

'But can we, in consistence with Paul's doctrine of the resurrection body, conceive Jesus saying, "Handle Me and see, for a spirit hath not *flesh and bones* as ye behold Me having"? Can we conceive that He took a piece of broiled fish and ate it before the disciples? . . . Meats for the belly and the belly for meats, Paul says, and God shall destroy both it and them. Eating is a function which belongs to the reality of this life, but not to that of immortality; and there does seem something which is not only incongruous but repellent in the idea of the Risen Lord eating. It makes Him real by bringing Him back to earth and incorporating Him again in this life, whereas the reality of which His resurrection assures us is not that of this life, but of another life transcending this. . . . But though we have to discount this, the resurrection itself, as the revelation of life in another order, is not touched. . . . To reject the eating is not to reject the resurrection of Jesus, it is to preserve it in its truth as a revelation of life at a new level—life in which eating and drinking are as inappropriate as marrying or giving in marriage.'[2]

[1] 1 Cor. xv. 50, 52, R.V.

[2] Op. cit., pp. 144–6. Denney discusses at length the apparent 'progressive materialization of the appearances of Jesus' as we go from the earlier to the later reports, and seems to accept the eating of the fish, but not the empty tomb, as an example of such materialization. Professor F. C. Porter of Yale writes: 'The Gospel stories of the resurrection of Christ disclose a tendency to make it increasingly unique by emphasizing its physical aspects and regarding it as the miracle of miracles. Paul saw a serious danger in this tendency to separate Christ from

The same point is temperately stated by Dr. Montefiore:

'It is doubtful whether Paul or any of the apostles would have admitted that Jesus, after his rising, would have been able to partake, or would have partaken, of "corruptible" mortal food, even though it were only to strengthen the faith of his disciples.'[1]

What St. Paul himself writes, still in the same chapter, is this:

'But some one will say, How are the dead raised? and with what manner of body do they come? Thou foolish one, that which thou thyself sowest is not quickened, except it die: and that which thou sowest, thou sowest not the body that shall be, but a bare grain, it may chance of wheat, or of some other kind; but God giveth it a body even as it pleased him, and to each seed a body of its own. All flesh is not the same flesh. . . . So also is the resurrection of the dead. It is sown in corruption; it is raised in incorruption: it is sown in dishonour; it is raised in glory: it is sown in weakness; it is raised in power; it is sown an animate (ψυχικόν) body; it is raised a spiritual (πνευματικόν) body. If there is an animate body, there is also a spiritual body.'[2]

It is clear that St. Paul is here following the view which we saw to have been long current in the Pharisaic tradition and to have been accepted also by Jesus, that in the next life we shall by God's almighty power be provided with a *new embodiment*—a body incorruptible, not 'of the earth, earthy',[3] but wrought of the texture of God's glory. His statement that

Christians' (*The Mind of Christ in Paul*, 1930, p. 243). Canon Streeter writes: 'In spite of the clear teaching of our Lord and of St. Paul, the early Church continued to be largely dominated by the pre-Christian idea of a flesh-and-blood resurrection; and there are clear indications that the influence of this pre-conceived idea has modified the tradition of what actually happened in this case' (*Immortality*, p. 115).

[1] *Synoptic Gospels*, 2nd ed., vol. ii, p. 643.
[2] 1 Cor. xv. 35–45, R.V. altered.
[3] Verse 47.

'flesh and blood cannot inherit the kingdom of God' is sufficient proof that he did not believe in the revivification of the present animal organism. Yet Dr. McGiffert goes too far when he says that St. Paul 'so spiritualized the resurrection as to make it practically no more than immortality, while most of the early Christians interpreted it in materialistic terms as the resurrection of the present fleshly body'.[1] Nothing, as we have seen, so much dismayed the Apostle as the prospect of being left with a 'naked' soul—left, as we should say, a mere ghost. And throughout the chapter St. Paul seems especially concerned to make it clear that his description applies alike to the body which Christ, 'the firstfruits of them that are asleep',[2] possesses since His Resurrection and to the bodies which 'they that are Christ's'[3] will have 'in their own time'.[4] So in another epistle we have the words: 'Who shall change our vile body, that it may be fashioned like unto His body of glory.'[5]

It should be noted carefully that to make the vision of the risen Christ conditional upon faith in Him is by no means the same thing as making it the fruit of faith. To say that I cannot see a certain star without lenses does not mean that the lenses create the star. To say that only a trained eye can find beauty in a certain picture does not mean that the trained eye puts into the picture a beauty that is not really there. What faith

---

[1] *A History of Christian Thought*, vol. i, p. 88.
[2] 1 Cor. xv. 20, R.V. altered.   [3] Verse 23.
[4] Verse 23. 'Nothing is more remarkable in this great chapter than the consistency and emphasis with which he insists on the identity of the experience of the Christian with that of Christ in the matter of life after death. . . . His assumption throughout is that the resurrection is the same thing in Christ's case as in ours, or in our case as in his.' F. C. Porter, *The Mind of Christ in Paul* (1930), pp. 243–5.
[5] Phil. iii. 21.

did for the disciples was not to make them subject to delusions but—as we are fain to think—to open their eyes to a Reality that was actively seeking to invade their consciousness. Indeed it is as wrong to speak of the vision growing out of the faith as of the faith growing out of the vision. The truth is rather that the vision and the faith are one. Perhaps visions are the form which faith assumes for exceptional natures or in exceptional circumstances. The theology of the Middle Ages taught, and the succession of the mystics has always believed, that *fides*, when it reaches its height, passes at last into *visio* —the *visio beatifica Dei*; so that, in rare instances, one who has long *trusted* in the Unseen World may now be given the grace actually to *see* it; though not, of course, with eyes of flesh.

The question is often raised whether the visions of the Risen Christ were 'subjective'. The answer, for all who believe in the reality of the Unseen World at all, must surely be an emphatic negative. The visions granted to the disciples were revelations of a genuinely extant reality. Neither their faith itself, nor the visions that accompanied and defined it, are capable of a purely 'subjective' explanation. They were what they were only under the pressure of the reality, now believed in, now seen. Behind the fact of their up-reaching faith lay the prior fact of God's down-reaching grace. Behind the fact of their strained seeing lay the prior fact of the invading presence of Him whom they saw.

There is every reason to class the appearances of the Risen Jesus with the many other 'visions and revelations[1] (ὀπτασίας

---

[1] 2 Cor. xii. 1. It is noteworthy that, according to Acts xxvi. 19, St. Paul spoke of his experience on the Damascus road as a 'heavenly vision'.

καὶ ἀποκαλύψεις)', as St. Paul calls them, which play so important a part throughout Biblical history, and not there alone. Modern writers who give over all the other visions and theophanies—including even the closely associated vision of the Ascension—to mere 'subjectivity', and yet insist on the appearances of the Risen Christ as entering in the ordinary way into the matter-of-fact historical order, create great trouble for inquiring minds. To make faith depend on the proved historicity of the appearances is to place a weight on the historical evidence which it cannot possibly bear and never was meant to bear; and it can lead only to perplexity. And this perplexity is increased when the Resurrection-appearances are separated from their natural context in the whole history of Biblical visionary disclosure. A story like that of Jacob wrestling with God at Peniel and seeing Him 'face to face'[1] is probably purely legendary. But what are we to say of Isaiah's vision in the temple; or of the visions of Ezekiel 'in the thirtieth year, in the fourth month, in the fifth day of the month', as he was 'among the captives by the river of Chebar'?[2] And again, what are we to say of the Transfiguration, of the Ascension, of St. Stephen's vision before he was stoned, of St. Paul's vision on the road to Damascus, and of many others recorded in the New Testament? These are clearly held by the Biblical writers to be 'objective' in just the same sense as were the Resurrection-appearances. St. Paul regards his own vision of the risen Christ as being on the same plane as those vouchsafed to the original disciples: 'and last of all, as unto one born out of due time, he appeared to me also'.[3] Yet are we to understand that what was seen in these

[1] Gen. xxxii. 30.   [2] Ezek. i. 1.   [3] 1 Cor. xv. 8.

cases was something that entered into the public and common order of events? 'And the posts of the door moved at the voice of him that cried, and the house was filled with smoke. . . . Then flew one of the seraphim unto me, having a live coal in his hand, which he had taken with the tongs from off the altar.'[1] So Isaiah describes the vision that made him what he was. But did the posts of the temple door move in such a way that all might see? Was the smoke such as would stain the walls? Was there a coal less on the altar when the vision was past? Again, was the 'cloud that overshadowed'[2] the three disciples on the Mount of Transfiguration on the same level of public material reality as were the clouds visible to other men? Was the 'light from heaven'[3] that shone round about St. Paul at his conversion a light that mingled with the lights of earth, being of one substance with them? Surely we must answer 'No' to all these questions. In *that* use none of the Biblical visions seem to have been 'objective'. But is that a proper use of the word 'objective'? I cannot believe that it is. I sometimes wonder, indeed, whether the word has *any* proper sense or use. The fashionable modern distinction, introduced by Kant,[4] between the objective and the subjective is a highly confused one and needs to be broken up into at least two separate distinctions, that between significant and merely illusory experience, and that between public and private experience. There is no reason to suppose that all private experience must be illusory.

The grounds of our Christian persuasion of the reality of

[1] Isa. vi. 4, 6.   [2] Mark ix. 7.
[3] Acts ix. 3.
[4] Cf. R. Eucken, *The Fundamental Concepts of Modern Philosophic Thought*, Eng. tr. (New York, 1880), p. 2.

eternal life may therefore be accurately expressed by means of an adaptation of our Lord's own words: 'But as touching the dead that they are raised; have ye not read that God is the God of our Lord Jesus Christ? He is not the God of the dead, but of the living.'

CHAPTER VI
THE LOGIC OF HOPE
I

SOME readers may feel that we have now, however haltingly, said all there needs to be said about the grounds and foundations of the Christian hope. Others may protest with a good deal of impatience that, on the contrary, we have hardly so much as made a beginning with our proper task—that we have been serving them with history where they had been encouraged to look for argument. I shall not judge between these two classes of readers, but will try now to do no less for the satisfaction of the latter than I have already tried to do for the former. In this chapter I shall set down, as well as I am able, the logic of the Christian belief in eternal life.

One thing, however, seems clear. It would surely be wrong in principle to attempt separately to deduce from any general and pre-religious premiss each of the several convictions of religion, of which the conviction of immortality is one. To do that would be to treat religion as a collection of detached beliefs rather than as an organic whole. Hence what ought to be expected of one who promises to set down the logic of his faith in immortality is, at least in the first place, that he should exhibit that faith as logically flowing from the idea of religion itself or from the primary act of faith in which all the further detail of religion may be taken as naturally contained— namely, belief in God. Whether, having (so far as may be) succeeded in showing that the reality of God necessarily carries immortality with it, I should afterwards be expected to show that God Himself is real—that is merely a question concerning the appointed range of our present inquiry. Some, who are anxious only to hear what I may have to say on the particular matter of immortality, would be very impatient of any attempt to carry them over into the other and wider field. Others might complain that if I stop short before the question of God's reality, there are a great many honest souls to whom I shall have nothing positive to contribute. Yet this latter opinion hardly seems reasonable. Every argument must begin somewhere, and it would be tedious and repetitive to start each separate argument from a point which all men have reached (i.e. from a proposition which would be denied by nobody), especially as such a point is nowadays exceedingly difficult to find. Surely it will be profitable if we succeed to any degree in making it clear from what initial major premiss, and through what process of subsequent reflection, the Christian doctrine of eternal life can alone be reached, even if we do not, at this writing, go on to inquire into the truth or falsity of that premiss. One cannot do everything all at once. And for my own part I have a still better excuse; for, having already in another place[1] written at length of the ultimate roots of our religious fellowship with God, I cannot now be reasonably expected to do more than show how the conception of eternal life is rooted in that fellowship.

But there are two other things that must be said with some emphasis before we proceed. We must point out, first, the temerity of hoping to be able to affirm the conclusion unless, or until, one is first able to affirm the major premiss from

---

[1] See my *Roots of Religion in the Human Soul* (1926) and my *Interpretation of Religion* (New York, 1928, Edinburgh, 1929).

which, historically speaking, the conclusion has alone been drawn. It is time there was an end to the expectation that anything even remotely corresponding to the Christian hope may be extracted from premisses of a purely humanistic kind. A continuance so established would, as we have already urged more than once, be what the New Testament calls eternal death rather than what it calls eternal life. It would be the continuance of Hades and Sheol—and it is a very significant fact that in the Christian tradition Hades and Sheol came to be alternative names not for heaven but for hell. 'Sooner than thus be separated from Thee', wrote the Blessed Henry Suso, 'I had rather suffer a thousand torments every day I live. If I do but contemplate such a separation, my heart for anguish is like to break.'[1]

The second thing requiring emphasis is that the disappearance of the hope of a life beyond the grave is far from being the saddest or most serious of the consequences that flow from disbelief in God. The denial of immortality always seems to me to be more disquieting for what it is a sign of than for what it is in itself. That a man should be doomed to go through this present life without any sense of God's accompanying presence is a much greater tragedy than that he should be faced with the prospect of extinction when at last he dies. There are indeed some men whose main reason for desiring to 'get religion' is that by means of it they may get assurance of immortality, just as there are others whose main reason for desiring it is that it should put them in possession of the secret of self-control. But true religion will not thus consent to be made a tool of. God must be sought and loved for His

[1] *Little Book of Eternal Wisdom* (c. 1338), Part I, ch. xi.

own sake, and not merely as a Purveyor either of moral power or of endless life. 'All human perversity or vice', says St. Augustine, 'consists in wishing to enjoy what we ought to use, and to use what we ought to enjoy'[1]; and here, if anywhere, is a case in point. At the heart of religion lies this significant paradox, that it is only by coming to care more about God than about either our own character or our own destiny that either our character can be transformed or our destiny in any wise foretokened. The transference of attention from self to God is the secret both of self-conquest and of hope. If in certain of the later mystery cults of Greece and Rome, and in those forms of early Christianity which were most open to this pagan influence, religion came to be thought of too narrowly as an agency for the purveyance of immortality—'medicine of immortality', as one Church Father has it, the experience of the Hebrew people here places at our disposal a most valuable corrective. The Hebrew psalmist's or prophet's absorption in God was no whit abated by his failure to rise to the thought of God as the guardian of his destiny after death. 'The Old Testament', writes Sir George Adam Smith, 'is of use as reminding us that the hope of immortality is one of the secondary and inferential elements in religious experience'.[2]

In the last chapter we were concerned to demonstrate the historical fact that all the hope of a blessed immortality which

---

[1] *Quaestiones*, 30.

[2] *Modern Criticism and the Preaching of the Old Testament* (New York, 1901), p. 214. See also W. Temple, Archbishop of York, *The Idea of Immortality*, &c., p. 9: 'If my desire is first for future life for myself, or even first for re-union with those whom I have loved and lost, then the doctrine of immortality may do me positive harm by fixing me in that self-concern or concern for my own joy in my friends.'

there has hitherto been in the world was born of the experience of fellowship with God. Our present concern is with the logic of this connexion. Let us begin by reminding ourselves what the experience of fellowship with God, which is the essence of religion, really is. Let us have a good look at our major premiss before asking whether any conclusion can validly be made to rest upon it. I shall state the matter in the most general terms possible. I shall say that the experience of religion consists in the perception of the supreme goodness or loveliness or friendliness or trustworthiness of the ultimate nature of things. Perhaps of the four words I have used 'trustworthiness' is the one that can be applied to the history of religion most generally. And the correlative of this character of trustworthiness in the nature of things is the attitude of trust on the part of the human soul. Religion has place in a man's life when the Eternal reveals itself (or rather Himself—for not to any 'it' can we entrust the things that matter most) to him as trustworthy and when he, in response to this revelation, puts his trust in the Eternal. Trust, however, is but another English word for faith, which thus becomes the name for the typical religious response to reality. There will, of course, be a few who will desire to use the word religion in a wider sense, so as to be able to include within it their own less believing variety of opinion; and some will even wish to use the word *God* more widely. But over this question of the 'Pickwickian' usage of words I shall not delay; for what I am anxious to exhibit in this chapter is the natural and necessary connexion which I take to exist between the conception of eternal life and the general religious tradition of our race. I am not concerned to inquire into its connexion, or lack of connexion, with what this or that individual may choose to call religion. As Professor Montague puts it:

'Religion is a eulogistic term, and many who have lost their faith in it, in any sense in which it matters, will cling lovingly to the word and use it as a designation for a devotion to their favourite ethical ideals. . . . When affection or disaffection for words is permitted to override their meanings, the wells of discourse are muddied and there ensues no advantage either ethical or logical.'[1]

Professor Montague's own conception of the essence of historical religion coincides closely with that suggested above.

'Religion, as we shall conceive it, is the acceptance neither of a primitive absurdity nor of a sophisticated truism, but of a momentous possibility—the possibility, namely, that what is highest in spirit is also deepest in nature, that the ideal and the real are at least to some extent identified, not merely evanescently in our own lives, but enduringly in the universe itself.'[2]

Or again,

'religion is taken to mean the faith, theoretical, practical and emotional, in something in nature that is making for the values that we cherish[3].'

Thus the issue at stake in it is

'whether the things we care for most are at the mercy of the things we care for least'.[4]

But indeed there is at the present time a very remarkable degree of unanimity among the leading writers of almost all

---

[1] W. P. Montague, *Belief Unbound* (1930), p. 7.
[2] Ibid., p. 6.   [3] Ibid., p. 26.   [4] Ibid., p. 66.

the schools concerning this elementary matter, and it would be easy to quote passages congruent with the above from a large variety of other sources.

What concerns us here particularly, however, is obviously not those putative embryonic beginnings of the racial religious experience over which the anthropologists are still engaged in hot debate, nor yet those earlier stages of its progress which are still open for our inspection in many parts of the world. Our concern is with religion in its highest actual embodiment, as mainly represented—for all likely readers of this book—by the Hebrew and Christian literature, but significantly foreshadowed also in ancient Greece and Rome and elsewhere. If then it is this highest development of religious experience, and especially the final culmination of it, that we have in mind, we can describe it in somewhat less abstract terms. Religion at this level becomes the experience of the love of God. The Eternal now discloses Himself to us as One who loves us with a love greater and more mysterious than our minds can comprehend, but to the depth and breadth and height of which the love that moved the heart of Christ is our best available clue. God, we believe, loves us better than we love ourselves. Our deepest interests are safer— beyond imagination safer—in His hands than they would be, had we ourselves the most unrestricted guardianship over them. And all the things that matter in the universe are safer in His hands than they could ever be in ours. Justice is safer. Friendship is safer. Love itself is safer. The cherished gains of the past are safer; and so also the promise of the future. 'So the All-great were the All-loving too.' The Omnipotence behind the universe is our Father and our Friend.

II

Our question now is whether, if this our major premiss be allowed, the conclusion of eternal life can be consistently denied. Is it possible to believe that the Eternal Father, if He veritably is, should consent to the annihilation of the souls He loves?

Theoretically, indeed, another possibility is open. Some may rob our premiss of its virtue, not by denying God's love, but by denying His power. From the fact that God is all-good, they may remind us, it does not follow that all things are ordered for the best, unless it be granted also that God is all-powerful. I confess this way of speaking produces on my mind an impression of unreality. The question I find myself asking is not whether God is omnipotent, but whether Omnipotence is God; not whether the Eternal Lover of our souls is truly in control of the universe, but whether that which is in control of the universe is truly such as to be a Lover of our souls. My own temptation, accordingly, has never been to doubt the power of a God unmistakably revealed as love, but rather to doubt the love of a God unmistakably revealed as power. The almightiness of reality is only too plain; it is the love that so often seems hidden. Hence I should say that the only grounds I know for believing in God would show Him omnipotent or not at all; and I should feel also that if some ground *did* appear for believing in the existence somewhere *within* reality of a being of loving purpose but finite power, I should not be moved to worship but only to admiration—I should applaud but I should not kneel. Nothing less than the Infinite can really slake the soul's thirst. I have difficulty, then, in adequately discussing this alternative form of denial. Yet perhaps this does not matter. Perhaps, after all, it does not present us with a genuinely 'live option' in the particular matter of eternal life. For though some would deny the omnipotence of God in the abstract, possibly none who believe in Him at all would hold Him so weak as not to be able to secure the immortality of the souls He loves, should He so desire.

Leaving this alternative on one side, then, we must ask again whether Omnipotent Love can be conceived as consenting to the annihilation of the souls of men after their brief span of life on earth. But what is immediately clear is that *this* question is an ethical one—in other words, a question of values. The minor premiss of hope's syllogism is thus, if we accept the common distinction, not a theological but an ethical proposition. It is a matter not of faith but of morals. Very abstractly we may state it thus: *Something of intrinsic value resides in human individuality.* For myself, indeed, I do not accept the distinction between theology and ethics as being an ultimately valid one, and I should accordingly prefer to retain in the statement of this ethical proposition a certain theological reference and to say: The souls of individual men are precious in God's sight. Or we might use our Lord's own words: 'Joy shall be in heaven over one.'[1] To this point we shall have to return at the end of the chapter, but for the moment the more abstract ethical form of the statement will serve our purpose equally well. It is, then, upon the various attempts to deny this minor premiss that we must now concentrate our attention. They are, as I believe, reducible in the end to two.

[1] Luke xv. 7.

There is first the view that the ethical demands of the situation are satisfied by what is called 'the immortality of influence'. One thinks of the now very hackneyed lines, by which their author is alone remembered as a poetess, about 'those immortal dead who live again in minds made better by their presence'. Or one thinks of Comte's 'subjective immortality' and George Meredith's 'Live in thy offspring!' and the fanciful doctrine in *The Blue Bird* that 'the dead live as long as we think of them'. The very able writer of a recent Ingersoll Lecture, on immortality, finds his only escape from an ultimate pessimism in the reflection that:

'My friend's ideals do not die when he dies. Indeed, as many have testified, his death may make possible for me a perfect loyalty to his ideals. A life which has been is not a non-existent thing. An achieved possibility is part of the nature of the real. The world is a very different place because of those who have left their mark upon us.'[1]

That the transmission of acquired spiritual values from one generation to another is a most precious fact, nobody will wish to deny. It is indeed the sole agency by which racial progress can ever be accomplished. But whether it has in it the virtue to save us from an ultimate pessimism is quite another question. There are two ways, as it seems to me, in which it falls short.

In the first place, I doubt whether anybody, when really

[1] Julius Seelye Bixler, *Immortality and the Present Mood* (1931), p. 36. The statement that 'his death may make possible for me a perfect loyalty to his ideals' is *of course* true, but seems irrelevant to the present issue. The fact that Christianity has always found a deep significance in death has not prevented it from having a lively belief in a life beyond the grave. Our Lord's disciples knew that by His death He had bestowed on them a gift He could not otherwise have bestowed, but that reflection did not in any way displace their faith in His continued life.

pressed on the ethical issue involved, will care to claim that more than a small part of the value of the individual is conserved by the continuance of his 'influence'. It is all a question, really, of where the value is held to reside. Is an individual human personality valuable as an exemplification of a certain type, as a carrier of certain abstract ideals, as an embodiment of 'an achieved possibility'? Or is it rather valuable *in itself* as a unique existent? Surely the latter is the only view that is either sensible or loyal. To take any other view is to sacrifice personality on the altar of the impersonal, and to prefer abstract nouns to living beings. Abstract universals are indeed involved in all ascriptions of value, but *that to which the value is ascribed* is not the universal itself but the individual in which it is embodied. Professor Sorley writes in his Gifford Lectures:

'When I say "love is good", or "justice is good", I mean that love as realized in a personal life is good, that justice as manifested in a man's character or in a social order is good. I do not mean than the mere abstract quality, love or justice, is also good. The mere quality love, conceived abstractedly and without any reference to its realization in personal life, is not good.... Good cannot be predicated of the abstract. It belongs only to the concrete . . . —to persons.'[1]

The same point is made by another Gifford Lecturer, Professor A. E. Taylor:

'When we speak of virtue, art, science, health, as having *value*, it is never virtue, art, science, health "in the abstract" to which we mean to refer, but always the actual virtuous conduct, artistic production, true thinking, healthy bodily functioning of persons conceived as existent, either in fact or *ex hypothesi*. The candid

[1] *Moral Values and the Idea of God* (1918), pp. 139–40.

utterances, generous acts and impulses, the creation or appreciation of beauty, the comprehension of truth, the vigorous performance of the physical functions of life by existents—in fact by
persons—are the real objects to which we are ascribing the
possession of value; we are not predicating value of the logical
"concepts", virtue, beauty, knowledge, or health.'[1]

'The truth, beauty, goodness to which we ascribe worth are in
all cases "concreted" in individuals of which they are the constitu-
tive forms, and . . . our ascription of worth is only significant in
view of this embodiment of the "universal" in the individual.'[2]

It is not therefore permissible to speak as if an abstract ideal
could be the bearer by which all the value residing in a certain
individual could pass, after his death, into other individuals.

Yet it is not on the absurdity of such a view that I would
dwell so much as on its disloyalty. Have I any *right* to treat
my fellow as if he were a means to some kind of impersonal
end? May I, for instance, hold that the state is the end, and
treat individual men as instruments to its welfare? Or may
I hold that the continuance of my name and family is what
matters and treat the individual members of my household
merely as links necessary for the continuity of the chain?
Surely the fundamental immorality of such a view is now
recognized by us all. It is certain that it has been the source
of much that we consider evil—of many inhuman practices
from suttee to hara-kiri and of the cruellest excesses of mili-
tarist and nationalist absolutism. As I look upon the fair boy
who is growing up to carry on my name, or upon the keen-
minded pupil who is growing up to carry on my influence,
I must not say to myself merely, 'He is a transmitter', or, 'He
is a stage in a process': I must say rather, 'In him is fulfilment',

---

[1] *The Faith of a Moralist* (1930), vol. i, p. 35.   [2] Ibid., p. 45.

'He is an end in himself.' Most of Kant's philosophy has had to bear the brunt of severe criticism, but there is one doctrine of his which, so far as I am aware, nobody has ever ventured to dispute—the doctrine that it is wicked to treat any human being as if he were of value merely owing to some end beyond himself that was being brought about through him or by means of him. 'So act as to treat humanity', he said, 'whether in thine own person or in that of any other, in every case as an end withal, never as means only.'[1] If this is good advice, then we have no right to take any *ultimate* comfort from the fact that 'my friend's ideals do not die when he dies', or that 'the world is a very different place because of those who have left their mark upon us'.

The advice which Kant here gives marks the culmination of an ethical development which took centuries and even millenniums to accomplish itself; and to deny the wisdom of it would be to retrace the march of history in a way for which few who understand what their undertaking implies, can really be prepared. Undoubtedly both the Hebrews and the Greeks did start out from the view that it was the race, not the individual, that mattered, and that therefore the essential values of human life could be conserved even if the individuals perished, so long as only the race survived. The patriarchs died and were gathered to their fathers, and their children

[1] *Grundlegung der Metaphysik der Sitten*, Abbott's tr., p. 56. Dr. L. P. Jacks has admirably applied this Kantian principle to the question of immortality in *A Living Universe* (1923), pp. 121 ff. There is also an interesting reminiscence of it in Unamuno's discussion of immortality. He paraphrases a saying of Sénancour's to read: 'If it is nothingness that awaits us, let us not so act that it shall be a just fate', and suggests this as a central principle of ethics, 'the firmest basis of action'. 'Act', he says again, 'so as to merit eternity.' 'Act as if you were to die to-morrow, but to die in order to survive and be eternalized. The end of morality is to give personal, human finality to the Universe.' *The Tragic Sense of Life*, Eng. tr., p. 263.

died, and their children's children until the present day; and soon you and I will die, and our children and our children's children; but there will always remain the chosen race, the peculiar people, the royal priesthood—and not only remain but multiply, until it is as the sand of the sea which cannot be numbered for multitude. I know well that this conception is one that has survived in many quarters almost down to our own day. I have often felt that in old England the conception of family continuance was allowed, in no small degree, to do the work of the conception of individual immortality. What made life worth living for many a loyal member of the old landed classes who was not perhaps very sure of his religion was not the hope of a life after death, but the hope of a family future that would be worthy of the family past. I have even myself known men who seemed to me to be saved from an ultimate pessimism by such a hope alone. The immortality of the ancestral acres was the real Rock of Ages in which their spirits found support. And I remember one friend who owned little land, but came of an old and honourable family and possessed considerable property interests of another kind, telling me sadly how his life had seemed to become aimless since he had realized that he was to have no son, but only a daughter. In this way, then, I have often reflected how a civilization based on a well-ordered family system and on the entailed ownership of land provided a real mental refuge from the tragedy of life, and made the question of individual immortality somewhat less immediately urgent.[1] And I have

[1] This kind of immortality is duly recognized by Plato and given its merited place. 'A man shall marry', he lays it down in his *Laws*, 'between the age of thirty and thirty-five, considering that after a sort the human race naturally partakes of immortality, of which all men have the greatest desire implanted in them, for the

found it sad that with the partial break-down of the old order, this refuge has seemed to become less and less available, so that many who in the old days would have felt their spirits upheld by their ancestral system, have in fact not known where to turn for help in time of trouble.

Yet of course the vast majority of those who found some support in the ancestral system of which I have spoken believed piously in individual immortality also, and derived their *main* support from this other-worldly hope. Their outlook on life thus gave large place to the intrinsic value of the individual personality—and this in spite of certain genuinely unethical (and frequently cruel) states of mind deriving from the other view, as when the first-born daughter was given a somewhat less joyful welcome than the first-born son, and when the son himself tended to be too much regarded in terms of his value as an instrument of family continuance. But if we go back to the early civilizations that preceded the appearance in the world of any true doctrine of individual immortality, we find an entirely different state of affairs. There it was quite definitely the group that counted, and the intrinsic value of the individual was not recognized in any explicit way at all. The family or the tribe was then the unit of justice, so that the deserts of the fathers, whether for good or evil, were visited upon the children unto the third and fourth generation. And it was the unit also of fellowship with God, so that private religion found little place. Nobody can deny that the progress

desire of every man that he may become famous, and not lie in the grave without a name, is only the love of continuance. . . . In this way men are immortal, leaving children behind them, with whom they are one in the unity of generation. And for a man voluntarily to deprive himself of this gift of immortality, as he deliberately does who will not have a wife or children, is impiety' (p. 721, Jowett's trans.).

of ethical and spiritual life has gradually left this old order behind and that the movement has been towards an ever greater and greater realization of the intrinsic significance of the individual. It has not indeed been felt that the social organism is of less significance than used to be supposed, but it has been felt that the individual personality is of much greater importance. And now, are we really prepared to surrender this hard-won insight and to pretend—as our forefathers of the last two thousand years, whatever other doubts they may have had, never for a moment pretended—that the individual personality may utterly cease to exist as an individual without a most precious value being lost from the world? Surely there is only one answer that can be given.

The second difficulty that stands in the way of the acceptance of the immortality of influence as a substitute for the immortality of the individual is of a very different kind; namely that, in order to be effective, it must be extended so as to include an eschatology which is even more difficult of acceptance than the eschatology which it presumes to displace. For the immortality of influence clearly implies the immortality of the race which is the carrier of influence. 'My friend's ideals do not die when he dies. . . . A life which has been is not a non-existent thing. . . . The world is a very different place because of those who have left their mark upon us.' Yet if the *race* dies, if human history itself comes to an end, then my friend's ideals do die; and the world will *not* be a very different place because of those who have left their mark on us, if ever there should be no more 'we' to whom the mark could be transmitted. *Something* of the ethical value of personality may pass from one person to another—though we found it necessary to insist that there was an inmost intrinsic value which can never thus pass; but *no* ethical value can pass from a world of persons to a world from which all personality is extinguished. 'An achieved possibility', said Professor Bixler, 'is part of the nature of the real.' But if the achieved possibility is an ethical value it cannot remain part of the nature of the real, after the real has ceased to be spiritual and personal. Ethical value is a function of personal spirit and cannot exist apart from it. Clearly it is only on men's minds that my friend's delicate sense of honour and scrupulous purity of heart can leave a mark. These things leave no mark whatever on the physical world. And certainly they do not leave any mark on 'the realm of essences'; for that realm, if such there be, is unchangingly the same and can have no 'marks' left on it. Hence, to Professor Bixler's assertion that 'a life which has been is not a non-existent thing', we can only reply that it *is* a non-existent thing unless either itself continues still to be or the universe be conceived as still containing something which is of such a nature as to be sensitive to the spiritual values which in the life in question were realized, i.e. as still containing a spirit or spirits. Some may say that this requirement is satisfied by belief in God or the Absolute Spirit, without the added belief in the immortality of the human race. With this view we shall be dealing in the next section, but clearly it is not what is in the mind of those who, like Professor Bixler, put their reliance on the immortality of influence. What they urge is not that their friend's ideals are absorbed into the Infinite Personality of God, but that they live on in other finite persons who come after them. As for myself, I do indeed believe that 'an achieved possibility is part of the nature of the real', and that 'a life which has been is not a non-existent thing'; but I am equally convinced that if the life and possibility in question are personal or ethical in nature, then the said belief carries with it both the reality of God and personal immortality. It cannot, I am sure, be intelligently held on any other terms. Indeed I should say that to believe that all the spiritual values of past history still 'exist', and will always continue to exist, is the same thing as to believe in God and immortality.

But for those whose substitute for personal immortality is not absorption in the divine life, but continued influence on the lives of those who come after them, a belief in the endless continuance of the human race on earth is surely quite indispensable. Apart from this, their proposed escape from an ultimate pessimism is no escape at all. For it would be very like trifling with a serious subject to suggest that we should find sufficient comfort in the thought that, though our friend's ideals must no doubt in the end perish utterly, yet they are quite likely to live on for some considerable time after his own death. This would simply be equivalent to adding to our present length of life the possibility of a certain extra span of existence, though of much less effective existence. But not in this way can death be robbed of its sting or the grave of its victory. The sadness of death is not only that it comes so soon but that it comes at all. For my own part I have no particular complaint to lodge against the present length of our allotted span. Threescore years and ten may, for aught I know, serve their appointed purpose as well as a little more or a little less. I cannot agree with Mr. George Bernard Shaw (in *Back to Methuselah*) that their extension to three hundred would turn the tragedy to triumph. Still less would my tragic sense of loss at my friend's death be removed by the reflection that his influence might perhaps continue yet awhile, until at last the race itself should utterly perish, leaving not a wrack behind. It would be a serious failure of imagination to suppose that the loss need not distress us because its incidence may be for some time delayed.

Let us therefore look somewhat closely into this eschatological doctrine that is implied in an immortality of influence. It should be realized that to accept this doctrine would, once again, be to unwind the spool of history and to go back to very rude beginnings. The children of Israel began by taking the view that it was racial, not individual, continuity that mattered; and they fully realized that this implied the endless continuance both of Israel as a nation and of the earth as a habitation. 'I will establish My covenant between Me and thee and thy seed after thee in their generations for an everlasting covenant . . . and I will give unto thee, and to thy seed after thee, the land wherein thou art a stranger, all the land of Canaan, for an everlasting possession.'[1] All this we saw in the foregoing chapter, and we saw also that when, at a much later time, the idea of a future golden age, a blessed and everlasting Kingdom of God, took shape in the Hebrew mind, it was at first held that this Kingdom would have place on earth. Why was this view at last given up? Why did it finally come to be held that, though the *beginning* of such a consummation would be on the present earth, yet its eternal continuance must be beyond the veil that divides the seen from the unseen world? And why has this remained the teaching of both

[1] Gen. xvii. 7–8.

Judaism and Christianity from that day to this? It was, writes R. H. Charles, because the Jews became conscious

'that the earth, however purged and purified, is no fitting theatre for an eternal Messianic Kingdom. If the Messianic Kingdom is to be of eternal duration, [it] . . . must be built, not of things earthly and corruptible, but of things heavenly and incorruptible.'

'This transference of the hopes of the faithful from the material world took place about 100 B.C. At this period the earth had come to be regarded as wholly unfit for this Kingdom.'[1]

And Mr. Edwyn Bevan writes:

'At the outset the consummation to which they looked forward may have been conceived simply as an ideally righteous and happy kingdom in Palestine. . . . As time went on and the thought of religious Jews became more mature, it was largely realized that no Kingdom of God limited by the essential conditions of earthly life could satisfy the spirit of man.'[2]

Finally, in the New Testament we read that 'here we have no continuing city, but we seek one to come'—a city 'whose builder and maker is God'.[3] Clearly, then, part of the difficulty leading to the change was the difficulty of conceiving the present earth as genuinely incorruptible and eternal. It was easier for the Jews and the early Christians to believe that a new Jerusalem would be provided by the power of God than that the old one would last for ever.

Now it can hardly be denied that the eternity of the earth, instead of being easier, is rather much more difficult to contemplate to-day than it was in 100 B.C. Scientific facts are now known to us which preclude the possibility that our little

---

[1] Op. cit., pp. 210, 179.
[2] *The Hope of a World to Come*, &c., p. 26.
[3] Heb. xiii. 14; vi. 10.

planet will always remain habitable by man. We know also that there is at any moment the chance of a stellar cataclysm by which it may be destroyed before the next moment arrives —a chance that was not within the purview of pre-Copernican thought. Moreover our immensely increased understanding of history makes it much more difficult for us to conceive of any one civilization or nation or city lasting even as long as the earth lasts, than it was for the men of ancient time.

> Troy town is covered up with weeds,
> The rabbits and the pismires brood
> On broken gold, and shards, and beads
> Where Priam's ancient palace stood.[1]

Yet it has often seemed to me that these facts and their consequences were being less honestly faced by those who denied personal immortality than by those who believed in it. It has been a merit of the Christian outlook that it has at least kept its eyes wide open to the plain facts of life. It has never minimized the uncertainty of human existence. It has looked death in the face without any blinkers. It has realized to the full the perishableness of all things earthly. It has put its hope in no earthly Jerusalem. It has not nourished the delusion that, although all previous civilizations have had their day and ceased to be, our present one is guaranteed to last for ever. It has ever warned us that this earth will one day come to an end. But are our humanists equally ready in their acknowledgement of these plain facts? The frankly pessimistic minority of them (such as Lord Russell and Mr. Krutch) are certainly so ready. But I think it is otherwise with the

[1] J. Masefield, *Fragments*.

complacently optimistic majority. *Their* humanism has it
eschatology just as surely as had traditional Christianity, and
it is a more difficult eschatology, one that takes more be
lieving, one that conflicts more abruptly with the teaching
of experience and of natural science. 'Posterity', as Diderot
admitted, 'is to *le philosophe* what the other world is to the
religious man.' The saying has been made the text of an
admirable chapter on 'The Uses of Posterity', by Professor
Carl Becker in his recent most illuminating book on *The
Heavenly City of the Eighteenth-Century Philosophers*. He
writes as follows:

'Without a new heaven to replace the old, a new way of salva
tion, of attaining perfection, the religion of humanity would
appeal in vain to the common run of men.

'The new heaven had to be located somewhere within the con
fines of the earthly life, since it was an article of philosophical
faith that the end of life was life itself, the perfected temporal life
of man; and in the future, since the temporal life was not yet
perfected. But if the celestial heaven was to be dismantled in
order to be rebuilt on earth, it seemed that the salvation of man
kind must be attained . . . by man himself, by the progressive
improvement made by the efforts of successive generations of
men; and in this co-operative enterprise posterity had its un
deniable uses. . . . Thus, the Philosophers called in posterity to
exorcise the double illusion of the Christian paradise and the
golden age of antiquity. For the love of God they substituted
love of humanity; for the vicarious atonement the perfectibility
of man through his own efforts; and for the hope of immortality
in another world the hope of living in the memory of future
generations.'

'I do not know why historians, who are ardently devoted to
noting exactly what happened, should so generally have failed

o note a fact that is writ large in the most authentic documents: he fact that the thought of posterity was apt to elicit from ighteenth-century Philosophers and revolutionary leaders a iighly emotional, an essentially religious, response.'[1]

Sometimes, when I have been discussing questions of belief vith groups of students who had been influenced by the modern humanistic temper, I have found myself in the posi- ion of a defender of the faith before an audience of shrewd ceptics, until some remark fell from me which indicated my incertainty as to whether our present civilization would last or ever, or whether our world would always remain habita- le, or whether a starry collision might not to-morrow make final end of all our toil and moil, or—it might be—whether ontinuous upward progress was really a law of human his- ory, or again whether natural science was really going to ucceed in abolishing all the ills that flesh is heir to; and then have found the situation to be suddenly and most amusingly eversed. It was now *I* who was the iconoclast, basely bring- ig the acid of my scepticism to bear upon the most sacred of uman beliefs; and it was my young friends who were hotly efending the faith once delivered to the—humanists!

Here are some weighty sentences from T. E. Hulme:

'By the perverted rhetoric of Rationalism your natural istincts are suppressed and you are converted into an agnostic. ust as in the case of the other instincts, Nature has her revenge. 'he instincts that find their right and proper outlet in religion iust come out in some other way. You don't believe in a God, o you begin to believe that man is a god. You don't believe in Ieaven, so you begin to believe in a heaven on earth. In other vords, you get romanticism. The concepts that are right and proper in their own sphere are spread over, and so mess up, falsify and blur the clear outlines of human experience. It is like pouring a pot of treacle over the dinner table. Romanticism then, and this is the best definition I can give it, is spilt religion.'[1]

I hold it true, then, that the doctrine of the immortality of ideals is not only less satisfying to our sense of value but is also, in view of the facts revealed by natural science, more difficult to believe than is the doctrine of the immortality of persons.

III

We can deal somewhat more briefly with the second principal attempt to evade the judgement, which we set down as the minor premiss of hope's syllogism, that something of intrinsic value resides in the human individual: I mean the doctrine of so-called 'reabsorption'. What is of value in a man is not, it is now held, his individual personality, but only his sharing in the general fund of impersonal spiritual being. Hence he may altogether cease to exist as a distinct person without any loss of value being involved, if only he be 'reabsorbed' into the spiritual universe, or into the life of God. This kind of view has been much appealed to of recent years by those who, for one reason or another, have found it difficult to follow the accepted Christian teaching. Our novels and our contemporary poetry are full of it.

Like the other alternatives to personal immortality, the doctrine of reabsorption also had its ancient history. But unlike the others its history was not in Israel, nor yet (except at a late date) in Greece, but in India. We need only remind our-

[1] *Speculations*, p. 118.

selves of the facts set down in the preceding chapter. All the Indian religions do indeed take it for granted that individual immortality, in the form of reincarnation in one body after another, is the natural and normal destiny of mankind; but since this destiny is always taken to be a doom rather than a blessing, each religion holds out the hope that by the adoption of a suitable religious discipline this doom may at last be avoided and the soul sink back into its one impersonal Source. According to the teaching of the Upanishads, the human soul *is atman* and *Brahma*—'not a product of it, nor a portion of it, but the whole'.[1] On this view, then, the value of a man is not anything peculiar to himself, but the abstract intelligence which he possesses along with others; and consequently nothing is lost when *he* dies, if only abstract intelligence remains. Professor Farquhar writes:

'Therefore, since this was the teaching of the earliest system of release (a system which has had an immeasurable influence in India), and since it taught the identity of man's soul with this abstract impersonal intelligence, the great stream of Hindu thought has always tended to conceive the human spirit as being essentially intelligence, to regard personality, will, and emotion as belonging to the lower reaches of human nature, because they are involved in action, which leads to *karma*, and to think of morality as a set of rules belonging merely to the social life of man and therefore having little relation to the nature of the soul.'[2]

The primary associations of such a view will always be with India, but it has frequently appeared also in European thought. Probably its first appearance is in Aristotle, though his few reserved utterances on the matter are notoriously

[1] See article 'Soul (Hindu)' in *Encycl. of Religion and Ethics.*
[2] Ibid.

difficult to interpret and have been subjected to many different interpretations during the past two thousand years. The most important part of us, he teaches, is our active intelligence (νοῦς ποιητικός). In some passages he seems, quite in the manner of the Upanishads, to identify this active intelligence of ours with the Divine Intelligence: at the very least he strongly emphasizes the kinship between the two. And this is all there is about us that survives death. The active intelligence, we read in his treatise *Concerning the Soul*, is 'separate from body, impassive, unmixed'.

'It thinks without intermission. Only when separated is it its own true self, and it alone is immortal and eternal. . . . The passive intelligence, without which there can however be no thinking, is perishable.'[1]

'Reasoning and love and hate are not states of intelligence itself, but of the organism that has the intelligence, though only by reason of its having it. Therefore, when that organism perishes, intelligence ceases either to remember or to love. For such states belong not to intelligence but to that union [of intelligence with organism] which has perished. Intelligence itself, however, being of a diviner nature, remains unaffected.'[2]

Yet it was the Stoics who really naturalized this view upon European soil. Their teaching was that originally nothing existed but universal undifferentiated Reason, which is God. But Reason, though undifferentiated, had in itself the possibility of differentiation. It was, in fact, a Germinative Reason (λόγος σπερματικός) and soon it differentiated itself into a large number of partial reasons. Such a 'detached part or shred' (μέρος καὶ ἀπόσπασμα) of the Divine Reason dwells in me. It is what I call my intellect. And it is the important part of me.

[1] *De Anima*, 430 A.   [2] Ibid. 408 B.

Hence I have no reality that matters over against God. The part of me that matters, my ruling part (τὸ ἡγεμονικόν), really *is* God. 'Quid aliud est anima', asks Seneca the Stoic, 'quam Deus in corpore humano hospitans?'[1] But the Stoics, believing as they did that Reason was a kind of flame, would sometimes express the same thing in a different way. Originally, they would now say, there was only the One Pure Flame which is God. Afterwards part of this Flame became condensed and debased into the material world we so familiarly know, but the rest of the Flame still continues to wrap itself around the world and interpenetrate it, and the human intellect is an example of such interpenetration. Our minds are sparks of the Divine Fire. Finally, however, at the end of the present world-cycle, all will once again be reabsorbed into the One Pure Flame. The Stoics did not indeed believe that the soul would necessarily cease to exist at the death of the body. It would retain its separate existence until the end of the present world-cycle, but then it would be reabsorbed into Reason's Universal Flame. And by such reabsorption nothing that was of any value would be lost.

After a long interval this view reappeared in the seventeenth century in the philosophy of Spinoza, according to whom all that is eternal in man (the *pars aeterna nostri*, as he calls it) is that in him which is also 'in God', namely, 'the essence of his mind'.[2] Spinoza had to wait for nearly a century and a half after his death before a generation was born whom he could profoundly influence—the generation of the Romantics. We need mention only Schleiermacher, and one other who believed himself critical of Romanticism but whose

---

[1] *Epp. Mor.* 31.   [2] *Ethica*, v, Prop. xxiii.

way of thinking was nevertheless deeply influenced by it, namely, Hegel. In his celebrated *Addresses on Religion to Its Cultured Despisers*, published in 1799, we find Schleiermacher saying:

'The immortality that most men imagine, and their longing for it, seem to me irreligious, nay, quite opposed to the spirit of piety. . . . Would they but attempt to surrender their lives from love to God! Would they but strive to annihilate their personality and to live in the One and in the All! Whosoever has learned to be more than himself, knows that he loses little when he loses himself. Only the man who denying himself sinks himself in as much of the whole universe as he can attain, and in whose soul a greater longing has arisen, has a right to the hopes that death gives. . . . In the midst of finitude to be one with the Infinite and in every moment to be eternal is the immortality of religion.'[1]

Hegel's position, though embedded in a very different metaphysical system, is much the same. 'Man as spirit' is said to be immortal; but not, apparently, the individual man as individual spirit. 'The radical error of Hegelianism', wrote Pringle-Pattison in his *Hegelianism and Personality* in 1887, is the 'identification of the human and the divine self-consciousness, or, to put it more broadly, the unification of consciousness in a single Self'.[2] In the English-speaking countries the Hegelian brand of Absolute Idealism enjoyed a very remarkable vogue in the latter part of the nineteenth century, the most distinguished of its more whole-hearted representatives being perhaps F. H. Bradley and Bernard Bosanquet. Thus an ethical valuation and a line of reflection

[1] At the end of the second address. The translation is Professor Oman's, made from the second edition.
[2] Op. cit., p. 226.

that had long been associated rather with India than with Europe found at last a considerable following 'in England's green and pleasant land'. The situation has been grasped with precision by Professor Whitehead:

'The absolute idealism so influential in Europe and America during the last third of the nineteenth century, and still powerful notwithstanding the reaction from it, was undoubtedly a reaction towards Buddhistic metaphysics on the part of Western mentality. The multiplicity of finite enduring individuals were relegated to a world of appearances and the ultimate reality was centred in an absolute.'[1]

Now behind this Indian, Stoic, Spinozistic, and Absolute Idealist view there undoubtedly lies a true religious insight. It has always been the office of high spiritual religion to shift the centre of attention and concern from one's self to God. True salvation has at all times been found in the knowledge that God alone matters and in the will to do all things for His greater glory. And we have ourselves repeatedly insisted that all everlastingness is in Him and of Him and unto Him alone. Nevertheless the main stream of Western religion, whether Greek, Jewish, or Christian, has never understood it to follow from this that the souls of men were without individual reality or importance in the scheme of things. Certainly they cannot be real or important in isolation from God. It is only in relation to God that they can be either. But the Christian teaching has always been that this relation is not one of identity, whether complete or partial, but is a unique relationship of created to Uncreate Spirit which may best be understood by means of such human analogies as

[1] *Religion in the Making* (New York, 1926), p. 14.

communion, fellowship, and sonship. It is not, then, as the Vedanta theologians and the Stoics and the Spinozists would have it, by *emanation* that God's immortality is communicated to us, but by *creation*. Our distinction from God must be emphasized no less than our oneness with Him. To speak of losing our personalities in the Personality of God may seem a deeply religious thought; and indeed it is deeply religious so far as it goes. But it is only half a thought; for personalities cannot really be *lost* in a Personality, but rather must they be retained and enriched and reinforced. Certainly this is the conclusion to which all our human experience of the relation of one personality to another seems to point. As a matter of fact, however, those who ask us to contemplate the loss of our personalities in God do not mean that we are to lose them in a divine Personality but in a divine Impersonal. Schleiermacher tries hard to make his doctrine sound Christian when he writes:

'Recall how religion earnestly strives to expand the sharply cut outlines of personality. Gradually they are to be lost in the Infinite that we, becoming conscious of the Universe, may as much as possible be one with it.'[1]

And how much eloquence Bosanquet was in the habit of expending to the same end! Yet this use of impersonal words like 'the Infinite' and 'the Universe' gives the case away too plainly. Their God is clearly as impersonal as their immortality. It would appear that you cannot retain personality in God unless you also retain it in man, and indeed no serious thinker has ever tried. But when this is understood the religious appeal of Schleiermacher's words disappears. The thought

[1] Op. cit., Oman's translation, p.100.

of losing one's personality in the infinite Personality is a thought that elicits a religious response so long as its inner inconsistency is not perceived; but the thought of losing one's personality in the impersonal infinite can never elicit any religious response in minds that have ever been influenced by the religion of the Incarnation.

For let us look only at the judgement of value in which this doctrine of reabsorption is implicated—the judgement that the individual human being can lose his individual identity at death without anything that matters being lost. Are any of us really prepared to accept that view with all its consequences? Are we prepared to hold that human individuality has, as such, no significance and can fade without loss into a general fund of spirituality? I cannot think that we are. The disloyalty of such a position is too manifest. Here, again, one must insist that it is quite unallowable to give one answer in the sphere of eschatology and another in the sphere of ethics.

> The wrong that pains my soul below
> I dare not throne above.[1]

If you tell me that my neighbour's personality may disappear at death without anything of value being lost, then you must absolve me from the duty of respecting my neighbour's personality *now*. You must allow me to argue that as individuals my fellow men do not count and that I am well within my rights in ignoring such individuality as they may seem to possess. You must allow me to deny the validity of the Kantian imperative that every human personality must be treated 'as an end withal, never as means only'. You must allow me to deal with humanity *en masse*, dispensing with

[1] Whittier, *The Eternal Goodness.*

individual discrimination. You must allow me to say with the Hindu, 'There is no difference between one *guru* and another, between one woman and another. The differences are the veils of *maya*.' And you must even allow that if I destroy my neighbour's personality, I am not doing any real harm. 'For', as Canon Streeter has it in one place, 'if the divine righteousness may lightly "scrap" the individual, human righteousness may do the same.'[1] Yet I believe there is not one of us that will really desire thus to unwind the spool of ethical progress, once we have grasped the real nature of the issue involved. Rather shall we agree with Canon Streeter that 'the most conspicuous mark of the moral level of any community is the value it sets on human personality', and that 'the moral height of a society is shown by its reluctance to sacrifice even its least worthy members'.[2] Hindu ethics is indeed in many ways congruent with Hindu eschatology, but what I find so incongruous in a writer like Bosanquet is his attempted union of Hindu eschatology with Christian ethics. One cannot consistently look forward with complacence to the reabsorption of all individual souls and at the same time take delight in such words as the following:

'And whosoever shall give to drink unto one of these little ones a cup of cold water only, in the name of a disciple, verily I say unto you, he shall in no wise lose his reward.'[3]

'Take heed that ye despise not one of these little ones.'[4]

'Inasmuch as ye have done it unto one of the least of these My brethren, ye have done it unto Me.'[5]

But as in the case of the immortality of ideals, so now in the case of immortality by reabsorption I am sensible not only of

[1] *Immortality: An Essay in Discovery* (ed. Streeter), p. 85.
[2] Ibid.   [3] Matt. x. 42.   [4] Matt. xviii. 10–11.   [5] Matt. xxv. 40.

the disloyalty, but also of the difficulty of the conception. It seems often to be implied by modern writers that it is some-how easier to conceive of my being reabsorbed at death into the divine life than of my continuing to possess my own individuality. But if reabsorption is to mean any real kind of persistence, I have never been able to see that this is so. Of course, if what is meant is simply that I cease to be, whereas God remains, no strain at all is then put upon my powers of believing, because there is really nothing regarding myself that I am asked to believe. But if more than this is implied, to what exactly does it amount? We seem to be asked to believe that all the minds of men, and of such other reasonable beings as may anywhere exist, are parts or modes of a single universal fund of mentality which is indestructible and eternal; and that, though during the life of the body they suffer a partial temporary isolation from this fund, yet they are once more merged into complete oneness with it when the body dies. Now it may be that for those who are already and antece-dently convinced of the truth of a system of Absolute Ideal-ism, such as that of Bradley, this conception presents no in-superable difficulty. But such are a small band; and I must submit that for the rest of us the difficulty is very great indeed. What does it really mean to say that this 'I', this thinking, feeling, and desiring centre of consciousness, this bundle of hopes and fears, of joys and of sorrows, is to be 'taken up' into a universal impersonal mind? I feel sure that to most of us it means less than nothing. And I think that what pre-vents some people from realizing this is the fact that they place a wholly uncritical reliance on the single material meta-phor of reabsorption. If the human personality were a fluid or a vapour, then indeed it could be reabsorbed. But the more steadily we keep it in mind that personality is of the nature of spirit, the harder does it become to imagine what possible kind of spiritual process such a metaphor could be taken to signify.[1] I think it is a most significant fact that Buddha, according to what is apparently as reliable a report as any that we possess about him, refused to answer his disciples' question whether *nirvana* meant an actual state of being or total extinction. It was a case, surely, in which silence was the better part of prudence.

Immortality by reabsorption is thus no more successful a means than is the immortality of ideals by which to avoid our minor premiss that the value of the human individual is inseparably bound up with his individuality. We can revert neither to Brahminism nor to ancient tribalism without imperilling our most cherished ethical ideals. And I know of no third way by which the attempt to avoid this premiss has ever been made.

[1] I am glad to find a similar comment in an essay by Professor A. E. Taylor. Speaking of the conception of reabsorption he writes: 'The expression seems to me highly ambiguous. We speak sometimes of a man as "absorbed" in prayer or in scientific work. But we do not mean that in such moments the man's individuality has ceased to be; we mean that his mind (*his* mind, and not another or an "impersonal" mind,) is wholly concentrated on what he is doing. "Absorption" in the Deity, so understood, would not only be consistent with, but would require, individual immortality. The "saints" so "absorbed" in God would no more forfeit their individual existence than the stars cease to be when the sun shines.' (*The Faith and the War*, ed. F. J. Foakes-Jackson, 1915, p. 157.) Compare with this Pringle-Pattison's comment: 'I believe that in the literature of mysticism there is often an unobserved transition from absorption in the sense of concentration upon one object to absorption in the sense of being sucked under, as it were, and physically incorporated in the being of the object. The higher mysticism, I should judge, rests upon the first sense; but with less speculative and less truly religious minds the material metaphor becomes more and more dominant. We never know how deep our materialism goes.' (*The Idea of Immortality*, p. 162.)

IV

If the truth both of hope's major and of its minor premiss be granted, then its conclusion of personal immortality cannot possibly be resisted. Hence it is of the utmost importance that those who doubt or deny this conclusion should make it clear to themselves and to others *which of the two premisses they are doubting*. It seems to me there is no small degree of equivocation in contemporary literature on this vital point. Every one who denies the doctrine of personal immortality is denying *either* the ultimate conservation by the universe of the values that emerge during its process *or* the intrinsic nature of the value that resides in personality. *Either* he is doubting the reality of God the Father Almighty *or* he is holding it possible that God should will the annihilation of the souls He loves—or at the very least the dissipation of their individualities. Yet I read many books in which a slighting reference is made to the Christian hope, but from which I can gather no clear notion as to which of these two things is being doubted. It is for this reason that, paradoxically, I often find myself in closer spiritual sympathy with the frankly and blankly pessimistic type of humanist than with those of merrier mood. There is no real but only a superficial affinity between humanistic optimism and Christian hope. Pessimistic humanists like T. H. Huxley, Thomas Hardy, Lord Russell, and Mr. Joseph Wood Krutch are at least unhesitant in their affirmation of *one* of hope's premisses, namely, the minor one. They do not pretend that the annihilation of personality is anything but a ghastly tragedy. They do not pretend to be reconciled to death. (When Spinoza wrote that the free man thinks of nothing less than of death, says Unamuno unanswerably, 'he did in fact think about death, and he wrote it in a vain endeavour to free himself from this thought'.)[1] I feel there is more hope of advancing to the Christian conclusion from such a clarified pessimism than from a position which, by facing a godless universe with all good cheer, seems to be denying both premises in the same breath.

And now we must add a further word to what was said at an earlier point in reply, not to those who deny the doctrine of immortality, but to a certain body of those who most unhesitatingly affirm it. The question will once again be pressed upon us whether there is not a way of presenting the case for survival that makes no direct appeal to our major premiss of belief in God. Is not a consideration of the soul's essential nature sufficient of itself to persuade us of the soul's continuance—though not perhaps of that more blessed consummation which is also part of the Christian hope? Can we really believe that, while the physical world of matter and energy are eternal, spirituality shall vanish into nothingness? Are protons and electrons to be eternal and the souls of good men to be but shadows in a dream? Is *this* the conception of the ultimate reality of things to which we are led by a broad and wise assessment of the intimations of experience? Must we not rather believe that the souls of good men have infinitely more of the true reality of things in them than any unspiritual thing can have, and that the conservation of souls is therefore more likely to be an ultimate principle of reality than the conservation either of matter or of physical energy? And so, may we not after all fall back on Plato's argument that souls,

[1] *The Tragic Sense of Life*, Eng. tr., p. 31.

which alone of all things are capable of apprehending Ideas, must alone of created things be held to share the eternity of the Ideas they apprehend? Or again, may we not argue that the experience of pure and loyal love reveals itself to us as having within it the seeds of eternity? May we not say that he who knows what love is knows that it can never die?

With those who thus speak I find myself in fundamental sympathy. Where they err is only in not setting forth the successive steps of their argument in a sufficiently analytic way. I do indeed believe that he who knows what love is knows it can never die, but that is only because he who knows what love is knows *first* that it is of God. It is because it is of God that it can never die. It is in God alone that the deathlessness resides. Our human loves are indeed felt to demand continuance. But how can we believe such continuance to be secured? I do not see that there is any answer, unless love be more than human, unless it be divine, unless *God* be love. Again, to be vividly impressed by the personalities of those around us is indeed (if no other inhibiting tendency enters into the case) to grow in the conviction that personality will survive death; but that, logically regarded, can only be by way of the intermediate conviction that in personality we are touching the core of reality; and to believe this—that reality is personal—is most assuredly to believe in God. Once more, it is only if, as persons, we are made in the image of Eternal Being that there is ground to think ourselves eternal. Once more it is in God alone that the eternity resides. My point then is that no argument for immortality which sets out from an analysis of the nature of the soul and its secular interests succeeds in convincing us unless it proceed by way of the establishment of the reality of Divine Being; and that such persuasive power as we do sometimes feel to be contained in arguments of this type derives from the fact that the suppressed premiss is really operative within them. That is why Plato's proofs fail of logical completeness and are yet deeply moving in the direction of belief.

There is, moreover, another consideration which may be adduced in support of this point. In the logic of hope we have distinguished a major premiss—that 'the All-great is the All-loving too' or that 'what is highest in spirit is also deepest in nature'; and a minor premiss—that what is highest in spirit is personality. The major premiss, we said, is theological and the minor ethical. But what was hinted at the beginning must now be repeated with emphasis—that the two premisses are not *ultimately* separable the one from the other. Theology and ethics do not represent two separate regions of spiritual life. The conviction that personality is our highest value did not come into the world independently of the conviction of God's reality, but by way of it. Historically speaking, it was in the theological realm that the ethical conception of personality was first discovered. Men spoke of personality in God before they began to speak of personality in man. 'Nay, it may even be said', Professor Webb declared in his Gifford Lectures, 'that it was the religious and theological interest in the Personality of Christ, conceived as being at once God and man, which actually afforded the motive and occasion of undertaking the investigation of the nature of Personality in men generally.'[1] It is, he points out, out of the Christian debate concerning the nature of the Triune God that the

[1] *God and Personality*, p. 20.

word 'personality' has been born into the world, there being no proper equivalent for the word in any ancient language. What this means, then, is that it is through their consciousness of God's reality that men have become conscious of their own status as persons. Which makes clearer than ever the helplessness of any argument which, entirely evading the theological issue, attempts to proceed directly from consideration of man's nature and value to the certainty of his eternal life.

In a striking passage in his *Speculations* T. E. Hulme goes even farther than this. I have myself urged many times that eternity ultimately resides in God alone, and that accordingly it is much more by thinking of God than by thinking of ourselves that the assurance of our immortality is likely to be born within us. I have suggested also how great a stumbling-block it might be to the development within our souls of a proper humility and God-centredness, if by looking at ourselves alone we could ever come to feel that we were deserving of immortality or that it was ours by inalienable right. What Hulme says is this:

'It seems paradoxical at first sight, that the Middle Ages, which lacked entirely the conception of personality, had a real belief in immortality; while thought since the Renaissance, which has been dominated by the belief in personality, has not had the same conviction. You might have expected that it would be the people who thought they really had something worth preserving who would have thought they were immortal, but the contrary is the case. Moreover, those thinkers since the Renaissance who have believed in immortality and who have attempted to give explanations of it, have, in my opinion, gone wrong, because they have dealt with it in terms of the category of individuality. The problem can only be profitably dealt with by being entirely restated.

This is just one instance of the way in which thought about these things, in terms of categories appropriate only to human and vital things, distorts them.'[1]

The context makes it clear that the categories which Hulme would have us substitute for the human or vital ones are those of the divine.

V

This chapter has been concerned with logic. Some may think it overdone, and that I have driven my adversary too hard: but, after all, it is the business of logic to be logical. Nevertheless, if the chapter would be true to the thought of the writer, it must end on a different note. I do indeed believe that within the movement of spirit which has led to the entertainment of the Christian hope an implicit logic is contained, and I believe also that this implicit logic may be made explicit, and its validity made entirely manifest, in some such way as has here been attempted. But I am quite sceptical about the likelihood of being able, by such a process of explicit argument, to persuade anybody of the reality of eternal life who has not already some degree of belief in it. This is not to say that argument is useless. On the contrary it may be of immense service in clearing the mind of various inhibitive tendencies, especially perhaps of *contrary* arguments, wrong and confused, such as might prevent the natural growth of positive conviction. But that this natural growth is itself likely to receive from argument its first impulse I find it very difficult to believe. There is no mystery in this state of affairs. The reason of it is apparent. For the argument is itself so simple as to be within the reach of even the most untutored

[1] Op. cit., p. 49.

minds, so long only as they have firm grasp of the premisses; hence, where the conclusion has not already been drawn, it is more likely (and this quite apart from the special case, just referred to, of the presence in the mind of inhibitive tendencies derived from philosophic or other prepossessions—a case in which I have allowed the great helpfulness of argument) that the defect is in the hold men have on the premisses rather than in their ability to put the two premisses together. Historically speaking, it is certain that failure to put the premisses together accounts for only a quite minor part of the delay in the emergence of the Christian hope, the main cause of delay being the slow development of the premisses themselves. The most unschooled of Christian saints, and indeed whole bodies of men, have made the deduction with ease and conviction, because they have had clear vision of the realities from which the deduction proceeds.[1] *Abscondisti haec a sapientibus, et prudentibus, et revelasti ea parvulis.*

The way to attain to a surer hope is thus not so much to attend to the sharpening of our wits, though that too may have its measure of importance, as to deepen our human experience of fellowship with God and, as a fruit, increase our sense of the preciousness of human souls. Here as everywhere the two great commandments are to love God with all our heart and our neighbours as ourselves.

[1] I have dealt with this matter fully in my *Interpretation of Religion*, Part II, ch. vii, and may be allowed to repeat here two sentences which I have written there: 'Argument is therefore here at this far-reaching disadvantage, that it carries conviction only in proportion to the depth of each man's moral consciousness, and that in that same proportion it is likely to have been already anticipated by the swifter processes of the intuitive understanding. For after all it i not as if the logic of religion were a very elaborate process of deduction requiring a clear head to follow it' (p. 362).

Chapter VII
THE NATURE OF ETERNAL LIFE
I

Having now laid bare the grounds of our Christian hope, we are faced with the task of more clearly defining its content. This task is sure to be pressed upon us. Granted that eternal life awaits us, what, we shall be asked, will it be like?

Yet it is, for the most part, a task which we must be excused from having to undertake. For this is a region in which agnosticism is assuredly the better part of wisdom. To nearly all the questions that are put to us we are constrained to answer that *we do not know*, yet this answer is given without any confusion of face and in such a way as to imply that not knowing does not matter, or even (though this a little less confidently) that it is better not to know. In this domain, as St. Paul said, we walk not by sight but διά πίστεως—by trust.[1] We willingly leave to the Eternal Wisdom the whole economy of the future. 'The souls of the righteous are in the hand of God',[2] and we are content that there they should remain. It is the true note of Christian agnosticism that is sounded in Whittier's familiar lines:

> I know not where His islands lift
> Their fronded palms in air;
> I only know I cannot drift
> Beyond His love and care.[3]

It was once my lot to visit an acquaintance, a fine Christian

[1] 2 Cor. v. 7.   [2] Wisd. iii. 1.
[3] *The Eternal Goodness* (1865).

gentleman, who was about to die. His mind was plainly working upon the great change that so soon awaited him and he spoke about it freely. But he told me how of all he had ever heard or read concerning the future life there remained most of all in his mind a simple story of which he had now quite forgotten the source. The story was of just such another dying man as himself who, when informed by his devotedly Christian doctor that the end was very near, asked the doctor if he had any conviction as to what awaited him in the life beyond. The doctor fumbled for an answer. But ere he could speak, there was heard a scratching at the door; and his answer was given him. 'Do you hear that?' he asked his patient. 'That is my dog. I left him downstairs, but he grew impatient and has come up and hears my voice. He has no notion what is inside that door, but he knows I am here. Now is it not the same with you? You do not know what lies beyond the Door, but you know your Master is there.' It is an artless tale, but it embodies the authentic Christian temper.

It is not true that this temper has always been preserved within the Christian Church. At many times and places the salutary agnosticism of which I have spoken has been replaced by a *gnosticism* such as has offered us extensive and detailed knowledge of the world to come. Many a celestial geography has been committed to paper, many a chart has been traced of the New Jerusalem, many a classified directory has been compiled of its various denizens! Yet it must in justice be said that such gnosticism has seldom met with any general or official sanction. It is true that in many sanctioned writings there is detail enough and to spare of a certain kind. The New Testament Book of Revelation seems to satisfy every inquisitive question we can ask about the city of God, even to the style of its architecture and the paving of its streets; and the same is, of course, true of the large body of Jewish apocalyptic literature on which this Christian apocalypse is based. And again, what knowledge of the future could be more complete than that offered us in the *Divina Commedia*? The answer, however, is evident. These are all works of licensed religious imagination and are not concerned at all with doctrinal or dogmatic statement. They are designed not to extend our knowledge but to nourish our piety. They are precisely what Plato would have called instructive 'myths'; and it is noteworthy that even a writer like Karl Barth here follows his lead.[1] Plato's teaching is that the description of events in time is not within the province of philosophic or theologic doctrine at all, but must be left to historiography; and that where historiography fails, as it must always do in the case both of the *Archē* and of the *Telos*, we have no resource left but to *tell a story*, which is in the Greek language a 'myth' (μῦθος). And so the Platonic dialogues are everywhere interspersed with 'myths', some of which are about origins, but many of which are myths of future destiny that are strictly parallel in their objective significance to the compositions of Dante and St. John the Divine. The seer of Patmos has not, of course, taken us into his confidence as the Greek philosopher has done, so that we know much less about the subjective side of his vision than we do of the philosopher's. And some will wish to claim, no doubt, that he understood his

[1] *Mythus* for Barth is either equivalent to what he calls *Urgeschichte* or is a part of it. See his *Lehre vom Worte Gottes* (1927), pp. 272 ff. Cf. Walter Lowrie, *Our Concern with the Theology of Crisis* (Boston, 1932), pp. 67 ff., for other references.

vision with a literalness quite foreign to the Greek philosophic mind. Against this there is, however, to be set the fact of the variety of contradictory images which the Hebrew and Christian apocalypses offer us without any apparent hesitation or scruple. 'Apocalypse', writes Dr. J. H. Leckie, 'had a reasonableness of its own, but it was not the rationality of logic. It was tolerant of the most opposing images and symbols, caring only that each of these expressed some truth of the spiritual order. The writings that embody its spirit resemble a picture-gallery wherein the most dissimilar presentations of Nature hang side by side, all being welcome which worthily reflect genuine aspects of the world. No teacher using the forms of Apocalypse was, or could be, careful to display the second-rate virtues of the systematic mind. All he could be expected to do was to see that each of his utterances was in itself an authentic message of truth.'[1]

Moreover it seems clear to me that the religious mind can never afford to dispense entirely with such imagery. It must always tell itself Platonic 'myths'. Where knowledge fails, it must weave itself a story. Where concepts are lacking, it must use pictures. The Christian Church will never tire of such a hymn as Bernard of Morlaix's

> Jerusalem the golden,
> With milk and honey blest,

with its pictures of the 'halls of Zion':

> The Prince is ever in them;
> The daylight is serene;
> The pastures of the blessèd
> Are decked in glorious sheen.

[1] *The World to Come and Final Destiny* (1918), p. 59.

Or of such another hymn as the sixteenth-century 'Hieru-salem, my happy home', with its even more detailed pictures:

> Noe dampishe mist is seen in thee,
>   Noe cold, nor darksome night;
> There everie soule shines as the sunne;
>   There God Himselfe gives light. . . .
>
> Thy walls are made of precious stones,
>   Thy bulwarkes diamonds square,
> Thy gates are of right orient pearle,
>   Exceedinge rich and rare. . . .
>
> Thy gardens and thy gallant walkes
>   Continually are greene.
> There groes such sweete and pleasant flowers
>   As noe where eles are seene. . . .
>
> There cinomon, there sugar groes
>   There narde and balme abound.
> What tounge can tell or heart conceive
>   The joyes that there are found?

Obviously to object to such details on the ground that they go beyond our knowledge is to be less than intelligent. To go beyond our knowledge is precisely their intention.

I have been dwelling upon the necessary extent of our ignorance regarding the nature and conditions of eternal life. Yet obviously it cannot be held that this ignorance is complete. There are several ways in which this can be made clear. For one thing, it is not really possible that we should know that we are to possess eternal life without having *any* knowledge as to what eternal life is. In knowing *that* a thing is, some knowledge of *what* it is is always contained. One cannot imagine any ground for believing in the existence of a thing which did not carry with it some determination of the thing's nature. It has often been argued that every separate proof of the reality of God which has ever been offered proved the reality of a different God, or of a God differently conceived; and the same is true of all possible proofs of immortality. If we look again at the grounds we have ourselves offered for believing in the soul's immortality, we shall find that the immortality so reached is immortality of a certain kind. Of what kind, then? It is to the answering of this question that the present chapter must be devoted. By a close re-examination of our premisses, we must draw out the subtler overtones of meaning contained in our conclusion.

Again, it is clear that if we have *no* knowledge of the nature of eternal life, it is impossible to sustain even such a justification of the use of apocalyptic imagery as I have offered above. I said it was precisely the intention of apocalyptic detail that it should go beyond our knowledge; but where we have no knowledge at all, it is meaningless to speak of going beyond it. The imagery, as it stands, is not to be mistaken for knowledge, but it must have some significance and meaning. It *stands for* something that we do know. Something that we do know is all the time controlling and testing it. If this were not so, there could be no standard of excellence in apocalypses and one description of the Heavenly Jerusalem would be as good as another—which nobody could hold who allowed to such description any place at all. I said it would be unintelligent to criticize the detail of the *Hora novissima* on the mere ground that it went beyond our knowledge; but we are quite at liberty, if we so desire, to say that it goes beyond it in a wrong direction—which must mean in a direction contrary to the indications of certain things that we already know. When Plato warns us that we must be content with a 'myth', he is very far from meaning that *any* myth will do, or that one myth is as good as another. No, all readers of the *Republic* know that Plato entertained the very strongest opinions about the misleading tendency of some of the old myths, and that he chose his own with the greatest care. If we tell a myth, he would say, it must be 'a likely myth (εἰκότα μῦθον)',[1] a myth that suggests the right meaning and contains the right moral values. The foundation of myth and apocalypse, then, can only be the possession of some measure, however small, of true knowledge. It is this knowledge we must now proceed to lay bare.

II

There is a poem of John Donne's, written in his sickness, which begins thus nobly:

> Since I am comming to that Holy roome
> Where, with Thy Quire of Saints for evermore
> I shall be made Thy Musique; As I come
> I tune the Instrument here at the dore,
> And what I must doe then, thinke here before.

The first thing to be noted is that eternal life stands primarily not for a greater length of life but for a new depth of it. This has emerged very clearly from our historical survey. The soul's hope has not been for more of the same, but for something altogether higher and better. The shortness of the

---

[1] *Timaeus*, 29.

present life is very far from being its most unsatisfying feature. And we are left in no doubt as to how much interest those who have hoped most for immortality would have retained in the prospect of it, had they been told it was to mean only an endless prolongation of the common life of earth. So far from being elated, they would have been crushed and terrified. This, as we noted in Chapter V, is what has actually happened in India, where it is believed that men are destined to pass through a long succession of lives not essentially dissimilar to the present one, and where, consequently, survival is looked upon not as a blessing but as a doom. *Nobody ever wanted an endless quantity of life until discovery had been made of a new and quite particular and exceptional quality of life.* In Greece this discovery was first made in the worship of Dionysus. In the holy frenzy of the ritual dance men first had experience of a manner of being which they could only describe as 'union with God'. Never until now had they tasted a kind of life that they wanted to last for ever. But here was a life which they not only wanted to last for ever, but which seemed to have in it the certain promise of so doing. For since the gods are immortal, whatever is ἔνθεος—whatever has God in it—must be immortal too. So the man who has once tasted of the life divine knows it can never die. And in Israel, as we saw, the case was strictly parallel. No Israelite either wanted resurrection to a deathless life or believed in its possibility until the prophetic movement had discovered to him the prior possibility of the communion[1] of the individual

---

[1] The difference, let it be repeated, between the Greek and the Israelite was that while the Greek spoke of being made divine by *union* with Dionysus, the Israelite spoke more modestly of being blessed by *communion* with Jehovah. This difference was due to the Israelite's far loftier realization of the divine transcendence.

soul with God; and then the desire and the faith were together born.

Our defective philosophical tradition, with its frequent meagre equipment of religious understanding and its lack of a proper historical-mindedness, has tended to strip the meaning of *athanasia* or immortality and of 'aeonian' or eternal life down to the bare idea of survival. And we have seen how both Plato and the exponents of the 'natural theology' of the Christian Middle Ages as influenced by Plato have their share of blame for this misunderstanding; because, though immortality meant far more to them than mere survival, yet the type of proof they brought forward in support of it was really capable of proving no more than this. But in actual religious usage, and especially in their original classic employment, both terms are primarily qualitative in their significance. In the ancient world everybody took survival to be a matter of course, but the promise of immortality and eternal life was a quite new promise of something altogether better. The Greek word for eternal (αἰώνιος, aeonian) goes back to Plato. It means 'pertaining to an aeon', and an aeon (αἰών) means a lifetime, age, or epoch. The natural meaning of 'aeonian' would thus be 'pertaining to an age' or 'lasting for an age'. But Plato uses it to denote that which has neither beginning nor end and is subject to neither change nor decay—that which is above time, but of which time is 'a moving image'. Eternal life would then mean, not a life that goes on and on, but a life that is not subject to temporal conditions at all. In the New Testament, however, the term 'aeonian' takes on a still more specialized significance: it tends to mean 'pertaining to one particular aeon—the αἰών μέλλων or Age to Come of Messianic expectation'. Eternal life, then, is *the kind of life characteristic of the Age to Come*. The simpler meaning of the word as 'lasting for ages and ages and never coming to an end' is commonly present in its usage, but it never holds the leading place. The primary reference is always qualitative: 'And this is eternal life,—to know Thee the only true God, and Jesus Christ whom Thou hast sent.'[1] The same has always been true of the Christian Church, in the orthodox dogma of which the opposite of eternal life has never been 'life that lasts only for a time', still less 'non-survival', but *eternal death*. That is to say, life itself has always been a transcendental term, as even the casual reader must feel it to be in the New Testament. It never, in this usage, signifies mere existence; it signifies rather a rare quality of existence the possibility of which is now opening itself out before men's minds. 'To be spiritually minded is life.'[2] 'In Him was life.'[3] 'I am come that they might have life, and that they might have it more abundantly.'[4]

III

But if immortal or eternal life means primarily a new dimension of life and only secondarily life that will go on for ever (as many inferior kinds of life might conceivably do also), then the question arises whether this new dimension of life cannot be enjoyed *now*, instead of waiting until we have died. To this question the experience of the ages returns an affirmative answer, though it is an affirmative of a definitely qualified kind. The conditions of the present life are indeed such that no full or uninterrupted enjoyment of the eternal

[1] John xvii. 3.   [2] Rom. viii. 6.
[3] John i. 4.   [4] John x. 10.

blessedness is possible while they continue, yet even now we may have a real 'foretaste' of that blessedness. And it is from this foretaste that men have learned what it is like, so that they have come ardently to desire its more complete manifestation. The worshipper of Dionysus found that he could, under the difficult conditions of the ritual dance, and for a moment, attain to a state of being quite unlike the ordinary life of earth. This state of being was, he believed, essentially that of union with the immortal life of the god, and his hope was that after his release from the body this life of union with God would be a constant and uninterrupted possession. The Greek mystical tradition, then, could speak of immortality as being in a real sense a present experience. And in the New Testament we have the same way of speaking with reference to eternal life, to the Kingdom of God, and even to resurrection. All these must in the main be thought of as future realities such as await our introduction to quite other conditions of life. But they are all spoken of as being, by foretaste, present realities too. The primary reference is not to the time but to the quality of them; and it is a quality which may in part belong to the time that now is. 'The Kingdom of God', says St. Paul, 'is not meat and drink; but righteousness, and peace, and joy in the Holy Ghost.'[1] 'Who hath delivered us from the power of darkness', he says again, 'and hath translated us into the Kingdom of His dear Son.'[2] And the Apostle, though looking forward to the resurrection as a future fact, is yet fond of regarding the essence of it as something which has already been realized in the consciousness of every Christian. He writes to the Colossians:

[1] Rom. xiv. 17.　　　　　　　　　　　　[2] Col. i. 13.

'You were buried with Him [Christ] in your baptism, and thereby you are risen with Him through faith in the power of the God who raised Him from the dead. . . . For you were dead in your sins . . . yet He has made you live with Christ. . . . If, then, you are risen with Christ, seek those things which are above, where Christ sits on the right hand of God. Give your mind to things above, not to things on the earth. For you died and your life is hidden with Christ in God.'[1]

But it is in the Gospel and Epistles of St. John that the thought of eternal life as a present possession comes most fully into its own. The author's presupposition seems to be that the real moment of transition to the new order of being is not the moment of physical death but the moment of spiritual rebirth. When in this life a man comes to know God, a far more radical change has taken place in his soul than will take place when he passes from this life with God on earth to the admittedly much fuller life with God in the world beyond.

'We know that we have crossed over from death to life, because we love the brethren.'[2]

'He who hears My word and puts his faith in Him who sent Me, has eternal life; no judgement will be passed upon him; he has already crossed over from death to life. Verily, verily, I say unto you, the time is coming, and now is, when those who are dead will hear the voice of the son of God, and those who hear will live.'[3]

'And this is eternal life—to know Thee, the only true God, and Jesus Christ whom Thou hast sent.'[4]

The essential discovery, then, for which the doctrines of immortality, resurrection, and eternal life stand is the discovery of the possibility of a higher kind of life for man and

---

[1] Col. ii. 12–13; iii. 1–2.   [2] 1 John iii. 14.
[3] John v. 24–5.   [4] John xvii. 3.

has nothing to do with the question of the everlasting continuance beyond the grave of such existence as all men familiarly know on earth. Yet, as we have perhaps already sufficiently argued, this higher kind of life appears to carry in itself the promise of its own everlastingness. Its imperishableness is a corollary of its quality. Because it is a life with God, it is a life that can never die; and it is in proportion to the depth and vividness of our present experience of it that the assurance of its continuance beyond the grave takes root within our souls. F. W. Robertson declared from his Brighton pulpit on Easter Day, 1853:

'There are men in whom the resurrection begun makes the resurrection credible. In them the Spirit of the risen Saviour works already; and they have mounted with Him from the grave. They have risen out of the darkness of doubt, and are expatiating in the brightness and sunshine of a Day in which God is ever Light. Their step is as free as if the clay of the sepulchre had been shaken off; and their hearts are lighter than those of other men, and there is in them an unearthly triumph which they are unable to express. They have risen above the narrowness of life, and all that is petty, and ungenerous, and mean. They have risen above fear—they have risen above self. In the New Testament that is called the spiritual Resurrection, a being "risen with Christ"; and the man in whom all that is working has got something more blessed than external evidence to rest upon. He has the witness in himself: he has not seen, and yet he has believed: he believes in a Resurrection, because he has the Resurrection in himself. The Resurrection in all its heavenliness and unearthly elevation has begun within his soul, and he knows as clearly as if he had demonstration, that it must be developed in an Eternal life.'[1]

Beside that I shall place some words spoken by Pringle

[1] *Sermons*, Second Series, p. 282.

Pattison from his Gifford Lecturer's chair at Edinburgh in the spring of 1922:

'It is, then, on the possibility of such experiences . . . that any valid theory of immortality must be based. . . . He who has tasted eternal life is not wont to be troubled in heart about the question of his personal survival; for such survival would mean nothing to him, if he were separated from the object in which he has found his true life. His immortality lies for him in his union with the eternal object on which his affections are set, and he seeks no other assurance.'[1]

IV

Eternal life, then, is life of a certain quality. But of *what* quality? This must be our next question.

Our answer may set out from the Platonic distinction, already referred to, between eternity and perpetuity. That which is perpetual merely persists endlessly through time, while that which is eternal transcends the conditions of time altogether. In true eternity, then, successiveness gives place to simultaneity or compresence. The Creator and Father of All, writes Plato in the myth of the *Timaeus*,

'in ordaining the universe, resolved to make a moving image of Eternity, hence of Eternity which abides in unity He made that eternal image which, in its measured advance, we call *time*. There were no days and nights and months and years before the universe was created, but in bringing the universe into being He brought these into being also. They are all parts of time, and *was* and *shall be* are created forms of time too, though we thoughtlessly and mistakenly ascribe them to the Eternal Essence. For

[1] *The Idea of Immortality*, p. 147.

we say that it *was*, that it *is*, and that it *shall be*, whereas in truth *is* alone applies to it.'[1]

This teaching passed from Plato into the best pagan thought and thence, with certain reinforcements from native Christianity itself, into the Christian schools. It is set forth with great precision of thought in the concluding section of Boethius's *Consolation of Philosophy*, written A.D. 523:

'That God is eternal is the common judgement of all who exercise their reason. Let us therefore think what eternity is. .... Eternity is the complete possession of unlimited life all at once. And this becomes clearer by the comparison of temporal things. For whatever lives in time is itself present and proceeds from past to future, and nothing which is in time can embrace all the space of its life at once—it has not yet attained to-morrow and it has already lost yesterday, and even in to-day's life you live only in that moving and passing moment. Whatever then is subject to temporal conditions, although (as Aristotle thought of the world) it should never have begun and never come to an end and its life be stretched out through an infinity of time, would yet not deserve to be called eternal. .... Hence those are wrong who, hearing that Plato thought this world neither had a beginning nor would have an end in time, think that in this way the created world becomes co-eternal with the Creator. For it is one thing to be drawn through an interminable life, as Plato thought the world was, and quite another thing to embrace the whole of that interminable life as a present, which is manifestly the prerogative of the divine mind. Neither should God be judged more venerable than created things by reason of His quantity of time but rather by reason of the simplicity of His nature. .... And so, if we would give things their right names, let us say, following Plato, that God is eternal and the world perpetual.'

[1] *Timaeus*, 37.

Boethius's definition of eternity in this passage as the complete possession of unlimited life all at once (*interminabilis vitae tota simul et perfecta possessio*) remained classical throughout the Middle Ages. But what Boethius did was only to give precision to a conception that was already fully present in Christian thought. All that is in Boethius is in St. Augustine more than a hundred years earlier. 'The things of to-morrow and of what is beyond it, the things of yesterday and of what is behind it', he cries to God in his *Confessions*, 'Thou hast done and wilt do in this Thy to-day.'[1] And again of the Eternal Wisdom he says: '*To have been* and *to be about to be* are not in her, but only *to be*, seeing she is eternal.'[2] Similarly, many centuries afterwards, Dante makes Beatrice gaze for a moment upon that point of light 'wherein are focused every where and every when' (*dove s'appunta ogni ubi ed ogni quando*) and which is God's 'eternity beyond time'.[3]

English-speaking students are fortunate in having had this conception of eternity worked over afresh by at least four eminent thinkers of our own day—in Philip Wicksteed's remarkable lecture on *The Religion of Time and the Religion of Eternity*, delivered at the Essex Hall in London in 1899, and afterwards in von Hügel's *Eternal Life* (1912), in Pringle-Pattison's *Idea of God* (The Aberdeen Gifford volume, 1917), and in Professor A. E. Taylor's *Faith of a Moralist* (1930). From these discussions certain further points of importance have emerged. Pringle-Pattison lays stress on the fact that the true eternal must be distinguished not only on the one hand from the perpetual, but also on the other hand from the

[1] i. 6.   [2] ix. 10.   [3] *Paradiso*, canto xxix.

213

timeless.[1] Abstract truths are timeless in their validity; but God is a concrete reality and His eternity is therefore not in this sense time*less* but, though transcending time, must yet somehow include it. Though God is not in time, yet time is in Him and has a meaning for Him. To take any other view would be to make the not unfamiliar mistake of regarding time as altogether illusory—to make the distinctions of before and after and of past and present *mean nothing*—as they certainly mean nothing when applied to timeless truths. The truth, however, must surely be that eternity is not the antithesis of time but its fulfilment—its *Telos* and also its *Archē*. Time is, as Plato put it, a moving image of eternity, in whose motion the features of eternity are reflected as in a glass darkly. '*Alles vergängliche ist nur ein Gleichnis*'—but a *Gleichnis* it truly is. Time, says Boethius, 'seems to imitate in part what it cannot embrace or express, tying itself to the presentness, such as it is, of this thin and winged moment, which presentness, because it bears a certain likeness (*imaginem*) to that abiding presentness, gives a semblance of true being to such things as it touches.'[2] This means that the successiveness of time represents, as in a broken reflection, some real feature in the organization of eternity. Yet only as in a broken reflection; for God's eternal vision of things cannot mean merely that He takes in the whole stretched-out span of time at a glance, unless we say also that in being thus taken in at a glance it loses its character of a stretched-out span.

Such, then, we must believe God's eternity to be, as over against our temporality. It is a mystery to us; yet, as St. Augustine teaches, its very incomprehensibility is deeply

---

[1] Cf. *Idea of God*, lectures xviii and xix. [2] loc. cit.

satisfying to those who feel they can never find full satisfaction in the bleak familiarity of 'one thing after another'. 'Let us delight to find Thee by failing to find Thee', he exclaims, 'rather than by finding Thee to fail to find Thee '(*non inveniendo invenire potius quam inveniendo non invenire te*).[1]

Nevertheless it is not *wholly* a mystery. Not even our human experience is *wholly* given over to temporality and successiveness. Even now we can have some part in the life divine. Karl Barth indeed speaks of 'the infinite qualitative difference between time and eternity' (*die unendliche qualitätive Unterschied zwischen Zeit und Ewigkeit*—a phrase borrowed from Kierkegaard)[2]; and T. E. Hulme speaks in an image of eternity as an infinite straight line perpendicular to the line of time's procession. Such expressions represent a healthy and much-needed reaction against the self-satisfied temporalism of much nineteenth-century thought; yet it is only to conceptual or clock time—'the Astronomer Royal's time', as it has been called—that they can properly be taken as applying. Time as measured by mathematics and by clocks is indeed pure successiveness; its present has no duration but is a mathematical point, without parts and without magnitude, separating the past from the future. Between such a mere chain of mutually exclusive moments and the compresence of all things in the divine mind there could only, of course, be complete opposition. Clock time, however, is but a convenient mathematical abstraction and is very different from the time of actual human experience. The essence of experienced time lies precisely in what clock time entirely excludes, namely duration—the *durée réelle* which plays so important

P   [1] *Conf.* i. 6.   [2] *Römerbrief*, 2nd ed., preface.

a part in the philosophy of Bergson, but which had (in one regard at least) already been made much of in the psychology of William James. 'The practically cognised present', James pointed out, 'is no knife-edge, but a saddle-back, with a certain breadth of its own on which we sit perched, and from which we look in two directions into time. The unit of composition of our perception of time is a *duration*, with a bow and a stern, as it were—a rearward- and a forward-looking end. It is only as parts of this *duration-block* that the relation of succession of one end to the other is perceived.'[1] What is present to me, then, is always a short stretch and not merely a point of time; and these successive short stretches overlap one another as mere successive points could not do. If this were not so, indeed, I could have no consciousness of succession, but only of one point at a time; for it is in the 'overlap' that the sense of past and future is contained. But it follows from this that in some small degree we do know, even in our human experience, what is meant by rising above mere succession into compresence and simultaneity. If for God the whole of time is 'present all at once', even for us a few moments are habitually so present. If for God a thousand years of clock time are as one day, for us a few moments may be as one moment. 'In the compresence which is thus an essential feature of our consciousness of time', writes Pringle-Pattison, 'we therefore already realize, though doubtless on an infinitesimal scale, the nature of an eternal consciousness.'[2]

But this is not all. Sometimes our ability to rise above successiveness to simultaneity seems to be of a still more

---

[1] *The Principles of Psychology* (1890), vol. i, p. 609 f.
[2] *The Idea of God*, p. 354.

significant kind. We have said that the very awareness of time's lapse involves a certain transcendence of temporality. A purely animal consciousness, we may imagine, is one of utter successiveness and is consequently without any awareness of the lapse of time at all. But at all events it would be allowed that as the spirit of man develops to ever higher and higher powers, and even as the individual man develops from babyhood and childhood to maturer personality, his awareness of the lapse of time and the pressure upon him of the burdens of temporality become ever more acute. 'The tragic sense of life' is the prerogative of human maturity alone. Yet it is obvious that this increased sense of the burdens of temporality must be the fruit of a correspondingly deepened experience of a simultaneity with which the temporality is being contrasted. A man can rebel against time only in proportion as he has 'eternity within his heart'. Now it is precisely in our highest experiences that such transcendence of temporal conditions does appear to go farthest. To see life only as a strung-out succession of happenings is to be poor in spiritual experience; to see it steadily and see it whole is to be rich. There is no surer mark of a great mind, in no matter what field of greatness, than the ability to combine in a single synoptic vision more of the detail of experience than the rest of us are able to do—to see each thing, not just in its separateness, but in all its bearings. In his book on *The Spirit of Modern Philosophy*, published in 1892, Josiah Royce gave as an illustration of this the words of a letter that is supposed to have been written by Mozart to one of his friends with reference to the manner of his musical composition.

'My ideas come as they will, I don't know how, all in a stream.

. . . Well, if I can hold on to them, they begin to join on to one another. . . . And now my soul gets heated, and if nothing disturb me the piece grows longer and brighter until, however long it is, it is all finished at once in my mind, so that I can see it at a glance as if it were a pretty picture or a pleasing person. Then I don't hear the notes one after another, as they are hereafter to be played, but it is as if in my fancy they were all at once. And that *is* a revel. While I'm inventing, it all seems to me like a fine vivid dream; but that hearing it all at once (when the invention is done), that's the best. What I have once so heard I forget not again, and perhaps this is the best gift that God has given me.'[1]

The illustration has been found by many a most apposite one. Royce himself borrowed it from von Hartmann, and it is made use of again in three of the four books I mentioned above as working over this topic afresh.[2] For the experience which Mozart had supremely, every amateur of music can enjoy in some small measure. Our appreciation of any tune depends on the fact that more than a single note is present to our minds at one time, so that what we have already heard is not merely remembered as a series of past events, but is grasped as part of a compresent pattern; and in the case of a tune which we know well the notes still to be sounded enter into the pattern as well as those which have been sounded already. Another illustration has been found in the field of literature. Wicksteed writes:

'Contrast the feverish excitement with which we follow a play or a story because we do not know what is coming, and our feeling as we read *The Agamemnon*, *The Divine Comedy*, or *King Lear*, when we *do* know what is coming. How crude, how

---

[1] p. 457.
[2] Wicksteed, p. 55; Pringle-Pattison, p. 355; A. E. Taylor, vol. i, p. 427.

shallow and immature, seems the successional excitement in the one case compared with the awful or beautiful sense of co-existing completeness in the other.'[1]

Professor Taylor writes:

'To any one who wants to appreciate the art of the story, or the play, the element of mere surprise is a hindrance; it is an advantage to him to know beforehand what the incidents are, that he may be free to concentrate his attention on the structure of the whole. . . . What shocks are there in the *Iliad*, or, again, in *Tom Jones?*'[2]

It may be suggested, however, that all this applies only to aesthetic experience, and not at all to moral experience. This latter, it will be said, is in its very essence a temporal process —a struggle, a strife, a growth, a progress, an endless quest of an endlessly elusive goal; and its characteristic glory is 'the glory of going on and still to be'. The large measure of truth in such a view is obvious enough, and yet it is equally certain that one of two other things must be true also. *Either* we must say that moral experience includes fruition as well as quest *or* we must say that, if it does not, then it points beyond itself to another sort of experience that transcends and completes it. Which of the two things we say is largely a matter of terminology. If the former alternative be chosen, the point must be made that the goal of the moral life cannot reasonably be envisaged as something altogether in the future, something which stands at the end of an infinite straight line of time and which therefore, in the nature of the case, cannot be realized in any finite stretch of time, however long. Surely the end is an end which indwells in the process. Surely realization is as authentic an element in morality as anticipation. The highest

---

[1] Op. cit., p. 56.   [2] Op. cit., vol. i, p. 428 f.

moral life known to man is not one of restless, straining effort *only*: there must be *some* resolution of such effort in calm serenity and pure contentment. 'The strenuous life', a favourite ideal of our age, is a noble ideal enough; but if unbalanced by any ideal of unhurried peace and enjoyment, it can only lead, as it appears to be doing, to an ever-increasing number of nervous break-downs and sudden deaths from heart disease.

It may be said, however, that morality itself can never provide us with this fruition, being in its very nature an unceasing warfare to the success of which even the briefest armistice must necessarily be fatal; and that it is to religion that we must look for a deliverance from the conflict and restlessness and endless unfulfilment of the moral life. This, perhaps, is the better way of speaking. Certainly it is the way of speaking which St. Paul has made current within the Christian Church. Christianity stood in St. Paul's mind for a deliverance from the life of endless moral effort after righteousness, yet this deliverance is wrought, not through the hope of righteousness being abandoned, but through righteousness becoming *now* a present possession; and this can only be accomplished by our laying hold through faith upon the eternally perfect righteousness of God in Christ. 'For the law of the Spirit of life in Christ Jesus hath made me free from the law of sin and death. For what the law could not do, in that it was weak through the flesh, God sending his own Son in the likeness of sinful flesh, and for sin, condemned sin in the flesh: that the righteousness of the law might be fulfilled in us, who walk not after the flesh, but after the Spirit.'[1] 'Therefore we con-

[1] Rom. viii. 2-4.

clude that a man is justified by faith without the deeds of the law. . . . Do we then make void the law through faith? God forbid: yea, we establish the law.'[1] This means that through religious faith a man is enabled to take hold *now* of something that is above the struggle, above the weariness of temporality, above the endless disappointment of the 'not yet', and have fruition of that which is truly eternal. 'But one day', so runs the famous passage in Bunyan's *Grace Abounding*, 'as I was passing in the field, . . . suddenly this sentence fell upon my soul, Thy righteousness is in heaven. . . . Now did my chains fall off my legs indeed.'[2] This is but one of the several respects in which the religious experience seems to combine in itself the characteristics of the two less completely satisfying orders of experience which we call the aesthetic and the moral. The essence of religion lies in its present possession and present enjoyment of a good which, regarded from the merely moral point of view, can be possessed and enjoyed only at the end of endless time. 'On examining what we find in the religious consciousness', writes F. H. Bradley, 'we discover that it is the ideal self considered as realized and real. The ideal self, which in morality is to be, is here the real ideal which truly is.'[3] Yet the religious experience differs from mere aesthetic contemplation precisely in the fact that it is always given in intimate union with the life of moral effort and has its proper being in the constant tension between these two attitudes of activity and receptivity.

It is supremely in the religious experience, then, that we are able, in the midst of temporality and without any denial of its true witness, to ascend to the vision of the Eternal Presence

---

[1] Rom. iii. 28, 31.   [2] § 229 f.   [3] *Ethical Studies*, p. 284.

and see all things *sub specie quadam aeternitatis*. In speaking of the Dionysiac ecstasy Professor F. M. Cornford says that it is doubtful whether the concept of eternity 'would ever have been formed, if states which appear to be timeless had not been actually experienced and taken as a warrant of the intrinsic divinity of the soul'.[1] It is in connexion with the same Dionysiac ecstasy that von Hügel writes:

'. . . All states of trance, or indeed of rapt attention, notoriously appear to the experiencing soul, in proportion to their concentration, as timeless; *i.e.*, as non-successive, simultaneous, hence as *eternal*. They appear thus to the soul, if not during, at least soon after, the experience. And hence the eternity of the soul is not, here, a conclusion drawn from the apparent Godlikeness, in other respects, of the soul when in this condition, but the eternity, on the contrary, is the very centre of the experience itself, and is the chief inducement to the soul for holding itself to be divine. The soul's immortality cannot be experienced in advance of death, whilst its eternity, in the sense indicated, is, or seems to be, directly experienced in such "this-life" states; hence the belief in immortality is here derivative, that in eternity is primary.'[2]

To know God is to know all things as He knows them and as they are in Him. To see God is to see all things with His eyes. Of this identification of 'seeing God' with 'seeing as God sees' Wicksteed remarks that it is perhaps the most fundamental conception of the developed religion of the Middle Ages. 'The medieval saint', he explains, 'believed that to see God is to see as God sees, and that just in so far as we rise into true communion with Him and do in truth see God, so far shall we see things not in their fragmentary imperfection, but in

[1] In *Immortality*, ed. Sir James Marchant (1924), p. 38.
[2] *Eternal Life*, p. 27.

their combined perfection.'[1] This is exactly St. Paul's meaning: *nunc cognosco ex parte: tunc autem cognoscam sicut et cognitus sum.*

Yet these words of the Apostle refer not to the present but to the future term of being. For indeed it is only by way of *arrhabo*, by way of brief and occasional and tantalizing foretaste, that we can enjoy eternal life within the conditions of this earthly existence.

'When in the midst of my soul the bright morning star rises . . . then I am as though I had overstepped the bounds of time and space, and stood in the ante-chamber of eternal salvation. Alack, Lord! who will grant that it might only be of longer duration, for behold, in a moment it is snatched away, and I am again stripped and forsaken?'[2]

This precisely, then, is the Christian hope, that after our earthly existence is ended, a further existence awaits us in which we shall be relieved of all the burdens of temporality through the uninterrupted enjoyment of the Eternal Presence. *Videmus nunc per speculum in aenigmate: tunc autem facie ad faciem.*

Not very often has the eternal world seemed so near to dwellers upon earth as in the conversation which Augustine had with his mother as the two leaned out of the window looking into the garden at Ostia a few days before Monica's death in November 387. Augustine afterwards reported the substance of their conversation in the following way:

'What we said, then, was this. If for any man the tumult of the flesh should be stilled—stilled the phantasms of earth and sea and air, stilled also the poles of heaven, and stilled within itself

---

[1] Op. cit., pp. 97, 25.
[2] The Blessed Henry Suso, *Little Book of Eternal Wisdom*, Part I, ch. ix.

the very soul so that by not thinking of self it should go beyond self; stilled also all dreams and imagined revelations, every tongue and every sign, and all transitory existences;—if for any man all these things (which indeed say to all who have ears to hear, "We did not create ourselves but were created by Him who abideth for ever") should be stilled utterly, having done no more than quicken our ears to Him who created them; and were He Himself to speak alone, not through them but through Himself, so that we should be hearing His word, not through tongue of flesh nor voice of angel nor sound of thunder nor puzzle of symbolism, but hearing Himself—Himself whom in all these things we love, but now hearing Him without hearing them (just as we two now strained ourselves upwards and in the rapid flash of thought touched the eternal wisdom that dwells over all things); *if now this were made continuous* and, other visions of a very different kind being withdrawn, this one should ravish and absorb and envelop its beholder in interior joys so that his life might eternally be such as that moment of intelligence (*hoc momentum intelligentiae*) which now we sighed after; then were not this, INTRA IN GAUDIUM DOMINI TUI—"Enter into the joy of thy Lord"? And when shall that be? When "we shall all rise again" though "we shall not all be changed".'[1]

And many years later we find the same Augustine writing in his treatise *On the Trinity* that

'Mayhap when "we shall be like him" our thoughts . . . will no more go from one thing to another, but in a single perception we shall see all we know at one and the same time.'[2]

But now again arises the final question whether we are to believe that in a future life man is destined *entirely* to put off every form of temporality and enjoy such eternal life as God Himself enjoys—pure simultaneity and 'the complete posses-

---

[1] *Confessiones*, book ix, ch. x.   [2] *De Trinitate*, xv. 26.

sion of unlimited life all at once'. Modern writers have occasionally seemed to answer this question in the affirmative—for example Dean Inge in the much-quoted final essay of his first volume of *Outspoken Essays* and perhaps Professor Karl Barth in his expository brochure on *The Resurrection of the Dead*.[1] But Christian thought generally has answered otherwise. So long, it has been held, as the finite spirit remains finite, it must in some degree continue to experience reality under the forms of duration and succession.

There are several decisive considerations which compel us to choose this latter view. For one thing, any other view would involve us in a contradiction of a very absurd kind—the contradiction of saying that *after* death there will be no before or after, that *in the future* there will be no past or future. Obviously it is absurd to refer to a particular time a life that is essentially timeless (i.e. that is not in time); hence we cannot speak of a *timeless* life *to come*. If we are ever to enjoy a timeless life, then we are enjoying it now and have always enjoyed it; or at least it is by putting the three tenses together that we least falsify that which is itself without tense. A life which is timeless is clearly no more future than it is past; and if eternity means pure timelessness, then it is no truer to say it is in store for us after death than to say we enjoyed it before birth. It was characteristic of the robust but somewhat prosaic mind of the late Dean Rashdall that he should utterly reject the conception of eternal life which we have here been at pains to set

---

[1] *Die Auferstehung der Toten* (1924). I am thinking of such a phrase as that on p. 58: '*eine Wirklichkeit so radikal überlegen allem Geschehen und aller Zeitlichkeit*.' It is curious that so characteristically Greek an idea as complete non-successiveness should be given so central a place in the theology of one who, following the Ritschlians, treats the Greek element in the catholic Christian system as a regrettable intrusion.

forth, and should be content to conceive of it as mere perpetuity; but his logic is at least effective against what he calls the 'self-contradictory assertion that at a certain date in the future *I* shall pass out of time into the timeless'.[1] The only sense, he argues, in which Dean Inge can, consistently with his own premises, ascribe eternal life to a man is simply that it will always be true that the man has lived; which of course is a mere triviality.[2] Schleiermacher carried out the position more logically when he said that the true immortality 'is not the immortality that is after time' but 'the immortality which we can now have in this temporal life. . . . In the midst of finitude to be one with the Infinite and in every moment to be eternal is the true immortality of religion.'[3]

Again, it would seem that to contemplate the enjoyment by ourselves of an entirely non-successional life would be to claim for ourselves the prerogative of deity. For successiveness is the very mark of finitude, the very mark of distinction between finitude and the Infinite. Why we experience some things before or after other things is that our experience is never complete. Only for an all-knower would there be no surprises in the universe. But the only All-knower is God.

The future state of the soul which we are thus led to contemplate is one in which, by such a steady vision of the pure eternity of God as in the present life is altogether beyond our reach, we are relieved of the intolerable burdens of temporality—its rude interruptions and tragic endings, but not less its *Langweiligkeit*, its *ennui*, the irksomeness of its petty

---

[1] *God and Man* (1930), p. 141.   [2] Ibid., p. 139.
[3] *Reden über die Religion* (Oman's trans.), p. 101.

pace; yet retain a certain form of successiveness. This is von Hügel's conclusion. He will admit that

'the sense of Time, in the most fully eternalized of human spirits, would be so durational as almost to lapse into Simultaneity',[1]

but yet he will retain to the end his sense of

'the most delicate difference within affinity between two, the deepest and most real of all realities really known to us, our finite, *durational* spirit, and the infinite, *eternal* Spirit, God.'[2]

He tells us that

'Here the special value lies in the double sense that we are indeed actually touched, penetrated, and supported by the purely Eternal; and yet that we ourselves shall never, either here or hereafter, be more than quasi-eternal, durational.'[3]

And

'in this way the vividness and dynamic force of man's ideal— Eternity, full Abidingness—is accounted for by man's real, how- ever obscure, diffused, and predominantly indirect, experience of it. And all fanaticism is excluded by the two admissions, that this full eternity is not, and never will be, man's own; and also that such experience as he has of it is never pure and separate, but ever of it only in, through, and over against, his various, ever more or less successive, directly human experiences.'[4]

This view of von Hügel's is accepted by Professor Taylor:

'The completest transformation of "this" world into the "other" of which we can reasonably conceive would not wholly abolish the successiveness of human experience. Even a heavenly life, such as we have tried to imagine, would still be a forward-looking life. . . . The blessed would always have new discoveries

---

[1] *Eternal Life*, p. 391. [2] Ibid., p. 3. [3] Ibid., p. 366.
[4] Ibid., p. 231 f. Cf. also the same writer's *Essays and Addresses on the Philo-sophy of Religion*, vol. i, p. 216; vol. ii, pp. 49–55.

awaiting them, more to learn than they had already found out of the unspeakable riches of the wisdom of God. . . . Hence I think von Hügel on the right lines in regarding the life of creatures as one in which successiveness and futurity never wholly vanish, though they may become of decreasing importance "beyond all assignable limits".[1]

V

And now in this conclusion a further insight seems to be contained, and the answer to a further question that is sure to be put to us. Is the heavenly state, we shall be asked, one of rest or one of activity? Are we to think of it in terms of fruition or in terms of continued progress?

There can be no doubt as to the answer returned by the Christian ages—or indeed by the pre-Christian ages so far as these occupied themselves with this problem. The life eternal has always been regarded as being essentially a life of fruition, that is, of fulfilled enjoyment. *Here* we strain and strive after that which is good, but *there* we shall rejoice at last in the complete possession of it. 'Man's chief end is to glorify God, and to enjoy Him for ever'; on earth we seek this end, but in heaven we shall attain it. The quest will then be over and we shall have entered upon our heritage. It follows from this that the heavenly state is a state of rest. Of toil and moil there has been enough and to spare during our earthly sojourn, but in heaven they 'rest from their labours; and their works do follow them'.[2] This is the familiar teaching of hundreds of our hymns.

---

[1] *The Faith of a Moralist*, vol. i, pp. 420 f., 431 f.
[2] Rev. xiv. 13.

It is enough; earth's struggles soon shall cease,
And Jesus call us to heaven's perfect peace.

When the day of toil is done,
When the race of life is run,
Father, grant Thy wearied one
Rest for evermore.

But in the nineteenth century an opposite sentiment began to declare itself. This was, of course, closely in connexion with the current glorification of the idea of progress and with the increasing reliance on human effort as over against divine grace. It now began to be said that quest is better than attainment, and labour than the release which follows its satisfactory performance. Such a position had, in ancient times, been most nearly approached by the Stoics, who had gone very far in insisting that our human business is only with the quest, the fulfilment being entirely in the hands of God. Life, they said, is like a game played with counters; the fun lies in trying to win as many counters as possible, but the counters are quite valueless in themselves, and nobody wants to keep them once they are won. But for the Stoics this was only a rule of action, not an ultimate philosophy. Their ultimate philosophy did allow that certain fulfilments were desirable in themselves and that God brought these about without our agency. Indeed, whatever happens we must accept as the fulfilment of God's will, because God and nature are one. A very different outlook was, however, represented in the ancient world by the Platonic and Aristotelian philosophies. The doctrine of the famous tenth book of the *Nicomachean Ethics* is that, just as the aim of war is peace, so the aim of all our busy-ness is the enjoyment of leisure. Ἀσχολούμεθα ἵνα σχολάζωμεν.[1] 'No one chooses to be at war, or provokes war, for the sake of being at war; no one is so bloodthirsty as that.'[2] Thus Aristotle is entirely at one with the Christian tradition in believing that man's chief end and supreme blessedness must be a state of σχολή (leisure, rest, peaceful ease, the Latin *otium*) which supervenes upon the toil and moil—only that Aristotle looks for it in this present life. It would be interesting to know at what date, in modern European literature, there appear the earliest protests against this conception of heaven as a place of fruition and of rest; but perhaps the most important single name is that of Kant. In the Kantian ethic the features of the Stoic ethic are very closely reproduced. Here again, what matters is said to be not the attainment, but the spirit of the quest. The *complete* good (or *summum bonum*) is, it is true, admitted to include a having as well as a seeking, and a being as well as a becoming; but it is held that this complete good cannot be attained within any finite time, but only throughout infinite time. Hence, since man is conceived as destined always to view his life under the form of time, the heavenly life must be regarded as an endless prolongation of our present moral struggle between duty and inclination. 'For a rational but finite being the only possibility is an endless progress from the lower to the higher degrees of moral perfection.'[3] Such an idea of immortality was, in 1788, a startlingly novel one, but the intervening century and a half has made it familiar enough. The nineteenth century was the century of busy-ness. Its characteristic gospel was the Gospel of Work, Carlylean and otherwise. Its ideal

---

[1] Op. cit., 1177 B.   [2] Ibid.
[3] *Kritik d. pr. V., Dialektik*, ch. ii, § iv.

has been the Strenuous Life. Its highest watchword has been Service. So the old impatience for fruition has given way to the zest of the struggle itself; and we find Stevenson, a typical spirit of his time, going so far as to suggest that 'to travel hopefully is a better thing than to arrive, and the true success is to labour'.[1] In these circumstances it is not surprising that the prospect of 'rest for evermore' has seemed to us a very unwelcome one, and that we have preferred to think instead of an endless future continuance of our present earthly 'progress', the thread of which we are to take up in the hereafter at the precise point where death obliges us to lay it down. Tennyson's lines about the soul are typical:

> She desires no isles of the blest, no quiet seats of the just,
> To rest in a golden grove, or to bask in a summer sky;
> Give her the wages of going on, and not to die.[2]

Is this nineteenth-century sentiment a complete aberration? I cannot believe that it is. I am convinced that it discovers a real weakness in the traditional outlook and enshrines a true insight of its own such as must be taken up into any view which is going to satisfy the men of the future. The mistake of our forefathers lay in their tendency to regard fruition as a state of mere passivity. They encouraged in the popular mind the idea that in heaven we should be all the time sitting down in a vast and serried circle, singing hymns; and the maid-of-all-work, 'who always was tired', objects even to the singing!

> I'll be where loud anthems is always a-ringing,
> But as I've no voice, I'm clear of the singing.
> Don't mourn for me now, don't mourn for me never,
> I'm going to do nothing for ever and ever.

[1] The last words of the essay on 'El Dorado', in *Virginibus Puerisque*.
[2] *Wages*.

But the wrong turn which thought has here taken is manifest enough. Our life on earth is an alternation of activity and relaxation, of working and resting, of term and vacation, of business and holiday; and if we are to conceive of a transcendent quality of life at all, it must be one in which this alternation is genuinely transcended instead of one pole of it being merely glorified at the expense of the other. Hence it is false to think of heaven as a mere period of relaxation, a vast holiday, or the endless Long Vacation of the lazy student's dreams. The peace of momentary respite, such as we must all allow ourselves, must not be confused with the peace that follows victory. A night at an inn is one thing and the journey accomplished is quite another. In the inn we sleep, but when the journey is accomplished, we are in a sense more active than ever. We are now actively enjoying something that is worth having for its own sake, whereas the journey was undertaken only for the sake of this to which it has led. It may be we are only talking with the friend to whose house we have travelled, and that only for love's sake; yet it cannot be denied that our souls are now much more active than when we were jogging along in the saddle, or being jolted in the train, or sitting behind the steering-wheel. *Fruition*, then, *is essentially an activity*—a higher activity than the activity of becoming or of unfulfilled quest. This, as is well known, is insisted on by Aristotle. Blessedness, he urges, cannot be a becoming (γένεσις); and on the other hand it

'is not a condition (ἕξις); for if it were, it might be in the possession of a man who spent all his life sleeping and living a merely vegetable life. . . . If then we reject that, we must make blessedness an activity (ἐνέργεια) . . . , and as to the two classes of activities that may be distinguished—those that are necessary and desirable for the sake of something else, and those that are desirable in themselves—we must obviously place blessedness among those desirable in themselves and not for the sake of something else; for blessedness must be self-sufficient, lacking nothing.'[1]

Aristotle's weakness is that when we ask him what this activity consists in, he answers that it can only be θεωρία or speculation; because, he says, the activity of speculation is the only one that is 'loved for its own sake alone'. Here, however, we see the philosopher unduly glorifying the philosophic life. Yet perhaps after all the necessary correction is one that is easily made. Aristotle's βίος θεωρητικός was translated into Latin, literally enough, as *vita contemplativa*; and the contemplative life came, within the Christian tradition, to include far more than philosophic speculation—it came to include the cultivation of human friendship, the pursuit of beauty, and, above all, the exploration of the divine love.

In our own time, then, the solution of this apparent antinomy of thought has usually been found in the conception of an activity which is essentially an activity of attainment rather than of progress; a growth *in* rather than *towards* that which is good. Professor Sorley concluded his Gifford Lectures in 1915 by urging that it was possible to think of free spirits

'as, themselves made perfect, still pressing forward into new and untried ways, enhancing the values of the world. It is not only evil (that is, moral evil) that has to be mastered. The artist or the man of science has not been fighting against moral evil in his effort to produce things of beauty or to enlarge the sphere of knowledge; and yet he has been producing values. In this way it is conceivable that moral evil might be overcome, and yet that

---

[1] *Eth. Nic.* 1176 A–B.

adventure would not cease. There would still be call and room for pressing further into the unknown and making all things subservient to the values which it is the function of free spirits to realize.'[1]

Another Gifford Lecturer, Professor Taylor, has developed the same view somewhat more fully. He eloquently inveighs against the assumption that moral action consists in putting wrongs right.

'The moral life would not disappear even from a world in which there were no wrongs left to be righted. Even a society in which no member had anything more to correct in himself, and where "Thou shalt love thy neighbour as thyself" were the universally accepted rule of social duty, would still have something to do; it would have the whole work of embodying the love of each for all in the detail of life.'[2]

Again,

'the elimination of evil and its source in unruly inclination would still leave the ultimate distinction between God and man untouched, and consequently could not affect the essential characteristic of the moral life, that it is a life of *aspiration*. With the passage from struggle to triumph, morality would no doubt undergo a transfiguration, but it would be a transfiguration and not a transformation.'[3]

There will thus be plenty of room for adventure, and even for social service, in the heavenly life, though it will be adventure and service of a different kind. Instead of development *towards* fruition there will be development *in* fruition.

'There would be no more progress *towards* goodness of en-

[1] *Moral Values and the Idea of God,* the closing sentences.
[2] *The Faith of a Moralist,* vol. i, p. 400.
[3] Ibid., p. 406.

vironment or character, but there might be abundant progress *in* good, onward movement in the manifestation of the principle of the good life in ever more varied and richer forms.

Professor Taylor illustrates this from the fact that an artist, even after he has achieved as complete a mastery as is possible to him, may still go on producing an infinite variety of masterly works of art, without necessarily even trying to make each *better* than the last.

'If we are to think morally of Heaven, we should, I suggest, think of it as a land where charity *grows*, where each citizen learns to glow more and more with an understanding love, not only of the common King, but of his fellow-citizens. In this respect, again, there would be one lesson mastered before the portals of Heaven would open to admit us. We should have learned to love every neighbour who crosses our path, to hate nothing that God has made, to be indifferent to none of the mirrors of His light. But even where there is no ill-will or indifference to interfere with love, it is still possible for love to grow as understanding grows.'[1]

It is, I feel sure, along such lines that further reflection on the matter must proceed.[2]

More than this we cannot concede to the enlightenment of the nineteenth century. The mistake of modern thought at this point, as at almost every point, seems to me to lie in its anthropomorphism. It has discovered the fact of evolutionary change in the biological realm—that is to say, in the realm of the protoplasmic scum that has appeared on the damp surface of this very insignificant planet. It has interpreted

---

[1] Ibid., p. 421.
[2] Reference may be made to Canon Streeter's essay on 'The Life of the World to Come', in the symposium on *Immortality* which he edited in 1917. 'The Content of the Idea of Heaven' is there expounded under the heads of love, work, thought, beauty, humour, and the vision of God.

this change as a movement towards perfection, as progress, and then it has at once jumped to the conclusion that such evolutionary progress is the law of all being. Human history, too, is an evolutionary progress, and so is each individual human biography. And after death our spirits will continue in evolutionary progress for ever and ever. Indeed the universe itself is progressing. And so is God—He is 'a growing God'. And we are all—the universe and God and ourselves —getting on famously! Thus is everything interpreted by the protoplasmic scum in the light of the laws of the protoplasmic scum. And any attempt to see farther than our noses is set down as 'medievalism'. The designation is not altogether inappropriate, for the medievals were one with the ancients in their ever-present sense of the unimportance of mere human history and the infinitesimal nature of human achievement as over against the infinite otherness of the final Reality, God. The medievals would have smiled at the idea of a gradual approximation to divine perfection on the part of man. They would have argued that in no finite time, however long a time it was—even unto millions of years—could sufficient progress be made to make any real difference. This is the true Christian doctrine. 'For there is no difference: for all have sinned, and come short of the glory of God; being justified freely by His grace, through the redemption that is in Christ Jesus.'[1] And it is sound mathematics. For all finite numbers are equally far removed from infinity. Dedekind and Cantor's definition of infinity, which lies at the root of so much modern mathematics, is that that number is infinite from which some units can be deducted without diminishing

[1] Rom. iii. 22–4, A.V.

the number of units it contains. This makes plain the parochialism and anthropomorphism of the attempt to reach infinity by approximation. Yet to lose sight of infinity altogether, by restricting our attention to the progression, is to be equally parochial. For we cannot long continue to cheat ourselves with the belief that progress is valuable only for the sake of its movement, and not for the sake of the goal to which it conducts us; or, in Aristotle's words, that it is the fight, not the victory, that makes life worth living. This is but the passing philosophy of a restless and excitement-seeking age; and it has in it no more hope of longevity than have its devotees, who usually die off in their forties and fifties with hearts overstrained and nerves over-taut. What the modern man needs is an outlook which, without impairing his effectiveness as a worker, will yet relieve his sense of pressure, and which will help him to 'relax' without ceasing to strive. But the only outlook from which this result can be hoped is one which speaks to us 'of a truth which is worth enjoying as well as worth seeking, of a life which is worth living as well as worth gaining'.[1] Our ultimate looking forward must be not to a continuance of the race, but to the secure possession of the prize.

VI

But this does not prejudice the question whether, for us all, the race comes to an end with the present term of life. Nothing that has so far been said necessarily excludes the view that for some the time of trial continues for a certain period beyond the grave. The question owes its importance to its

[1] Wicksteed, op. cit., p. 39.

bearing upon another question, which we must now proceed to discuss.

This is the question whether eternal life is in prospect for all men or only for some. Here, as we have seen, is the main issue on which, from the very beginnings of the immortal hope in Israel and in Greece, earnest thought has been divided. Nor is there any difficulty in seeing how the issue arises. The present life has always been held to be a time of testing and of preparation. The enjoyment of eternal life in the future has always been made conditional upon the use we make of the present. Only those whose lives are now lived in such fellowship with God as earthly conditions permit can look forward to the fuller fellowship hereafter. There is here an insight which we can never afford to surrender. If our consciences tell us anything they tell us that it matters *eternally* what we do with our lives *now*—that 'behold, now is the accepted time; behold, now is the day of salvation'.[1] No form of other-worldliness could be more offensive to our sense of values than one which, by offering us the prospect of an infinitely extended opportunity, would rob the present moment of its urgency; and here, if anywhere, our modern hither-worldliness will be justified in its protest. Yet we are haunted by our doubt concerning the destiny of those who have misused their opportunity on earth and have lived out of all fellowship with God.

Three different possibilities are presented to us by the history of thought. *Either* we may believe that only those who have here been initiated into the divine fellowship will survive at all, and that all other souls will be annihilated.

[1] 2 Cor. vi. 2.

This doctrine was entertained by a number of the Jewish apocalypse-writers and by not a few of the early Christian fathers, and it is difficult to believe that it is entirely unrepresented in the New Testament.[1] *Or* we may believe that, instead of being annihilated, the souls of the unregenerate live on everlastingly in utter exclusion from all blessedness, if not in actual torment. This was the doctrine of many Jewish apocalyptists who, as we saw, spoke of a place called Gehenna that was as far below Sheol as heaven was above it. The Jewish Gehenna became, with a difference, the Christian Hell, a conception the later career of which is well known to all. But it has its close parallels in Greek thought too, in the Orphic sects and in Plato.[2] *Or again* we may believe that those who in this life have not found fellowship with God will have their time of preparation and testing extended beyond the grave until at last all souls realize their true destiny and enter into the society of the blessed. This 'larger hope' is neither Greek nor Jewish, but seems to have made its first definite appearance within the Christian Church. Again, it is hard to believe that it is entirely absent from the New Testament, but it is in Origen that it makes its first definite appear-

[1] Many scholars of the first rank hold that St. Paul definitely taught this doctrine. 'At this point', writes Dr. McGiffert, 'Paul was in disagreement with Christ and with most of the early Christians, for he accepted the resurrection of believers only, basing it upon their union with Christ' (*History of Christian Thought*, vol. i, p. 88). 'But if', writes Dr. William Morgan, 'a study of these terms leaves the question of annihilation or endless suffering an open one, the general tenor of the Apostle's thought points conclusively to the former. . . . The universe he contemplates as the goal of redemption is one reconciled to God in all its parts. . . . The vision which the Apostle leaves with us is that of a world which is without a devil and without a hell, without a shadow on its brightness or a discord in its harmony' (*The Religion and Theology of Paul*, p. 238).

[2] Cf. Plato's phrase in *Laws*, 905: 'If thou art transported to Hades or to a still more dreadful region (ἀγριώτερον ἔτι . . . τόπον).'

ance in systematic form. The three competing views have commonly been known by the names of conditional immortality, eternal punishment, and universal restoration.[1]

How are we to decide between the three possibilities? There is indeed little that we can say. A careful theologian like Dr. H. R. Mackintosh warns us against 'infringement of the nearly complete agnosticism with respect to the lot of the impenitent which ... is ordained for faith'[2]; and such agnosticism is, no doubt, the better part of wisdom. Yet some things must be said.

It is by Plato that, in the form of an Orphic myth and without particular emphasis on its everlastingness, the doctrine of eternal punishment has been given its most persuasive statement. His doctrine is that by God's appointment each soul finds its own place, like going to like. Thus the most unrighteous souls 'sink into the abyss (βάθος) and the so-called lower regions of Hades, the very names of which make men greatly afraid'. He goes on:

'And when the soul, either by its own resolve or by the influence of the company it keeps, changes greatly in virtue or vice, then, if, through communion with Virtue Divine, it becomes pre-eminently virtuous, it is changed to a pre-eminent region, another and better region to which it is borne along a holy road, whereas if it changes in a contrary direction, then the change of its abode is also of a contrary kind. ... O boy, O lad, that think yourself forgotten by the gods, know that as you become more evil, you join the company of more evil souls, and as you become better, the company of better; and that both in life and in all that follows death you will do and suffer exactly as it is meet you should, like

[1] By far the best presentation of them in English is Dr. Leckie's *The World to Come and Final Destiny* (1918).
[2] *Immortality and the Future* (1915), p. 205.

going to like. For this is a divine judgement which neither you nor any other luckless lad will ever boast of having escaped.'[1]

The bracing moral quality of such a view will be felt by all. The corner-stone of the doctrine of eternal punishment has always been the conviction that distributive, retributive justice is the ultimate law of the spiritual universe, and nowhere have we a nobler statement of that conviction, or one more completely purged of petty vindictiveness, than this of Plato's.

The later doctrine of hell, on the other hand, is made suspect by much of its history. Vindictiveness and hardheartedness have undoubtedly had some part in the fashioning of it. Had the doctrine been worked out, from the beginning and steadily, in terms of what its proponents felt *themselves* to deserve, it would have to be taken very seriously; but in fact it bears the taint of having been worked out in terms of what its proponents felt to be the deserts of their neighbours, or rather of their enemies. Many, it is true, have feared hell for themselves, but many also have wished it for others. And except when we begin to reflect on our own merits, our human thinking is never so prone to err as when we begin to reflect on our neighbour's defects.

We have seen that the doctrine of hell has its ancient sources, both Greek and Hebrew; but it was undoubtedly in the early Christian centuries that the conception now so familiar to us took definite and final shape. This was the age of persecution and of the first struggles with heresy, and it is difficult to avoid the conclusion that it was as a fit place for the persecutors that the conception gradually formed itself in the minds of the Christians, when it did not rather form itself in

[1] *Laws*, 904–5.

241

the minds of the orthodox as a fit place for the heretics. 'The growth of the belief in hell', writes one historian, 'was largely due to a very intelligible indignation at the cruelty of persecutors and a desire to stem heresy.'[1] Shortly after the close of the second century we find Tertullian writing as follows:

'What a spectacle is that fast-approaching advent of our Lord. . . . Yes, and there are other sights: that last day of judgement. . . . How vast a spectacle then bursts upon the eye! What there excites my admiration? what my derision? Which sight gives me joy? which rouses me to exultation?—as I see so many illustrious monarchs . . . groaning now in the lowest darkness . . . ; governors of provinces, too, who persecuted the Christian name, in fires more fierce than those with which in the days of their pride they raged against the followers of Christ. . . . I shall have a better opportunity then of hearing the tragedians, louder-voiced in their own calamity, . . . of beholding the wrestlers, not in their gymnasium, but tossing in the fiery billows . . .'

—and much more of the same kind.[2] It is well known how important was the influence of St. Augustine in finally establishing this doctrine in the mind of the church. 'He teaches', writes Dr. Leckie, 'that the fire of Gehenna, though not that of the Intermediate State, is a material flame, and that the lost will be furnished with bodies able, like the salamander, to live for ever in the furnace.'[3] And he adds that 'it is difficult to be patient with the inhuman urbanity of the Bishop of Hippo when he discourses elegantly of the value of human suffering in embellishing the ages by supplying an artistic shadow in the spectacle of the world'.[4] Mr. Bevan goes still farther in his

[1] *Immortality* (ed. Streeter), p. 203 f.
[2] *De Spectaculis*, ad fin.; translation in *Ante-Nicene Fathers*.
[3] Op. cit., p. 122.
[4] Ibid., p. 125.

accusation of St. Augustine, yet not too far: 'Where his theology led him to terrible conclusions, his hard logic so eliminated natural human feeling that his personality strikes a chill, as contact might with a being from another planet.'[1] Yet the same has been true of many other believers in hell, both before and since. 'In the oldest part of the *Book of Enoch* things are said which indicate a joyful conviction that everlasting torments await the unrighteous.'[2] And in the Christian ages, 'preachers of great repute for sanctity and zeal painted their pictures of Gehenna in colours of a crude vulgarity. Their imagery revealed often a singular acquaintance with the worst horrors of human life. . . . And over all this scene of sordid cruelty the saints of heaven watched and were glad.'[3]

But even when hell is conceived as a place suited rather to one's own deserts than to the deserts of one's neighbour or enemy, the doctrine is still open to serious objection. For its essence, as has been said, is to make distributive (and therefore also retributive) justice the ultimate law of the spiritual universe; and though that is a high conception relatively to many others that have been entertained, it can hardly be held adequate to the truth of Christianity. The Christian teaching surely is that the highest spiritual attitude is not justice but forgiveness. We may, if we choose, speak of forgiveness as a higher kind of justice—a justice which judges men not in the light of what they are, but in the light of what they have it in them to become; but then we shall have to distinguish this higher justice in which 'the last shall be first and the first last' from the lower justice which rewards 'each man according to his works'. The difference between the two is that the latter

[1] *Christianity* (1932), p. 100. [2] Leckie, op. cit., p. 15. [3] Ibid., p. 119.

makes good stand opposed to evil in equal and opposite re-action, whereas the former makes good overcome evil and blot it out. What the doctrine of eternal punishment does, then, is to make evil an eternal element in the universe, no less positively real than the good itself; a result which must always follow from the attempt to regard punishment as an end in itself, instead of as a reformatory discipline. But this is Manichean dualism; and how can St. Augustine have coun-tenanced it? He could do so only because he was able to per-suade himself that whereas unpunished sin was an evil, sin properly punished was not an evil but a good. This explana-tion, however, is entirely unacceptable in spite of its having been piously repeated by many a Christian divine. For it does nothing but lead us back to that side of St. Augustine's thought which we have already found so repellent—his bland assurance that the universe is no less admirable and beautiful a place for having a chamber of horrors eternally present with-in it, so long only as each horror of pain perfectly matches and balances each horror of sin. It is like saying that a state which was obliged to keep half its citizens perpetually in prison would be as ideal a fatherland as one in which complete absence of crime kept the prisons perpetually empty—pro-vided only that the penal laws were administered with equal justice in the two cases.

If we reject the doctrine of eternal evil, then we have to choose between the alternatives of conditional survival and universal restoration. And this choice is likely to be deter-mined by our judgement on a single issue. The conditionalist holds that complete annihilation is the natural fate of souls from which every trace of the divine image has been effaced, and it may be that in this the conditionalist is right. But the question is whether we may believe that there are any souls of which this is true. Are there men and women from whose natures all possibility of higher desires have disappeared and whom no appeal of divine love could ever hope to touch? Jesus Himself has encouraged us to think otherwise—to find the seed of faith in the most unlikely places, and to look upon the lost sheep as being often the most promising subjects for redemption. 'Verily I say unto you, the publicans and harlots go into the Kingdom of Heaven before you.'[1] And the career of His Gospel in the world has lent much support to an outlook of this kind. To take any other view is to set a limit to the power of divine love over the recalcitrant will of created spirit. And it is doubtful whether the final supremacy of the Good would be less compromised by the power of evil finally to destroy souls that had been created in the divine image, than it would be by the perdurance to all eternity of souls in which sin remained for ever active but for ever under punishment.

But if we decide for universalism, it must be for a form of it which does nothing to decrease the urgency of immediate repentance and which makes no promises to the procrastinating sinner. It is doubtful whether such a form of the doctrine has yet been found. But one has the feeling that in this whole question of the fate of the unrepentant we are touching one of the growing-points of Christian thought at the present time.

[1] Cf. Dante, *Purgatorio*, xvii.

> Ciascun confusamente un bene apprende,
> nel qual si quieti l'animo, e disira:
> per che di giugner lui ciascun contende.

VII

One other issue must be briefly touched upon. We have found eternal life to be a higher order of living which, though foretasted during our earthly term, cannot be fully enjoyed by us until we are released from earthly conditions. This seems to mean, on the one hand, that each individual who is worthy is caught up at death into the Heavenly Kingdom, there to enjoy the fullness of God's presence for evermore. On this view the Kingdom of Heaven is, as it were, *always there*; but as time goes on, more and more individuals are admitted into the fruition of its blessings. The march of earthly history might continue through unending time, on the same lines as now, without progress or any tendency to culminate; and yet the Kingdom of Heaven would be everlastingly present above it. To each individual biography there would be culmination, but to the history of the race there would be no culmination. And should the earthly story, instead of going on *ad infinitum*, come one day abruptly to an end, still the essential situation would not be changed; the last individual would now have passed into glory—that would be all.

But there is another conception of the Heavenly Kingdom that is entirely different. The interest is now centred not in the biographies of individuals but in the history of the race. We are dealing now with a philosophy of history; that is, with the conviction that not merely the lives of individuals, but also history as a whole has a meaning and is leading up to some culmination—some 'one far-off, divine event to which the whole creation moves'. The Kingdom of

Heaven, on this view, is essentially a future order of things —a transfigured society which cannot have place *alongside* of the present social order, but which can be inaugurated only after the present order has at last been completely transformed.

Which of the two views are we to follow? It is, I think, impossible to choose between them. What we must do is to find a composite view which will take up into itself the positive elements contained in the two one-sided views before us. We must not be misled here by the contemporary cry for the simplification of dogma. Better have no eschatology at all than one so over-simplified that it destroys the delicate and difficult balance of the deepest spiritual experience. One main reason for the elaborateness of the orthodox Christian eschatology is that it has attempted to combine its hope for the individual and its hope for society into a single expectation.

We have seen how in the beginning of the Hebrew-Christian development it was the hope for society that chiefly held men's thoughts. Their dream was of a culmination of the racial history rather than of the individual biography. The Kingdom of God was a future order which would be the end of history. For history *had* an end and was leading up towards a grand climax. That, we saw, was what distinguished the Jews, together with the Persians, from all the other peoples of the earth. And, as we saw, such a conception is bound to appeal to us modern Westerners who incline to look into the future with so confident an optimism, whose habitual picture of human history is of a steady and continuous upward progress, and who find it hard to speak of ideal perfection except in terms of a time to come. But the Jews came to feel that this climax *at the close* of history was not enough by itself. The consummation must not be looked for simply in the last term of the series, it must be found in the series as a whole. If the Kingdom of God means simply the transfigured and perfected order of human society which some day in the far-distant future will at last be realized, then it is only *the last generation* that will enjoy its blessings. And what of the generations that perish by the way? It is here that the development of Jewish and Christian thought, in close agreement with the thought of the Greeks, parts company with our contemporary futurism. It came to be felt, as we saw, that the Kingdom of God, if it is to be a satisfying object of hope, cannot be a mere earthly paradise[1] to be enjoyed by the final generation, but a transcendent order of being in which all generations have a part. The Jewish teaching was that, when the Kingdom came, the righteous dead would share equally with the final generation in the blessings of its appearing. But where are they meanwhile? To this question there were three possible answers: (*a*) that they remain, awaiting revivification, in the virtual non-existence of Sheol—as it were 'asleep'; (*b*) that they are in some intermediate state—as it were of incomplete blessedness; and (*c*) that they are already enjoying the blessings of the Heavenly Kingdom, having been admitted into it immediately after death, though not until the end of history will they be conjoined to their own bodies, and the cup of their blessedness be full. All three

---

[1] Or if ever the scene of eternal life was thought to be earth, it was an earth utterly and miraculously renovated by the act of God—'a new heaven and a new earth; for the first heaven and the first earth were passed away; and there was no more sea' (Rev. xxi. 1).

views are represented in the apocalyptic books;[1] and no clear agreement was ever reached.

But the very uncertainty has behind it an important grasp of truth. For here we have an attempted synthesis of the two one-sided views which we have been concerned to distinguish. Within the framework of a grand-scale philosophy of history room is being made for a philosophy of the single soul. There is a consummation for society and a consummation also for the individual; and yet the two consummations are not two but one.[2] Even here and now (so it has come to be felt) I as an individual in the presence of God, *solus cum solo*, may begin to live the eternal life of the Heavenly Kingdom; and after release from the present life I shall enter into the fullness of its joy; and yet can my joy be full, while perhaps my friends still live on earth and I am separated from them, while our human society lives a broken and divided life, while the company of the redeemed remains incomplete? The Christian Church has steadily replied that it cannot. Its teaching, both Roman and Protestant, has been that *there can be no complete consummation for the individual until there is consummation also for society*. This is the real significance of the conception of 'the Last Day'. It is not really for the sake of the 'Judgement' that 'the Last Day' is important, for it is taught that men will be judged and (except, for the Roman Church, in the case of those who must pass through purgatory) sent to their final destination, *at death*, so that the Great

---

[1] See Paul Volz, *Jüdische Eschatologie von Daniel bis Akiba* (Tübingen und Leipzig, 1903), pp. 248–50.

[2] 'Die Auferstehung in ihrer früheren Form ist eine Kombination von Gemeindeeschatologie und individualisierter Eschatologie; neben das Bedürfnis der Gemeinde hat sich das Bedürfnis der Individuen gestellt.' Volz, op. cit., p. 133.

Assize is no more than, as we might say, a public announcement of a sentence that has already, except in the case of the final generation, been passed and put into effect. But the orthodox teaching, both Roman and Protestant, is that until the last day the souls both of the blessed and of the damned remain *disembodied*, though already dwelling in what is to be their final place of abode; but that on the Last Day there will be a General Resurrection whereby the souls of both are re-united to their old bodies. This, of course, *had* to be taught, so long as it was also taught that in the life eternal we are to have the same bodies of flesh and blood and bones (though rendered incorruptible) that we now possess; because these bodies were known to be meanwhile in the graves where they were buried. But the true significance of the teaching comes out only when we are told that the spirits of the blessed, though now enjoying the heavenly bliss *substantially*,[1] will not possess it *in the fullness of its accidental*[1] *nature* until after the Last Day; for the deepest reason of this delay is not really that until then they will be disembodied, but that until then their society will be incomplete. The words of the Westminster Confession will serve as well as any other statement of the received doctrine:

'The bodies of men after death return to dust, and see corruption; but their souls . . . immediately return to God who gave them. The souls of the righteous, being then made perfect in holiness, are received unto the highest heavens, where they behold the face of God in light and glory, waiting for the full redemption of their bodies. . . . At the last day . . . all the dead shall be raised up with the selfsame bodies, and none other, although with different qualities, which shall be united again to

---

[1] The scholastic usage of the words.

their souls for ever. . . . Then shall the righteous go into everlasting life, and receive that fullness of joy and refreshing which
shall come from the presence of the Lord.'[1]

Whatever else we may think about such a statement, we must
at least sympathize with its earnest endeavour to envisage a
single ultimate consummation that will include the complete
satisfaction both of our individual and of our social strivings.
It is not enough to believe that history has a goal, and again it
is not enough to believe that individuals are immortal. Rather
must we agree with the fine words of von Hügel that 'we
each of us already form, at our best, one particular link in but
one great chain from earth to heaven; yet each little link is
also, severally, already linked directly to Heaven itself'.[2]

And if we want a definition, we can find none better than
von Hügel's: 'Eternal Life consists in the most real of relations between the most living of realities—the human spirit
and the Eternal Spirit, God; and in the keen sense of His Perfection, Simultaneity and Prevenience, as against our un-
perfection, successiveness and dependence.'[3]

VIII

It comes, then, to this—that the only knowledge we can
have of eternal life is that which comes to us through our
present foretasting of its joys. All that we know of the other
life *there* is what we know of it *here*. For even here there is
another life that may be lived, a life wholly other than that
which commonly bears the name and yet one which may be
lived out in this very place where I now am, be it desert or

[1] cc. xxxii–xxxiii.
[2] *Essays and Addresses on the Philosophy of Religion*, Second Series, p. 52.
[3] *Eternal Life*, p. 378.

tilled field, office or market-place, study or sick-bedroom—
and may be begun to-day. This other life is the life everlasting.

'Heaven', says Whichcote the Platonist, 'is first a Temper
and then a Place.'[1]

Of the specific conditions of its future manifestation there
is nothing that we can know. Many questions may be asked
but none can be answered. There is, however, one question of
this kind that must not go quite unmentioned—the question
whether the life everlasting is to be an *embodied* life. We have
already studied the waverings of the thought of the past concerning this issue. On the one hand it has been felt that since
the life we hope for is a life which will altogether transcend
the present material and temporal and spatial order, material
bodies like our present ones would be wholly unsuited to the
conduct of it. On the other hand there has been the difficulty
of conceiving how a soul can have any effective life, or can
indeed exist at all, without the co-operation of its bodily
organism. The Greeks were more acutely aware of the former
difficulty, the Jews of the latter. But in the end the Jews were
really conscious of *both* difficulties, and in that they seem to
have definitely the advantage over the Greeks. Their reflection led them in the end to the position that the citizens
of the Heavenly Kingdom would indeed possess bodies, but
that they would be 'transfigured' bodies, 'angelic' bodies,
bodies 'made of the light and glory of God'; and this was
the view followed by our Lord and St. Paul. If we press the
question whether the body of glory is to be the same body
transformed or another body which replaces it, we receive no

---

[1] *Moral and Religious Aphorisms.*

clear or united answer. Not even St. Paul, who has set out his judgement at considerable length, can be pinned down to a certain pronouncement on this point. And perhaps this is no surprise. For which of us was ever pinned down to a certain pronouncement on the parallel question at what point a stocking that has been darned and darned again ceases to be the same stocking and becomes a new one? Perhaps St. Paul will not answer us because the question we put to him is too trivial for there to be any answer. Do not the bio-chemists tell us that even in the present life there is an almost complete renovation of our bodily tissues within each seven-year period, so that there is no material but only a formal identity between the body I now have and the body I had seven years ago. The change to a heavenly embodiment would no doubt be of a still more radical kind—a change, as St. Paul says, to something that is not flesh and blood at all: 'flesh and blood cannot inherit the Kingdom of God'.[1] And if it be true that in heaven 'they neither marry nor are given in marriage', then indeed it is difficult to believe that we are to retain to all eternity bodily organisms that have plainly been contrived for marital ends and some members of which would thus for ever remain without further function.[2] But on the

[1] 1 Cor. xv. 51.

[2] St. Thomas Aquinas argues that when St. Paul said that 'flesh and blood cannot possess the Kingdom of God', he meant only that they could not possess it until they were rendered incorruptible. Thomas therefore holds himself justified in believing that our fleshly bodies rise, and remain as fleshly, animal, and material throughout everlasting life, though being 'glorified' in certain other specified ways. The sexual members will rise with the rest of the body. 'Nor', he goes on, 'is this obviated by the fact that there will be no use for those members'; because though these members will be without use, they will not be 'without purpose, since they will serve to restore the integrity of the human body'. (*Summa contra Gentiles*, iv. 98; vol. iv, p. 300 f. of the translation of the English Dominican Fathers.)

other hand most of us will shrink no less than did St. Paul from the conception of an entirely disembodied (or, as St. Paul says, 'naked') spirit. The Apostle found it impossible to conceive how his spirit could live that fuller life in the hereafter to which he so eagerly looked forward, unless it were provided with some kind of bodily organization by means of which it might express itself; and the conduct of the psycho-physical debate from his day to ours has, if anything, made the entertainment of such a conception more difficult for us than it was for him. 'I know', he writes, 'that if this earthly home of my bodily frame [literally, tent] be taken down, I get a building from God, a home not made with hands, eternal in the heavens. And to this end I groan; I yearn for the putting-on of this heavenly structure of mine, being assured that, having put it on, I shall not be found naked.'[1] St. Paul's hope, then, is for a bodily endowment far more perfect in its organization, and adapted to a far higher mode of life and a far more intimate mode of intercourse, than any earthly or material body could ever be; and such, it would seem, is still the most reasonable hope for us to-day.[2] Yet about the nature of such a body nothing of a positive kind can ever be imagined by us. We can only say with the Apostle, 'God giveth it a body as it pleaseth Him.'[3] Our discussion may

[1] 2 Cor. v. 1–3.
[2] Cf. Edmund Spenser, *An Hymne in Honour of Beautie*:

> So every spirit, as it is most pure,
> And hath in it the more of heavenly light,
> So it the fairer bodie doth procure
> To habit in, and it more fairely dight
> With chearefull grace and amiable sight;
> For of the soule the bodie forme doth take;
> For soule is forme and doth the bodie make.

[3] 1 Cor. xv. 38.

fittingly be concluded with some familiar words from the First Epistle of John: 'Beloved, now are we the sons of God, and it doth not yet appear what we shall be; but we know that, when He shall appear, we shall be like Him; for we shall see Him as He is. And every man that hath this hope in Him purifieth himself, even as He is pure.'[1]

[1] 1 John iii. 2–3.

Chapter VIII

STRANGERS AND PILGRIMS

I

WE began our study by taking sympathetic cognizance of that hither-worldly temper which, though it had its roots in the humanism of the Renaissance and achieved apparent maturity in the eighteenth-century Enlightenment, has in our own time been carried out to altogether new extremes and has also been made effective in the thought and life of an immensely greater number of men. We gladly acknowledged the important insight into truth from which that temper must be taken as proceeding, and argued that no form of Christianity which fails to profit by it is likely to hold the future in these Western lands. But if we set out from this recognition of the partial justice of the modern hither-worldly rebellion, the tendency of our study has rather been to bring the opposing claims of the traditional other-worldly temper more and more to our attention. It must therefore now be our task to attempt a final estimate of these claims, and to inquire how the two apparently opposite attitudes of mind may be fused into the unity of a single harmonious outlook.

We considered the rebellion against other-worldliness as based upon two connected but distinguishable charges—the charge of 'puritan' blindness to the glories of the secular and the charge of 'quietistic' indifference to the preventable outward evils of our earthly existence; and we admitted the partial right of both charges. It is now our duty to guard against the equally serious, or indeed more serious, opposite error of giving earthly things first place in our thoughts and finding in the sphere of secular interests the final satisfaction of our souls.

II

As regards the former charge, the reader may well have gained the impression that in saying what I did I was really surrendering the whole case. I granted to Renaissance human- ism the right of its protest against the traditional opinion that secular interests, where they cannot be seen to be directly instrumental to the eternal salvation of the soul, are no more than *toys*, that is innocent diversions. I allowed to the pursuit of beauty and of knowledge an independent importance of their own, and argued that this emancipation of the arts and sciences from their too exclusively ancillary position must continue to be regarded as a definite advance. We must not, I said, turn our backs on the great *Quattrocento*, repudiating its treasures. Art has received immense permanent enrich- ment from Michelangelo's delight in the muscular forms of the human body and Andrea della Robbia's delight in the lovely faces of Florentine maidens and Verrocchio's delight in the shape of a horse. Science has received no less per- manent enrichment from the geographical curiosity of Diaz and Columbus and Vasco da Gama and from the curiosity (coming a little later) of Copernicus and Tycho Brahe and Kepler and Galileo about 'the revolutions of the celestial orbs'. The extent of this latter enrichment is vividly brought home to us when a historian reminds us that 'In the Dark Ages Arithmetic and Astronomy found their way into the educational curriculum chiefly because they taught the means of finding Easter.'[1]

Now I do indeed believe that all this must be allowed and insisted on; but I am aware also, and I believe a great many people are becoming increasingly aware, of another side to the case. If something was gained at the Renaissance, *was not something lost also?* The sundering of the secular from the eternal resulted in a far fuller understanding of secular detail, but did it not tend also to rob life of its highest and austerest glory? Men learned how to paint and carve perfect likenesses, but something of the old exaltation—as seen in the Byzantine ivories and in the Gothic stained glass—had disappeared. The systems of philosophy showed a great expansion of factual detail, but something of their sublimity, their immense seriousness, was gone and could not, apparently, be recaptured. In gaining its freedom thought had lost its sense of direction. In gaining its self-reliance it had lost its unity. A rare Christian spirit like the Roman Catholic Professor Karl Adam of the University of Tübingen feels the loss keenly when he writes that:

'Almost overnight whole ranges of human civilisation arose, profaned and separated from the jurisdiction of Christ. They had lost their inner nobility, their relation to the Logos, and therewith their Christian soul, their supernatural life and their intimate unity of existence with and for each other. Inevitably these sub-Christian, even non-Christian, products of culture isolated themselves from each other, combated each other, became idolised as ends in themselves, and ended by tyrannising over mankind like a Moloch. We are nowadays in the middle of this phase of development. *Numeri sumus*: we human beings are henceforth

[1] H. Rashdall, *The Universities of Europe in the Middle Ages*, vol. i, p. 35.

but ciphers before those autocratic, self-complacent, soulless things which we call State, Political Economy, Industry, Science. By setting them free from the jurisdiction of Christ, by making into an absolute end what is merely the part of a whole, and useful only as a part, the western mind has itself become the slave of these new absolute entities.'[1]

If this tendency had gone no farther than it did in the *Quattrocento* itself, so much could not indeed be said. For in that age, as Professor Adam himself goes on to say, the process of secularization was still for the most part 'below the threshold of consciousness' and not yet 'clearly grasped and asserted with emphasis and insistence'.[2] Moreover, as we saw at the beginning of our study, it made its first appearances only in certain peripheral regions of thought where men were 'off their guard'. But the Renaissance led in time to the Romantic Movement. Humanism had its real fruitage in the *Aufklärung*. When we think of the new movement in art we must think not only of Giotto and Michelangelo and Donatello and Raphael, but also of Correggio, of Paolo Veronese, of Tiepolo, of Guido Reni, of the masters of Baroque, of Watteau and Boucher—and even, as T. E. Hulme reminds us, of Greuze! 'Just as humanism leads to Rousseau', he says, 'so Michael Angelo leads to Greuze.'[3] In the realm of literature the fair comparison would perhaps be of Dante with Goethe —literary giants of high medievalism and high romanticism respectively. Yet who can fail to be sensible of the loss involved in the transition from the one to the other? From a splendidly unified personality we pass to a divided one. From peace (found 'in His will') we pass to struggle and confusion.

[1] *Two Essays*, translated by E. Bullough (1930), p. 31.
[2] Ibid.   [3] *Speculations*, p. 62.

From a nobly objective vision we pass to a consciousness turned inward upon itself. And withal we pass from a classic economy and inevitability of diction to a rich and luxuriant verbosity. It may be felt that a fairer comparison would be with Wordsworth, who was perhaps as great as a Romantic poet could be, or even greater—being (as in a moment we may have occasion to notice) much more than a mere Romantic—and whose autobiographical *Prelude* is a vastly nobler thing than *Dichtung und Wahrheit*. But are we not still aware, in comparison with Dante, of what is essentially the same loss ?[1]

If then the modern movement of thought since the Renaissance stands for loss as well as for gain, the question is how we can recover the one without surrendering the other. I believe this can be done only by the frank recognition that the autonomy which we allow to the secular must be relative and not absolute. The devotion to the glories of earth must, within the most generous possible limits, be allowed to be a law unto itself, but in the last resort it must take its law from beyond itself. 'When thou wast young, thou girdedst thyself, and walkedst whither thou wouldest; but when thou shalt be old, thou shalt stretch forth thy hands, and another shall gird thee, and carry thee whither thou wouldest not.'[2] Literature and music and all the arts, the love of nature, science, and philosophy—these must be granted a radical independence of

[1] I do not here concern myself with the important respects in which Romanticism, in giving the primacy to feeling, was the enemy rather than the ally of the rationalistic *Aufklärung*. Romanticism had an other-worldliness of its own—but of an *immanental* and not (like the Christian view) a transcendent kind. But on any large view both movements alike (and alike Rousseau and Voltaire) represent the extreme development of a tendency of thought which had its birth in the Renaissance.

[2] John xxi. 18.

a certain kind within their own spheres, yet such independence cannot be regarded as the ultimate fact in the case. The true end of their being has not been attained when they have pushed to the limit their own departmental curiosity, but only when they have 'brought in their sheaves' to the harvest of a riper wisdom and a profounder love, so laying them at the feet of Christ. It is to such a result as this that much of the deeper thought of the last few years seems to me to have been leading us.

Look at the realm of art. It is not very long—the 'gay nineties' are only a generation behind us—since 'art for art's sake' was the latest cliché of the schools. But how banal it sounds now, how weak and empty! For art for art's sake is simply art that is turned inwards upon itself instead of outwards upon the real and eternal world; it is self-conscious art, subjective art; in a word, bad art. It is indeed as necessary as ever to protect the *relative* autonomy of the aesthetic quest, and to insist that the artist's effort shall not be made *too directly* ancillary to the unity of the spirit—that would be bad art of another kind; but it is becoming ever clearer to us that what we want in the end is not art for art's sake, which were mere meaningless decoration, but art for the sake of something not itself which it is humbly serving—or, as Aristotle would put it, 'imitating'. And, theory quite apart, it seems difficult to doubt that as a matter of fact the greatest works of art have been produced in the service of ends other than merely artistic. Indeed I should go farther and say that the greatest art of all has been produced within the framework of a definitely other-worldly outlook. It is as if the beauties of eternity had proved, even when judged by purely aesthetic standards, to be the greatest beauties of all. There is no other beauty like unto the beauty of holiness. Could Gothic architecture, could the *Divina Commedia*, could the prose of our Authorized Version conceivably have come into being for their own sakes or of their own momentum alone—as mere masterpieces of decorative loveliness? No, when we say 'art for art's sake' we think rather of—Swinburne! And about Swinburne I can only feel that he might have been a great poet, if he had ever found anything substantial to say; if, that is, the loveliness of his language had ever been made sincerely subservient to something other and greater than itself.

It would be easy to quote extensively from the more significant writing of the last decade in support of such a view as is here indicated, but I must content myself with a few haphazard references such as are ready to my hand. Mr. Lawrence Hyde writes in his excellent book on *The Prospects of Humanism*:

'The only safe attitude towards aesthetic pleasure is to regard it as something which offers itself by the way, as a delicious, but subordinate, element in the process of orientating oneself to external reality.'[1]

Of Mr. Yeats and Mr. Gordon Bottomley a reviewer in the *Times Literary Supplement*[2] recently said:

'Both of them have, in their best work, escaped the decorative dangers incident to any conscious use of beauty as an end, by

[1] p. 121. He says also: 'The truth is that only very few people are capable of developing their aesthetic sensibility without paying for the privilege by becoming blind to the more profound, but very much less vivid, delights which it is open to them to derive from their workaday experience' (p. 123). And again he writes that it is characteristic 'of the more highly educated person to-day, to attach an altogether excessive significance to the aesthetic element in experience' (p. 218).

[2] 17 Nov. 1932.

seeking to recover and express a spiritual consciousness which was once the inspiration equally of art, of heroic action, and of the life of the folk. It is thus that, although living "in the shadow of death" or of our modern clamorous discord, they have recalled us to those hushed but tense regions of life where imagination, and not fact, is sovereign, and the timeless invades and overrules the narrow world of time.'

And here are some sentences from the *Letters to a Doubter* of M. Paul Claudel, lately French ambassador to the United States:

'Art first!—art for art's sake! Are we really back there? After all these years of frivolous literature, is that foundered old hobby-horse still in our path? Art for art's sake is not a creative doctrine at all. Something else besides a genteel system of callisthenics is needed to draw anything profound or essential out of a man. The relation of art to religion is an excessively grave, delicate and complicated problem. A few smart sayings will not help to solve it.'

'Ask any artist to-day who does not believe in God—who does not work solely for the glory of God, *for whom does he work?* For himself? If so, he is in a vicious circle. Oneself is the means, but cannot be the end. For others, then? For their pleasure? For their amusement?'

'Do you believe for a moment that Shakespeare, or Dostoievsky, or Rubens, or Titian, or Wagner, did their work for art's sake? No! They did it to free themselves as best they might from their burden, to deliver themselves of a great incubus of living matter, *opus non factum*. And certainly not to colour a cold, artificial design by borrowings from reality.'[1]

What is true of the arts is true also of the sciences. The doctrine of science for science's sake has as important a relative justification as the doctrine of art for art's sake, yet if

[1] Eng. tr. (1927), pp. 235, 238, 239.

elevated to the standing of a final truth it becomes no less barren and unsatisfying. Our modern era has heard enough about 'pure theoretic curiosity', about *voraussetzungslose Wissenschaft,* about interest in facts without regard to their values, about positivistic historiography, and about *die Philosophie reiner Erfahrung,* to have grown very suspicious of the utility of such view-points to the actual furtherance of the scientific task. It is surely possible to investigate facts with a purpose, and to enlist the results of our investigation in the service of that purpose, without allowing our purpose to interfere with our perception of the facts actually revealed. There is no intellectual sin in hoping that a certain thing may be true, or in having an interest in proving it to be true; there is sin only when we 'cook' our proof to accommodate our interest or hope. All proper autonomy may thus be allowed to factual inquiries without going on to rob them of their vital interest and significance by severing their natural relation to the purpose of life as a whole. Only to the cloistered scholar, to the pundit buried in his papers, does it seem at all obvious that the mere knowledge of facts about the transient earthly order of things is worth possessing for its own sake. What, after all, does it matter how many species of two-winged flies have been hatched on the surface of our particular little planet during its present brief spell of temperate climate, or how many Greeks were engaged at the battle of Marathon, or in what year the earthquake shook Lisbon, if these facts bear no relation to anything more enduring than themselves? Aristotle did indeed teach that knowledge was an end in itself, and therein he too may have committed the philosopher's fallacy; but at least he did not, like so much modern positivism, teach that particular bits of knowledge were separately ends in themselves; but rather that the only End-in-Himself was that eternal and all-embracing 'Knowledge about Knowledge' which is God; so that Spinoza is but following up the master's meaning when he testifies that 'love turned toward an Object eternal and infinite feeds the mind with a joy that is pure with no tinge of sadness'.[1] No more of science than of art, then, can autonomy be quite the last word; it too must bring its final thoughts into captivity to the apprehension of eternal life and to the obedience of Christ our Light.

The suggestion which I am here making for the settlement of the relative claims of secular and religious interests is one for which I am myself mainly indebted to the writings of von Hügel, who (like M. Claudel in the passage quoted above) always felt this problem to be so delicate and complex that no *simple* solution of it could ever be likely to succeed. Again and again throughout his various volumes we find him insisting on the autonomy that must be allowed to the non-religious interests within their own boundaries, and arguing that the cultivation of this autonomy—and especially the recognition of what he describes as the grim impersonality and mechanistic determinism of the 'thing-world' of science—is not only important for its own sake but exercises a valuable astringent and purgative influence upon religious development; yet insisting no less urgently upon the ultimate inclusion of these interests within a total mental attitude for which God and eternity are alone supreme. In one of his published letters he writes:

'Yet though God and Christ are not simply things or forces

[1] *De intellectus emendatione*, opening paragraphs.

within and amongst *other*, simply and absolutely independent things or forces, yet we cannot, I am persuaded through and through, show our apprehension of the secret of His law of spiritual life for us all, or co-operate in building it up, better than in ever remembering, ever vividly realising, ever practising, ever suffering the (within our world of relatives) *true and real independence* which God has chosen to give Creation, by the very fact of creating it, and still more by incarnating Himself in its head and centre, man. Never, as truly as creation will never be absorbed in the Creator, nor man, even the God-man, become (or become again) simply and purely God, will or can science or art, morals and politics be without each their own inside, their own true law of growth and existence *other than, in no sense a department or simple dependency of,* religion.'

This recognition that the secular interests have each their own inside is, he goes on to say,

'immensely difficult to the natural man. For the very minute you have a deep and vivid religion, that very minute you have, almost irresistibly, the omnipresent conviction that either *religion is everything*, since it is admittedly the most important and most universal of all things; and doesn't the greater ever include the lesser; or, at all events, that, if the other departments require religion, religion does not require them. At most, it is felt that, since a man cannot be directly thinking about religion all day, he ought to have some non-technically religious occupation for a rest and hobby . . .'[1]

In another letter written eighteen years later von Hügel illustrates the difficulty of the spiritual disposition that is here demanded of us by quoting the report of a friend:

'That Dr. Pusey, at least at the stage of his life when my friend was under him . . . was incapable, or had made himself incapable,

[1] *Selected Letters, 1896–1924,* ed. B. Holland (1927), p. 93.

or deliberately acted as though he were incapable, of taking any interest in anything that was not directly, technically religious, or that was not explicitly connected with religion. And that this was quite uncatholic, quite unlike the greatest of the Catholic saints, quite unlike the Jesus of the Synoptists, with all of whom God is the God of Nature as of Grace—a God deeply interested —if this be not profane—also in not directly religious things— grace things. Two movements—of attachment and detachment, of particularity and of abstraction, of sense and of spirit, of time and of eternity, of place and of ubiquity, etc.: one thing in and with another thing: only these together yield the full blossom, the richest fruit and fascination of Catholicism.'[1]

It will be seen at once how far distant we are here from the notion that mathematics and astronomy are chiefly of use as enabling us to find the date of Easter; and yet how much insistence there is upon the necessity of an ultimate unity of the spiritual life! Such a unity must, of course, be a complex and difficult 'unity in multiplicity and multiplicity in unity'—in short, it must be the unity of *organism*. Von Hügel takes the Trinity of Persons in God and the duality of natures in Christ to be the transcendent expressions of this kind of togetherness. In one of his books he writes:

'Thus from a lichen or seaweed up to God Himself—the unspeakable Richness (because the incomprehensibly manifold Unity and complete Organization)—we find ever increasingly rich, organised societies. And the great social complexes of Society and the State, of Economics, Science, Art, are all similarly possessed of specific laws of organisation. They are strong and beneficent only as special wholes possessed of special parts, which wholes again have to grow and fructify in contact, contrast,

[1] Ibid., p. 254.

and conflict with other such complexes without, and the ever more or less disorderly elements within, themselves.'[1]

And his conclusion in his *magnum opus* is as follows:

'Over and beyond the specifically religious life—though this, where genuine, is ever the deepest, the central life—every soul lives, and has to live, various other lives. And indeed—and this is the point which specially concerns religion—the soul cannot attain to its fullest possible spiritual development, without the vigorous specific action and differentiation of forces and functions of a not directly religious character, which will have to energise, each according to its own intrinsic nature, within the ever ampler, and ever more closely-knit, organisation of the complete life of the soul.'[2]

III

It has been the better worth our while to set down at such length these deliverances of von Hügel because the insight which they embody can, with certain necessary modifications, be made to apply also to the adjustment of the second charge brought against Christian other-worldliness, and was always vigorously so applied by the Baron himself. We shall accordingly be able to say what is necessary under this head in much briefer compass.

The charge, it will be remembered, was one of 'quietism'. It was argued that the entertainment of the heavenly hope must always result in a culpable indifference to external evils during the term of our earthly sojourn, and so prevent the progressive removal of these evils from one generation to

---

[1] *Eternal Life*, pp. 369–70.
[2] *The Mystical Element of Religion* (2nd ed. 1923), p. 393. For the Barthian view of the relation of *Profanität* to *Heiligung* see Barth's *Die kirchliche Dogmatik*, erster Halbband (1932), pp. 47–9.

another. And that such a result had to a considerable extent actually manifested itself in the early and middle Christian ages we showed ourselves very ready to allow. It cannot really be denied that the presence of an ardent and lively apocalyptic expectation has again and again tended to dull men's interest in the possible improvement of their lot during the present life. Those who looked forward to an eternity of bliss might very naturally develop a stoical indifference to sufferings which were, by comparison, of hardly more than momentary duration. If the streets of the Heavenly City were to be of shining gold and its walls of precious stones, then what matter though the streets of the earthly city *were* some-what ill paved and the walls of the cottage tumbling about one's ears? Moreover, we found it dificult to avoid the con-clusion that the beginning of our modern zeal for the improve-ment of the earthly city—not only as to paving and housing, but also as to sanitation, health, food, wages, and the general pattern of society—synchronizes very closely with the first marked occultation of the heavenly vision. Here again the turning-point may be dated roughly about the fifteenth cen-tury, perhaps with the Conciliar Movement, though the beginning has sometimes been found a century earlier in such a writing as Marsiglio of Padua's *Defensor Pacis*.[1]

Yet we must be very careful not to misunderstand the significance of these facts. What we are saying is simply that the natural man has in the past found it difficult to keep the interests of time and eternity in proper balance one with the other, having usually tended either in affirming the import-

[1] For the whole matter see E. Troeltsch, *Die Soziallehren der christlichen Kirchen und Gruppen*, pp. 377–426 (Eng. tr., *The Social Teaching of the Christian Churches*, vol. i, pp. 343–82).

ance of eternity to mock at the things of time, or in reawaking to the importance of the latter to make light now of the former. This is not to say, however, that a balance of the two interests must always remain impossible, still less that it is not the ideal attitude of mind, representing the truth of the situation with which we are here actually presented by the structure of reality itself.

We had already, at the beginning of our study, advanced so far as to realize that in such a balance of the two attitudes of other-worldliness and hither-worldliness, of acquiescence and rebellion, lay the true and original genius of the Christian religion, in contrast with Stoicism and almost all pre-Christian systems on the one hand and with modern humanism and humanitarianism on the other. It is the excellence of this view that I am now concerned to commend. I know no better statement of it than in the phrase already quoted from von Hügel—'a sufficient other-worldliness without fanaticism, and a sufficient this-worldliness without philistinism'. The Baron writes further:

'This double sense is ... a deep help in all our trials. For thus we are pricked on to labour energetically at the improvement of man's earthly lot, in all its stages and directions; but we do so without philistinism, impatience, or fanaticism, since we are fully convinced (even before beginning) that these attempts, could they all succeed, would not, could not, ever satisfy man, when once he is fully awake.'[1]

The outlook which we are here asked to maintain is one which is continually awake to the fact that only in eternity can the true objects of our desire be accomplished, without in the least degree allowing this awareness to slacken our zeal for such

[1] *Eternal Life*, p. 367.

little approaches to these objects as may indeed in this life be possible of attainment. The good life is seen to be essentially a life of *tension* between the will to earthly progress and the foretasting by faith of the heavenly fruition. The problem, says our author in another of his volumes, is one which must be dealt with not by the statics of the intellect, but by the dynamics of the will:

'And this dynamic system is so rich, even in the amount of it which can claim the practice of the majority of souls, as to require definite alternations in the occupations of such souls, ranging thus, in more or less rhythmic succession, from earth to Heaven and from Heaven back again to earth.'[1]

Similarly, Barth likes to speak of *die Spannung des Glaubens*, 'the tension of faith'.[2]

It is clear, then, that what is here called for is anything but a rubbing down of the other-worldly and hither-worldly attitudes against one another, or a whittling down of both by means of such a third agent as impartial reflection, until they can be made to dovetail without effort. Rather must each of the two attitudes be allowed its full natural development and most unrestricted scope, and then something like an *alternation* be maintained between the two. It will obviously not do at all to say that our zeal for the improvement of terrestrial conditions is to be *limited* by the recollection that here we have no continuing city; nor again will it do to say that our longing for the heavenly Jerusalem is to be limited by the discovery that we can make things moderately comfortable for ourselves even here. The result, surely, must be all the

---

[1] *The Mystical Element of Religion*, vol. ii, p. 360.
[2] *Die Auferstehung der Toten* (1924), p. 125.

other way: our works intensifying our faith and our faith in its turn lending power to our works. It would indeed be idle to deny the great difficulty and (in von Hügel's word) 'costingness' involved in the maintenance of such an attitude—*der Gratweg des Christentums*,[1] as Barth calls it, the 'knife-like ridge' which alone is the way of Christian thought and life. But there is no reason to deny it. For who, after all, has informed us that reality is constructed on so simple a pattern that we can adjust ourselves to its demands without going into complexities? The indications are all to the contrary. Χαλεπὰ τὰ καλά.[2]

If a few pages back I seemed to be less than fair to Wordsworth in contrasting him with Dante, let me now make amends by setting out his verses addressed *To the Skylark*, in which the balance of Christian wisdom on this matter is perfectly preserved.

[1] *Die Auferstehung der Toten* (1924).

[2] Professor Tillich expresses what is essentially the same teaching by insisting on the necessity of both a *horizontal* and a *vertical* movement in all true religion. In *Die religiöse Verwirklichung* (1930) he writes on p. 209: 'No religious attitude possesses inward justification at the present time in which the religious principle does not work itself out as it were horizontally, in a line that leads forwards, or in which the making of a better world is not an element of determinative significance. Christian piety, especially in its Lutheran form, has neglected the forward-looking line in favour of the line that leads upwards. It has rightly insisted that from every point of space and time there is a line that leads directly upwards; but it has failed to see that the upward-leading line without the forward-leading one (i.e. without the active will to remake) issues in self-contained piety which puts the individual's quest of salvation in place of a direct relation of God to the world. The proletarian is entirely justified in withdrawing himself from such an attitude and in denying the ultimate sincerity of an upward-looking tendency from which a forward-looking tendency is absent. . . . On the other hand, the socialists must be reminded of the complementary truth that the forward-leading line without the upward-leading one can end only in disillusion.'

Ethereal minstrel! pilgrim of the sky!
Dost thou despise the earth, where cares abound?
Or while the wings aspire, are heart and eye
Both with thy nest upon the dewy ground?
Thy nest which thou canst drop into at will,
Those quivering wings composed, that music still!

To the last point of vision, and beyond,
Mount, daring warbler!—that love-prompted strain
—'Twixt thee and thine a never-failing bond—
Thrills not the less the bosom of the plain:
Yet might'st thou seem, proud privilege! to sing
All independent of the leafy Spring.

Leave to the nightingale her shady wood;
A privacy of glorious light is thine,
Whence thou dost pour upon the world a flood
Of harmony, with instinct more divine;
Type of the wise, who soar, but never roam—
True to the kindred points of Heaven and Home.

IV

But here, in this very necessity of being true to the kindred points of Heaven and Home, there is suggested a third problem which has more than once come into sight during the course of our discussion and to which some final attention must now be given. It is the problem of the relation of the love of our fellows to the love of God.

To love one's neighbour as oneself and to love God with all one's heart, these have always been regarded as the twin commandments of the Christian way of life. But are they to be thought of as two separate commandments, each of which is valid in its own right, independently of the other? Are we to love men for their own sakes? Or is it only for God's sake that we are to love them?

It will be seen at once that this is but one aspect of the general problem with which we are confronted by the development of humanist thought since the Renaissance. Human love and friendship and the other pleasures of social intercourse are among the chief of those delights of our earthly sojourn for which the modern spirit has shown itself anxious to claim an autonomous position. Our forefathers wrote hymns in praise of God, but the humanists have often preferred to write them in praise of man. Perhaps the true humanist position has never been more ably represented than by J. M. E. McTaggart with his insistence that human personality existed and was immortal *in its own right* and his argument that this could only be if God does not exist *at all*. He could not see how there could be two absolutes, and as for himself his absolute was man. Man was for him eternal in the full sense which Christianity has attributed only to God; not only will man's life have no end but it has had no beginning; he has pre-existence as well as immortality. In one of his letters already referred to, we find McTaggart writing:

'But it can't be nice to believe in God, I should think. It would be horrible to think that there was any one who was closer to one than one's friends. I want to feel, and I do feel, that my love for them and the same love that other people have for their friends is the only real thing in the world. . . . I should say, as the Mahometan girl did in Kipling's story, "I bear witness that there is no God save thee, my beloved."' [1]

The position directly opposite to McTaggart's was defended

[1] *J. M. E. McTaggart*, by G. Lowes Dickinson, p. 87.

with equal ability by his contemporary and fellow-idealist, Bernard Bosanquet, whose view it was that the only being who exists in his own right, or is indeed real at all, or can possibly be thought to be immortal, is the One Absolute Being—who may be taken to correspond to what religion means by God. This latter, as we saw, is a view that has long been domesticated in India.

Now it seems clear that the true Christian position lies *between* these opposites of humanism and Brahminism and is perhaps *equidistant* from each. And yet we cannot settle the matter by the simple device of adopting two independent absolutes and saying that *both* man *and* God exist and have value and are immortal, each in its own independent right. We cannot say that I must love God for His own sake alone but must also, as another and separate exercise of my love, love men for their own sake alone. The two commandments cannot represent two different spheres of duty in that way. Religion and morality are not adjacent departments of the spirit's life, each with a final autonomy of its own; rather is it true that morality simply is the side of religion that concerns itself with duties to be done. God, certainly, must in every possible sense be an End-in-Himself. And we are constrained to follow Kant in believing each individual human person to be an end-in-himself. In arguing for this latter position and for the implied 'autonomy of the moral will' Kant was, it is true, a child of the Renaissance; but this is precisely the aspect of humanistic thought on which we feel that we can never again turn our backs—which indeed now seems to us to be drawing out the true genius of the Christian religion rather than doing anything to hinder or obstruct it. Yet it will not

do at all to conclude that because not only God but also my
fellow men are ends-in-themselves and immortal, they must
therefore be these things separately, each in its own separate
right, so that I have separate duties towards each. The fallacy
of such a way of thinking lies, as was said at an earlier point,
in its anthropomorphism, in its assumption that God and my
fellows are realities of the same order and on the same plane
—as if God were merely *somebody else*, just as my brother or
my friend is somebody else.

The truth seems actually to be far more complex and
mysterious than anything contemplated by so facile a scheme.
For in truth the relation between God and the soul seems
rather to be such that when He most controls my will, then
am I most free; that when the law I obey is His law, then am
I most autonomous; and that when I love my fellow men for
God's sake, then and then only do I begin to love them for
the sake of the deepest thing in themselves; that heteronomy
in which God is the Έτερος being itself the highest of all
autonomies—as in George Matheson's well-loved hymn:

> Make me a captive, Lord,
> And then I shall be free . . .

> My will is not my own
> Till thou hast made it thine . . .

Humanism elevates the human individual to the status of
creator, while Brahminism denies him intrinsic value or reality
of any kind at all. Christianity, in occupying an intermediate
position, demands a more complicated scheme which, while
attributing true being and immortality to the souls of men no
less than to God, insists at the same time that the being and

immortality of the latter is a *derived* being and immortality—the being and immortality of a creature rather than of a creator.

In a notable recent discussion of the subject Professor Lyman writes:

'Real love for one's neighbour means loving him for his own sake and not simply for the sake of God—as a matter of religious duty. Any other view is incompatible with Jesus' idea of God, who on his part loves men for their own sakes. Likewise real love for God is something more than the sum of one's love for men; it is also the devout response of one's being to a Being of Infinite Wisdom and Love. Neither love for God nor love for man, then, is merely a derivative from its counterpart; yet each nourishes the other. When we love our fellow-man for his own sake the life of God flows through us, and when we are responsive to the God of Infinite Wisdom and Love we are better able to discover and foster the moral and spiritual capacities of our fellow-men.'[1]

To such a statement we can, I think, give our almost whole-hearted consent. Such insistence upon the mutual involvement of the two great commandments is indeed what we most stand in need of. My own only hesitation would be as to whether God and man are not here too much treated as realities on the same plane—realities which might therefore enter as it were into *competition* with one another for the allegiance of my heart. The truth seems to be not merely that love towards God and love towards man 'nourish' each other, but that they are not properly separate loves at all. It is not as if my duties towards God were a different set of duties from my duties towards my brother. The command to love my brother is God's command. 'If a man say, I love God, and

[1] *The Meaning and Truth of Religion* (1933), p. 214.

hateth his brother, he is a liar.'[1] My relation to God and to my brother are not then so parallel to one another as appears from the symmetry of Professor Lyman's statement that 'neither is derivative from the other'. At bottom, the question is perhaps one of making more of our human creatureliness and less of our new-discovered 'creativity'.[2] But I should insist again that to love my brother for God's sake is the same thing as to love him for his own deepest sake; because the deepest thing in him is not his either by inherent right or by conquest, but only by the gift of God. It is only in the possibility which is open to it of personal intercourse with God that the value of the individual human personality can be held to reside—even as it is upon this possibility alone that its claim to immortality rests. 'Thy love for thy friend', we read in the *Imitation*, 'should be grounded in Me, and for My sake shouldst thou love whosoever seemeth to thee good and is very dear to thee in this life. Without Me friendship can neither thrive nor endure; neither is that love true and pure which is not knit by Me.'[3] Or, as it has been finely said by Karl Adam: 'True love can be found only where the absolute, the divine, is somehow co-involved; in other words, true love is at the same time love of God.'[4]

[1] 1 John iv. 20. What Dr. Lyman objects to is not, I think, loving one's neighbour as a matter of religion, but loving him as a matter of *duty*. His equation of loving one's neighbour for God's sake with loving him 'as a matter of religious *duty*' seems therefore to be unfair and to obscure the real issue. What religion does, as over against mere morality, is precisely to give us relief from this point of view of duty and to lead us into the realm of spontaneity and vision.

[2] But perhaps Karl Barth goes too far in saying that 'the discovery of the free creative individual, as it has been manifesting itself in every sphere of thought since the middle of the sixteenth century, was in itself undoubtedly nothing more than a piece of paganism coming to life again'.—*Die kirchliche Dogmatik*, erster Halbband (1932), p. 75.

[3] *De Imitatione Christi*, iii. 42.   [4] Op. cit., p. 71.

Adam would not for a moment allow Professor Lyman's appeal to the teaching of Jesus in support of the view that we are to love men for their own sakes. Yet however salutary his reminder may be, he seems himself to err in the opposite direction when he writes that 'Jesus was no philanthropist with an enthusiasm for the cult of the merely human. He was too profound and too whole to feel any enthusiasm for man. He perceived too clearly beneath the varnish of the purely human the all-too-human sides of him. If we look closer, we might even detect in His attitude to man something like a restrained disgust.'[1] That, surely, is not the impression we receive! But Adam's positive doctrine seems admirably true and wise:

'The human value is not the ultimate, but only the penultimate value; the last, the highest value is God the Father. He alone is the cause and the measure of all things, cause and measure of all valuations, cause and measure of all love. . . . My relation to men has therefore its roots in a transcendental fact, namely, in that fundamental relation of love in which God includes men, all men. . . . I shall never reach man by starting from the earth, I must first reach to heaven to find man through God. . . .

'It may be that one or other, who loves truly, knows nothing of this absolute, of this love in God; he may even be short-sighted enough to imagine that he acts reasonably, when he loves selflessly, without consciously believing in God, as the absolute value. But if his love is true love " in deed and in truth", as St. John expresses it, then his experience of love contains implicitly, at least, whether he knows it or not, the positing of God. . . . The lover can reach his beloved only through God. God alone can carry him over that dead point which lies between the *ego* and the *alter* and cannot be transcended by mere logic.'[2]

[1] Ibid., p. 60.   [2] Ibid., pp. 61 f., 65 f.

It will, I think, be felt that it is to a conclusion of this kind that our whole study has gradually been leading us.

What we have to do is to hold fast to the sole absoluteness of God, without, like the Hindu, thereby ceasing to believe in the immortal personality of man; and to hold fast to man's immortal personality, without, like the humanist, thereby elevating him to the rank of independent divinity. Such is the difficult balance which the Christian view has in all ages striven to maintain.

V

If then all these things be true, it is clear that we who are Christians can never think to find ourselves quite fully and comfortably at home in this present life, but that our deepest mood must always be that of those ancients spoken of in the eleventh chapter of Hebrews who, being persuaded of the promises and having embraced them, 'confessed that they were strangers and pilgrims on the earth'—*peregrini et hospites super terram*, as the Vulgate grandly has it. And we can also apply to ourselves the words that follow: 'For they that say such things declare plainly that they seek a country'—'a better country, that is, an heavenly'.[1] Our dissatisfaction with the life of earth is of too fundamental a kind to permit of its being removed by any number of minor readjustments. It is not really the shortness of life that saddens and offends us, it is its temporality—not that it ends so soon, but that it ends at all; and still more deeply the fact that, even while it lasts, it is made up of nothing but endings, of meetings and partings, of memories and longings, and of 'one thing after another'. How our poets have insisted on this fact!

[1] vv. 13–16.

To-morrow, and to-morrow, and to-morrow,
Creeps in this petty pace from day to day,
To the last syllable of recorded time.[1]

> We look before and after,
> And pine for what is not.[2]

> There is not any hour complete
> Nor any season satisfied![3]

And it has been finely insisted on also by such a philosopher as Professor Whitehead: 'The ultimate evil in the temporal world is deeper than any specific evil. It lies in the fact that the past fades, that time is a perpetual perishing.'[4] In such a situation there can be no ultimate basis for optimism, or for joy, or for any lightness of heart, save in the transcendent hope of an utterly transfigured life beyond the veil. We have indeed, in the course of our study, found ample reason to warn ourselves against such an intemperate over-indulgence in this mood of expectation as would leave no place for a properly discriminating apprehension and treatment of present actualities, and we have been led to realize something of the immensely delicate balancing of spiritual potencies that must be brought into play for the successful avoidance of this danger. But the opposite danger of *resting* in the present temporal order of things is of at least equal gravity; and this, and not the other, is the danger to which we are nowadays so prone to succumb. Therefore, while taking every possible delight in the lovely things of earth and immersing ourselves deeply in its manifold interests and allurements, while giving up our hearts without let or stint to earthly loves and attach-

---

[1] *Macbeth*, Act v, Sc. 5.   [2] Shelley's *Skylark*.
[3] Gerald Gould, 'The Search'.   [4] *Process and Reality*, p. 482.

ments, and while using every power we possess in the loyal service of our earthly citizenship, let us yet keep it ever in mind that we are 'men of the road', *viatores, peregrini*, who have here no continuing city. We remarked at the outset how this qualified and sombre view of our earthly existence was largely out of fashion in our time, and how it was regarded by many as a morbid inheritance from the perverse and peevish past of our human race—an inheritance of which at last we are about to rid ourselves for evermore. But as our inquiry has proceeded, we have found much reason to doubt the wisdom of such a view of the matter, and have come to regard this contemporary mood of ours as an extreme and somewhat belated manifestation of a reactionary tendency whose presence can be traced in European thought since the Renaissance; so that there is no particular reason why we should regard it in too solemn and serious a light.

Perhaps it will be permissible in our search for some final expression of a satisfying view to appeal once again to the poets. There is first that much-admired lyric, *The Pulley*, in which George Herbert describes how 'when God at first made man', He poured on him all the blessings He could: strength, beauty, wisdom, honour, and pleasure, but then made a stay and withheld one last blessing—the blessing of rest.

> For if I should (said He)
> Bestow this jewel also on my creature,
> He would adore my gifts instead of Me,
> And rest in Nature, not the God of Nature,
> So both should losers be.

Yet let him keep the rest,
But keep them with repining restlessness;
Let him be rich and weary, that at least,
If goodness lead him not, then weariness
May toss him to my breast.

Or we may do worse than go once more to Wordsworth—
to the lines he wrote at Milton's Vallombrosa:

For he, and he only, with wisdom is blest
Who, gathering true pleasures wherever they grow,
Looks up in all places, for joy and for rest,
To the Fountain whence Time and Eternity flow.

But perhaps it is to some verses of an even more homespun
beauty that the minds of some of us will most readily turn
—to the familiar hymn in which Adelaide Ann Procter,
having thanked God for this bright and beautiful world so
full of splendour and of joy, thanks Him also that 'all our joy
is touched with pain',

So that earth's bliss may be our guide
And not our chain.

And then goes on:

For Thou, who knowest, Lord, how soon
Our weak heart clings,
Hast given us joys, tender and true,
Yet all with wings,
So that we see, gleaming on high,
Diviner things.

And proceeds to a conclusion almost identical with Herbert's:

I thank Thee, Lord, that here our souls,
Though amply blest,
Can never find, although they seek,
A perfect rest . . .

Joys tender and true, yet all with wings, so that earth's bliss may be our guide and not our chain—no words could more accurately express the Christian view of the life that now is.

A concluding remark may, however, be looked for about the Christian attitude to death. Here again Christianity seems to occupy a difficult intermediate position. On the one hand it refuses to take death lightly. Shakespeare's 'There's nothing serious in mortality' has much more taste of sixteenth-century humanism in it than of Christian contrition. Rather would the Christian say with St. Paul, 'The last enemy that shall be destroyed is death.' There is deep sincerity in this refusal to be lured by the beguilements of a cheap and easy optimism such as has lately been so common in our Western lands. For what indeed could be shallower than to face the partings and bereavements of which every life is full, and the dissolution and corruption in which every life must end, with mere *cheeriness* of this kind? Unless it be to refuse to look these realities in the face at all, as was lately suggested by an eminent American literary critic who included in his published creed the article, 'Never allow oneself even a passing thought of death'. No, there has been in the Christian religion all through its history as deep a tragic sense as has ever appeared in the world. It has always given death a vitally important place in its scheme, refusing to regard it as a thing of secondary consequence, whether as a natural ending or as a mere milestone on a longer journey—or 'a door to another room'. Rather has it insisted on death as a most solemn crisis and extremity, a threshold of eternal judgement, on the brink of which we are all at every moment standing.

It is not for nothing that the striking theological move-ment which has now appeared among us in express reaction against our prevalent shallow optimisms has called itself 'the Theology of Crisis', and in a journal bearing the title of *Zwischen den Zeiten* ('Between the Ages') continues to commend to us the faith and practice of 'living on the brink'.

And yet it is not by this note of crisis and tragedy that the Christian spirit has ever allowed itself to be finally dominated but by the note, precisely, of joy and good cheer. To it the ultimate fact is not death but life, not the Cross but the Resurrection and the Crown. It is what it is only because it is persuaded that the sting of death has been drawn and the grave robbed of its victory; so that death has no more dominion over us. It is frankly recognized that in its own self-enclosed and untransfigured nature, as it must present itself to those who do not share any such persuasion, death must be a ghastly and terrible thing; and indeed it is thus that death always *has* presented itself to sincere and profound unbelief. To see one's beloved stamped into the sod for his body to rot and the worms to eat him . . . and then to be of good cheer! No, there can be no good cheer unless it be true that that to which this dreadful thing has happened is not really one's beloved *himself* but only his earthly tabernacle: unless it be true that 'the world passeth away, and the lust thereof: but he that doeth the will of God abideth for ever'.[1] Whereas, therefore, it would be nothing but shallowness of spirit for one who had no hope beyond the grave to cease to be obsessed by the fact of death (whether by facing it cheer-

[1] 1 John ii. 17.

fully or by refusing to make it the object of his too constant thought), such a result in the soul of a Christian must rather be the mark of a great depth and maturity. At the beginning of our study I quoted Spinoza's saying, spoken in defiance of Plato, that 'The free man thinks of nothing less than of death; his wisdom is a meditation not upon death but upon life.' Let me now say that of the man who stands fast in the liberty wherewith Christ has made him free this may well be true—truer than Plato's 'studying nothing but dying and being dead'; since he can now cry with St. Paul, 'For the law of the Spirit of life in Christ Jesus hath made me free from the law of sin and death.'[1]

During the course of our inquiry four, and only four, genuinely sincere and robust alternatives have emerged to claim our attention. Of these four, two are not really 'live options' for ourselves to-day, namely, tribalism with its purely corporate ethic and immortality, and Brahminism with its still more thoroughgoing denial of the claims of individuality and its contented reabsorption of all finite spirits into the one general fund of spiritual life. We are accordingly faced with the choice between the two remaining alternatives—on the one hand a radical and consequent pessimism and on the other hand the hope of everlasting life with God. The former is represented at its noblest in the writings of such a one as Thomas Hardy, who could find, as he put it in one of his letters, no support for his spirit save in the hope that 'there may gradually be developed an Idealism of Fancy; that is, an idealism in which fancy . . . is frankly and honestly accepted as an imaginative solace in the lack of any substantial solace

[1] Rom. viii. 2.

to be found in life'.[1] Such an outlook deserves to be honoured with our most deep and sympathetic and even affectionate understanding. It is a dark night of the soul at which none of us can afford to sneer; remembering that if we ourselves have indeed passed out of it into the marvellous brightness of the Christian expectation, the praise is not to us but to the grace of God in our Lord Jesus Christ, to whom be all praise and glory and merit throughout all ages world without end.

[1] *The Later Years of Thomas Hardy*, by Florence Emily Hardy, p. 90. Compare the fine passage on pp. 40–2 of Lowes Dickinson's *Religion and Immortality*, with its conclusion that 'Western optimism, in my judgment, is doomed, unless we believe that there is more significance in individual lives than appears upon the surface; that there is a destiny reserved for them more august than any to which they can attain in their life of threescore years and ten.'

INDEX

Absolute Idealism, 184–9.

Acquiescence, philosophy of, 30–46, 268–72.

Acts of the Apostles, the, 132, 139, 153 n., 155.

Adam, Karl, 258 f., 278 f.

Addison, J. T., 65 n., 67, 68, 116 n., 118 n.

Agnostic element in Christianity, 198–202, 240.

Alexander the Great, 131.

Ancestor-worship, 64–5, 71, 73–4, 97, 118, 135.

Animism, 67–9, 76–7, 80–3, 85–100 *passim*, 118, 119, 126.

Anthropomorphism, 235, 237, 276.

Apocalyptic literature, Jewish, 119, 123–33, 176, 200–4, 239, 247–8, 252.

Aquinas, St. Thomas, 253 n.

Argument, *vide* Proofs.

Aristophanes, 84.

Aristotle, 52, 92, 113, 181, 212, 229 f., 232 f., 237, 261, 264.

Art, 11 f., 24–7, 257–67.

Ascension of Christ, 154.

Athanasius, 61.

Augustine, St., 160, 213, 214, 223 f., 242–4.

Aufklärung, 13, 256, 259, 260 n.

Autonomy of the secular, 24–7, 257–80.

Babylon, 129.

Bacon, Francis, 95 f.

Baedeker, Karl, 12.

Baroque art, 259.

Barth, Karl, 146, 200, 215, 225, 268 n., 271, 272, 278 n., 285.

Bax, Ernest Belfort, 36.

Becker, C. L., 14 n., 178.

Bergson, Henri, 32, 67, 89 f., 94 n., 216.

Bernard of Morlaix, 201 f.

Bevan, Edwyn, 43 f., 127 n., 176, 242.

Bixler, J. S., 166 n., 173.

Blake, William, *quoted*, 30, 185.

Body, the, 17–23, 39, 40, 86–94, 103–10, 114, 117; and *vide* Resurrection.

Boethius, 212–14.

Boissier, G., 72 n.

Bosanquet, Bernard, 184, 186, 188, 275.

Bottomley, Gordon, 262.

Boucher, F., 259.

Bradley, F. H., 50, 184, 189, 221.

Brahe, Tycho, 257.

Brahminism, 114–18, 188, 190, 275, 276, 280, 286.

Browning, Robert, *quoted*, 163, 194.

Buddhism, 115, 117, 190.

Bunyan, 4, 221.

Burkitt, F. C., 45 f.

Burnet, John, 20 n., 84 f., 101, 111.

Butler, Joseph, 55.

Byzantine art, 11 f., 258.

Cairns, D. S., 43, 144 f.

Cantor, Georg, 236.

Carlyle, Thomas, 230.

Chamberlin, W. H., 36 n.

Chapman, Maristan, 18.

Charles, R. H., 74, 77, 119, 123, 127 n., 132, 136 n., 176.

Charvakas, 115.

Chesterton, G. K., 51.

Christianity, *passim; vide* Table of Contents.

Cicero, 71, 101.

Claudel, Paul, 263, 265.

Clement, First Epistle of, 31.

Coffin, H. S., 147.

Coleridge, S. T., 86 n.

Columbus, Christopher, 257.

Comte, Auguste, 166.

Conciliar movement, the, 269.

Conditional immortality, 105, 238 f., 244 f.

INDEX

Copernicus, 257.

Cornford, F. M., 222.

Corporate immortality, 123, 137, 169–180, 190, 286.

Correggio, 259.

Creation, doctrine of, 185 f., 277 f.

Crisis, theology of, *vide* Barth, Karl.

Daniel, the Book of, 125–7.

Dante, 4, 137, 200, 213, 245 n., 259 f., 262, 272.

Darwin, Charles, 26.

Death, attitude towards, 6–13, 16–22, 52–4, 58–61, 284–7; life after, *vide* Table of Contents.

Dedekind, J. W. R., 236.

Deists and Deism, 12–14, 33.

Democritus, 90.

Denney, James, 147 f., 150.

Diaz de Novaes, B., 257.

Dickinson, G. Lowes, 95 n., 274 n., 287 n.

Diderot, 178.

Dionysiac mysteries, 105, 108–10, 114, 119, 205, 208, 222.

Divina Commedia, 4, 137, 200, 213, 245 n., 262.

Donatello, 259.

Donne, John, 204.

Douglas, Norman, 28.

Einstein, Albert, 26.

Eleusinian mysteries, 103–5.

Elijah, 79, 126.

Eliot, George, *quoted*, 166.

Eliot, T. S., 16.

Elysian Fields, 69 f., 78, 103 f., 126.

Endocrinology, 88.

Engels, Friedrich, 35.

Enlightenment, the, *vide Aufklärung*.

Enoch, 79, 126.

Enoch, the Book of, 126, 136, 243.

Epicureanism, 113.

Erebus, *vide* Hades.

Eternal Life, *vide* Table of Contents.

Eternity, 63, 81, 85, 95, 204–28, 251 f.

Eucken, R., 155 n.

Euripides, 111.

Evil, doctrine of eternal, 240–4.

Evolution, 87, 90 f., 235–6.

Exile, the, 129–31.

Ezekiel, 154.

Faith, the nature of, 139–55, 161–2, 198–9.

Fall, doctrine of the, 108 f.

Family, continuance of the, 170–1.

Farquhar, J. N., 181.

Fowler, W. Warde, 102.

Frazer, Sir J. G., 63–6, 73, 76–7.

Free-thinkers and free thought, *vide* Deists and Deism.

French Revolution, 13, 33 f., 37.

Fruition, 98, 134, Ch. VII *passim*.

Fuller, Thomas, 13.

Galileo, 257.

Gama, Vasco da, 257.

Garden of Epicurus, 113.

Gautama Buddha, 117, 190.

Gehenna, 239, 242 f.

Genesis, 122, 154, 175.

Ghiberti, Lorenzo, 25.

Ghostly survival, Ch. IV and *passim*.

Gibbon, Edward, 25, 113.

Gilbert Islanders, 65.

Giotto, 11 f., 259.

Gnosticism, 199.

God, *passim*.

Goethe, *quoted*, 214; *discussed*, 259 f.

Goguel, Maurice, 143 n., 146 f.

Gospel according to St. Matthew, 135 n., 188.

Gospel according to St. Mark, 132 n., 133, 135, 137, 138, 155.

Gospel according to St. Luke, 135 n., 142, 148, 165.

Gospel according to St. John, 134, 149, 207, 209, 260 n.

Gould, Gerald, 281.

Gourmont, Remy de, 64, 66–7.

Gray, Thomas, 49.

Greek religion and philosophy, 19–21, 34, 36, 38, 41–4, 58, 68–74, 76–9,

86, 90–94, 100, 118, 119, 126, 131–2, 160, 163, 169, 180–3, 185, 205–6, 208, 238–41, 252.

Greuze, J. B., 259.

Hades, abode of, 69–75, 103–5, 110, 126, 159, 240.
Hadfield, J. A., 90 n..
Hadrian, 72 f.
Hardy, Thomas, 191, 286 f.
Harnack, Adolf von, 40.
Hartmann, E. von, 218.
Heaven, *passim*.
Hebrew religion, 44 f., 58, 68 f., 73–9, 92, 100, 109, 113, 118, 124–32, 138, 160, 163, 169, 175–6, 180, 185, 205, 238–9, 241, 247–8, 252 f.
Hebrews, the Epistle to the, 141, 176, 280.
Hegel, 184.
Hell, 15, 95, 98, 239–44.
Herbert, George, 282, 283.
Herbert of Cherbury, Lord,. 14.
Heroes, the, 104.
Herrmann, W., 146.
Hesiod, 69, 103.
Hinduism, *vide* Brahminism.
History, philosophy of, 43–5, 236, 246–51.
Hither-worldliness, Chs. I, II, and VIII.
Homer, 19, 69–71, 83, 103.
Hook, S., 35 n.
Hopi Indians, 68.
Hügel, Friedrich von, 45, 213, 222, 227, 251, 265–8, 270–2.
Hulme, T. E., 5, 11, 179, 195 f., 215, 259.
Humanism, 10–16, 24–7, 120, 159, 177, 191, Ch. VIII *passim*.
Hume, David, 58 f.
Huxley, T. H., 191.
Hyde, Lawrence, 262.

Ibsen, 26.
Imitatio Christi, 4, 26, 39, 45, 97, 278.
Immortality, *vide* Table of Contents; meaning and usage of the word, 77–82, 84.

Indian religions, 42, 100 f., 113–18, 180–2, 185, 188, 190, 205, 275, 276, 280, 286.
Influence, immortality of, 166–80.
Inge, W. R., 225, 226.
Isaiah, the Book of the Prophet, 74, 75, 125, 155.
Islands of the Blest, 69 f., 103 f.
Israel, religion of, *vide* Hebrew religion.

Jacks, L. P., 169 n.
Jackson, F. J. Foakes-, 190 n.
Jainism, 115, 117.
James, William, 216.
Jesus Christ, *passim*; *vide* Resurrection of Christ; *vide* also Table of Contents.
Job, the Book of, 74, 124.
John, the First Epistle General of, 38 f., 60, 209, 255, 278, 285.
Joseph, H. W. B., 90 n.
Josephus, Flavius, 128, 136.
Judaism, *vide* Hebrew religion, Apocalyptic literature, &c.
Judgement, The Last, 129.

Kant, 155, 169, 187, 230, 275.
Karma, 114–16, 121, 181.
Keats, 25, 26.
Kempis, Thomas à, 4, 26, 39, 45, 97, 278.
Kennedy, H. A. A., 21 n.
Kepler, 257.
Kingdom of God, 124–36 *passim*, 208 f.
Kierkegaard, 215.
Krutch, J. W., 177, 191.

Lamb, Charles, 13 n.
Last Day, doctrine of the, 249 f.
Lateran Council, the Fifth, 140 n.
Leckie, J. H., 201, 240 n., 242, 243 n.
Lenin, 35, 37.
Leucippus, 90.
Levirate marriage, 135.

Lewis, Day, 41.
Love, nature of, 53–61, 163 f., 273–9.
Lowrie, W., 200 n.
Lyceum, the, 113.
Lyman, E. W., 277–9.

Macdonnell, A. A., 118 n.
Mackintosh, H. R., 240.
Maeterlinck, Maurice, 166.
Manichaeism, 244.
Marcus Aurelius, 113.
Marett, R. R., 77.
Marillier, Léon, 64.
Marsiglio of Padua, 269.
Marx, Karl, 34–7.
Masefield, John, 177.
Matheson, George, 276.
McDougall, William, 83.
McGiffert, A. C., 152, 239 n.
McTaggart, J. M. E., 95, 120, 274.
Meredith, George, 166.
Messiah, 133.
Metempsychosis, vide Transmigration of souls.
Meynell, Alice, 33.
Michelangelo Buonarotti, 25, 257, 259.
Millennium, the, 127, 175 f.
Milton, 4, 283.
Miracles, 144 f.
Moffatt, James, 74 n., 125 n., 141 n.
Monica, 223.
Montague, W. P., 162, 194.
Montefiore, Claude, 131, 136 n., 142 f., 151.
Morgan, William, 239 n.
Mozart, 217 f.
Myers, F. W. H., 97.
Mystery cults in Greece, vide Eleusinian mysteries, Dionysiac mysteries, Orphism.
Mysticism, 111, 116.
Myth, 200–4, 240.

Neoplatonists, the, 19, 113.
New Guinea, native tribes of, 66.
Nietzsche, F., 56.
Nirvana, 117, 118, 121.

Oman, John, 184, 186, 226.
Omar Khayyam, 38.
Omnipotence of God, 163 f.
Origen, 239.
Orphism, 19–21, 107–16, 132, 239 f.
Other-worldliness, passim; vide Table of Contents.

Padua, Chapel of the Arena at, 11 f.
Palaeolithic man, eschatology of, 62, 82.
Paradise Lost, 4.
Parry, J. D. C., 129 n.
Paul, St., 19–23, 30, 38 f., 59, 101, 133, 139–41, 148–55, 208, 220 f., 223, 239 n., 252–4, 284, 286.
Pauline Epistles:
  Romans, 22, 59, 60, 139, 141, 207–8, 220–1, 236, 286.
  1 Corinthians, 19, 21, 31, 139, 149, 151, 154, 253, 254.
  2 Corinthians, 20–2, 139, 153, 198, 238, 254.
  Philippians, 22.
  Colossians, 59, 208, 209.
  1 Thessalonians, 38.
Persian religion, 44 f., 100 f., 129–32, 247.
Personality, 165–95, 274–80.
Pharisees, 101, 128, 131, 132, 134, 136, 139, 140, 148, 151.
Phidias, 90.
Philosophes, les, 13.
Pilgrim's Progress, The, 4.
Pindar, 69, 78.
Plato, 13, 38, 41 f., 79–87, 90–4, 101–2, 111–14, 131, 139, 170 n., 192, 200–1, 204, 206, 211–12, 214, 229, 239–41, 286.
Plotinus, 19.
Porphyry, 19.
Porter, F. C., 150 n., 152 n.
Poverty, 30, 33, 40–2.
Pre-existence, 274.
Presland, John, 52.
Primitive peoples, eschatology of, 62–8, 73 f., 96.

INDEX

Pringle-Pattison, A. S., 68 f., 184, 190 n., 210 f., 213, 216, 218 n.

Procter, A. A., 283.

Progress, idea of and zeal for, 27–45, 229–37.

Proofs of immortality, 77–99, 105 f., 111, 137, Ch. VI passim.

Proofs of the existence of God, 79 f., 157 f., 203.

Prophetic movement in Israel, 119–25, 136, 160.

Psalms, the Book of, 75, 124, 160.

Psychical Research, 96–9, 120.

Psycho-physical relationship, 86–94, 103, 254.

Punishment, eternal, 239–45.

Purgatory, 239, 249.

Puritanism, 24–7, 256–68.

Pusey, E. B., 266.

Pythagoras, 108 f.

Queensland, native tribes of, 66 f.

Quietism, 24, 30–46, 256, 268–72.

Rabbinic books, 127, 131, 136.

Raphael Sanzio, 25, 259.

Rashdall, H., 32, 225, 258.

Reabsorption, 173, 180–90, 286.

Reincarnation, vide Transmigration of souls.

Religion, general nature of, 157, 159–63.

Renaissance, 9–12, 24–7, 32 f., 43, 256–60, 274 f., 282.

Reni, Guido, 259.

Reprobate, destiny of the, 238–45.

Resurrection, General, 20, 21, 92–3, 125–56, 208–10, 249–55, 285.

Resurrection of Christ, 58–61, 139–56.

Revelation of St. John the Divine, the, 127, 199–201, 228, 248.

Ritschl, Albrecht, 146 f., 225 n.

Robbia, Andrea della, 257.

Robertson, F. W., 210.

Robespierre, 34.

Robinson, C. H., 149 n.

Rohde, Erwin, 70, 84, 102, 103, 105, 106, 107, 112.

Roman religion and philosophy, 42–68, 71–3, 76, 78, 92, 101, 119, 1[?], 163.

Romantic Movement and Romanticism, 179, 183, 259 f.

Rousseau, J. J., 259, 260.

Royce, J., 217.

Russell, Bertrand, Lord, 177, 191.

Sadducees, 101, 133–6, 138.

Sankhya philosophy, 117.

Savages, vide Primitive peoples.

Savonarola, 25.

Schleiermacher, 183 f., 186, 226.

Schweitzer, Albert, 113.

Science, natural, 24–7, 86, 92–9, 263–4.

Self-analysis, 50–5.

Senancour, 169 n.

Seneca, 183.

Shakespeare, 281, 284.

Shaw, G. B., 174.

Shelley, 96, 281.

Sheol, 73–5, 119–35, 159, 239, 248.

Shipp, Horace, 12.

Sikhism, 115.

Simultaneity, vide Eternity.

Smith, George Adam, 160.

Social reform, 27–45, 268–73.

Socrates, 38, 51, 80 f., 84, 102, 11[?], 141.

Söderblom, Nathan, 44, 129 n., 130.

Sophists, the, 34 f.

Sorley, W. R., 167, 233.

Soul, passim.

Soviet Russia, its attitude to religion, 34–7.

Spencer, Herbert, 65.

Spenser, Edmund, 254 n.

Sperry, W. L., 99.

Spinoza, 13, 183, 185, 186, 191, 265, 286.

Stephen, St., 154.

Stevenson, R. L., 231.

Stoics and Stoicism, 42 f., 113, 182 f., 185 f., 229 f., 270.

Streeter, B. H., 90 n., 151 n., 188, 235 n.

Subjective and objective, 153–5.

ulpicius, 71.
urvival, *passim*.
uso, Henry, 25, 159, 223.
winburne, A. C., 262.

almud, the, 136.
aylor, A. E., 97 n., 167 f., 190 n., 213, 218 n., 219, 227, 234 f.
aylor, Jeremy, 85.
e Deum Laudamus, 58.
emple, William, 99, 160 n.
ennyson, 28 f., 62-3, 65, 76, 121, 231.
ension, 271.
ertullian, 242.
hompson, Francis, 56 f.
horeau, H. D., 24.
iepolo, G. B., 259.
illich, Paul, 6, 272 n.
ime, nature of, 206-28 *passim*.
imothy, the Second Epistle to, 58-9.
ransfiguration, the, 155.
ransmigration of souls, 68, 114-17.
ribalism, *vide* Corporate immortality.
rinity, the Holy, 194, 267.
roeltsch, E., 269 n.
ylor, E. B., 26, 82-3.

Unamuno, Miguel de, 62, 86 n., 169 n., 192.
Universal restoration, 240, 245 f.
Upanishads, 114, 116, 181 f.

Value and the individual, 165-74, 180-8, 274-80.
Vauvenargues, 13.
Vedanta theology, 116, 186.
Vedas, 114.
Veronese, Paolo, 259.
Verrocchio, 257.
Vision, 141-55.
Voltaire, 33, 37, 260 n.
Volz, P., 127 n., 249 n.

Walpole, Hugh, 56.
War, the Great, 15.
Watteau, Antoine, 259.
Watts, Isaac, 25.
Webb, C. C. J., 7 f., 101, 144 n., 194.
Wellhausen, J., 130.
Westminster *Confession of Faith*, 95, 250.
Westminster *Shorter Catechism*, 3, 228.
Whichcote, B., 252.
Whitehead, A. N., 185, 281.
Whittier, J. G., 98, 187, 198.
Wicksteed, P. H., 213, 218, 222, 237.
Wisdom, the Book of, 198.
Wordsworth, William, 55, 260, 272 f., 283.

Yeats, W. B., 262.
Youth and age, 47.

Zarathustra and Zoroastrianism, 44 f., 129-32, 247.

Printed in Great Britain by Lowe and Brydone Printers Limited, London, N.W.10